I Was There

AN AUTOBIOGRAPHY

Frank Proctor

Edited by
William N. Tindall & Pamela Proctor

CANADIAN CATALOGUING IN PUBLICATION DATA

Proctor, Frank, 1902–
I was there

ISBN 0-9686544-0-1

1. Proctor, Frank, 1902– 2. Mission (B.C.)—Biography. World War, 1939–1945—Personal narratives, Canadian. 4. Painters—British Columbia—Biography. I. Tindall, William N. II. Proctor, Pamela. III. Title.
FC3849.M56Z49 2000 971.1'37 C00-910271-X
F1089.5.M57P76 2000

Editing and contributions by:
Dr. William Tindall
Pamela Proctor
John Roper
Ray Hammond
Betty Johns
George Cooper

Cover design by Rosemary Hanna
Production design by Patty Osborne
Map and Cap Badge reproduced with permission from The Royal Regina Rifles
Printed and bound in Canada by Printcrafters

For information about this book and to order copies please contact:
tmi publications
P.O. Box 692,
Gibsons, B.C. V0N 1V0
Tel: (604) 886-0540
Email: tmi@intouch.bc.ca

Contents

Foreword

My dad began writing his autobiography shortly after my mother died in 1981. At that time he held a strong desire to chronicle his life so that younger generations, born into different circumstances, could benefit from his experiences and insights. His story is one of extraordinary personal development through some exceptional periods in the twentieth century, including economic depression, war, peace and prosperity, events that have formed the fabric of our society.

Born in 1902 in a small coal mining town in Durham County, northeast England, he emigrated to Canada in 1928 to work the grain harvest in Saskatchewan. He later settled in Regina, married my mother Anne, and started a family. In 1939, at the outbreak of World War II, he joined the Regina Rifle Regiment and became its Quarter Master Sergeant. On D-day, June 6, 1944, he landed with his regiment on the beaches of Normandy and participated in the liberation of France and Holland. His eyewitness account of these events will fascinate the reader as they are told from the perspective of a front-line infantryman.

Following the war, Mum and Dad decided to relocate from Regina to British Columbia and settle in the Fraser Valley town of Mission. There, with Mum's help, Dad started his own independent business. They also bought a house on 3rd Street where I, my sister Joanne, and my younger brother, Mark, grew up. Dad's autobiography ends with his retirement in 1961 and the activities surrounding a year-long trip to England and Holland the following year.

Following his retirement, my father turned to his love of oil painting and became quite renowned for his nature studies. He has created over 350 paintings, mostly of Fraser Valley river and mountain scenes. He has also painted old buildings and machinery but his signature pieces include tree stumps. When asked why he painted tree stumps, he invariably replies, "I paint stumps because they are elegantly balanced, point upwards with meaningful significance, and are quiet witnessess. To me, tree stumps display the joy and character of old rugged individuals." "Further," Dad would say, "I like stumps. They give me a lift from earthly things to the spirit of Jesus who puts all things in perspective and balance."

This philosophy is found throughout my dad's autobiography. As you read it, you will find that he, too, like an old stump, displays the quiet elegance of a rugged individual who finds strength and balance through faith in Jesus.

Dad's paintings received many awards and honours and his works hang in many homes throughout Canada and other countries. He was also an active member of the Canadian Legion and has served as its President. Under his leadership, an apartment building for retirees was constructed in downtown Mission. He has travelled both to Holland and Regina to celebrate anniversaries of the Liberation and has always participated in Remembrance Ceremonies in Mission, even in 1998 at the age of ninety-five.

Dad became a warden and lay preacher in the Anglican Parish of All Saints Church, where for many years he published the All Saints' Parish Magazine. It was at All Saints in 1983 that he married Ruth Webber, a longtime family friend and retired nurse, several years after the passing of my Mother.

During the summer of 1995, Dad suffered a stroke, paralyzing his right side and affecting his speech, although fortunately not his sense of humour. With Ruth's love and great care he made an amazing recovery. During the summer of 1996, Dad and Ruth moved into a top-floor apartment in a building overlooking our old family home. From this apartment they are also provided terrific views of their beloved Fraser Valley. It was in this apartment, on December 9, 1998, Dad, Ruth, and many loving family and friends, celebrated his ninety-sixth birthday.

Thank you, Dad, for putting your wonderful story into words that can be shared and treasured by many. Also, thank you to Betty Johns for transferring Dad's words onto a computer. Finally, thank you to our cousin, Dr. William (Bill) Tindall, for his skills and the many hours spent editing Dad's story into the book you now hold.

Pamela Proctor
Gibsons, British Columbia, Canada
November 1999

Dad and Ruth at an exhibition of his paintings at the Harrison Gallery in 1989.

CHAPTER ONE

The Early Years

My NAME IS FRANK PROCTOR. I was born in England on December 9, 1902. My earliest recollections of Mum, Dad and older brother Ernest are from about the age of four. Ernest was three years and three months older. We lived at Number 14 Temperance Terrace, in the Village of Ushaw Moor, County Durham, England. Across the street from our house was Ushaw Moor County School. A boy named Billy Greathead became my first playmate.

Registered in the County School at the age of five, I was in the Infant School. My teacher's name was Mrs. Potts. I remember playing after school near Mrs. Hope's candy shop where sweets like cachous, sherbet and aniseed balls were sold. I have few recollections of my first year in the Infant School, other than the blackboard and A-B-C's, but I was happy and liked my teacher.

By the age of five, I knew that my Mum's name was Jenny, and I became fully aware of family, Mum, Dad, and baby sister, Amy. My father worked as a bricklayer and my mother stayed at home. I had four uncles on my mother's side, and two on my father's. Other than by marriage, I had no aunts on either side, and I never knew my grandparents. I can remember Uncle *Big Ernest*, Uncle Bennett, and Uncle Thomas, who was married to Aunt Lizzy and lived at New Brancepeth, called

Sleetburn by many. There were also Uncle Jack and Uncle Bill, Dad's brothers, and Aunt Maggie who lived at South Moor. Jack, Dora, Jessie and Mopsy were my cousins. Uncle Bill's adopted daughter, Jenny, and Uncle Thomas's son, Arthur, completed my extended family.

Ushaw Moor was like most other coal mining villages where practically all income came from or was associated with the *pits*. My father, even as a bricklayer, was employed at the Ushaw Moor coal mine. In the Deerness Valley there were coal mines at Littleburn, Esh-Winning, Waterhouses, Cornsay, Langley Park, New Brancepeth, Brandon and Bearpark. I remember my Uncle Ernest had only one arm. Mum told us that before I was born he got his hand and lower arm caught in the cog wheels of a hauling engine while trying to oil its wheels. She related to us the horror of seeing Uncle Ernest being brought home with his arm *stump* wrapped in newspaper. When what was left of his arm finally healed, I remember his empty sleeve folded back and pinned up to keep it out of his way. Naturally, Uncle Ernest could no longer work at the *pit*, so he became sort of an odd-job man at the Station Hotel, called the Bottom House Hotel and Pub. It was owned by a Mr. Woods.

When I was seven, my family moved from Temperance Terrace to Number 8 Middlefield Terrace further down on Station Road. My father found employment at New Brancepeth colliery working on the *Patent Ovens*. Here he worked on the *surface* in a new method of *coking* coal that had been introduced by the Germans. Middlefield Terrace had been so named because it was built on a sizeable field acquired by the New Brancepeth colliery owners who had built a street of eight colliery houses. These houses were literally in the middle of the field, therefore its name. In those days there were no electric lights in most houses. Each house had a big kitchen, a landing, and two bedrooms upstairs. Off the back kitchen was a pantry, and under the stairs was a large cupboard. At the bottom of each back yard was a *midden*. Our house, being the last house on the street, was walled-in by a wall that ended the property. The *midden* was situated about fifteen yards from our back door. It was both ash-pit and toilet. We used a kerosene lamp with a tall lamp-glass and globe for household purposes, and candles for going to bed or for going outside to the *midden*. I recall how us youngsters, and even Mum, would have someone go with us, for ghosts were the tone for flickering candles. Pranksters often took advantage, playing all sorts of tricks and scares, so we usually hung on to each other. In the winter we used chamber pots at night. A kitchen fire was our only heat source, using coal from the colliery.

As we practically lived in the kitchen, and as our fireplace was back-to-back with the house next door, we could always hear our neighbours poking their fire. The fireplace was brick with heavy iron grates. All iron parts were black-leaded, even grates and bars. The grates and top could be lowered to a bar, on which cans could be placed. The fire could be spread under an oven when Mum was baking. There was also a hot water tank on one side of the fireplace. One could lift the lid and have hot water for washing. There was no hot water in the back kitchen taps.

Also, in the back kitchen corner was a boiler with a built-in small fireplace for use on wash days. The front door entered right into the kitchen which was furnished with a large table, about five-foot square, with an oil lamp placed in the middle. We owned eight wooden kitchen chairs. A *settle*, about six-feet in length, was placed under the front window, and it was thinly packed with a shiny material similar to oil cloth table covers. We also had a wooden rocking chair. All furniture was wood except the fire irons, *Tidy-Betty* and *fender*, and these, being coated metal, were cleaned and shined weekly. I remember cleaning them many times as I could not play football until this chore was done. Of course, taking out the ashes was another frequent chore.

Opposite the kitchen wall nearest the street window was a press. It was made of mahogany, with large glass doors in its upper part, and three chests of drawers in its lower portion. This press was where Mum stored our Sunday clothes after brushing and folding them on Mondays. Various articles could be hung in a cupboard under the stairs, but mostly this cupboard was used as a catch-all. I remember that near the cupboard door was a flour bin. Mum baked every Friday: bread, tea-cakes, and pastry. There were no bakeries in the village, and if one ran short, one borrowed a loaf from the neighbour. Mum would bake sixteen-to-twenty loaves at a time. She had a large knead bowl, and watching her knead the dough with her sleeves rolled up past her elbows was fascinating. She always wore a clean apron.

On the floor in front of the fireplace was a huge mat which our family had made on frames of stretched canvas. I remember we would begin in the autumn, first cutting clippings from old clothing. Then nightly at every opportunity we got out the prodders and worked a design of some kind. Clippings were cut to about three inches in length. Mum would show us, one hand on top, prod down on end, other hand underneath, pulling clipping down to half-length, then prodding the other end from the top and pulling even underneath. Our stone floor coverings were mostly our home-made mats.

Much of our evenings were spent sitting around the fire on these home-made mats, usually doing homework. Sometimes we did homework by lamplight on the kitchen table. As coal often had to be carried in, "Go fetch in a scuttle of coal" was a common remark to my ears. The coal house was an outside shed attached to the building. Coals were brought from the colliery every three weeks by a delivery man using a two-wheeled cart pulled by a horse. The coal was tipped at the coal house door and us lads then shovelled it into the coal house. Coal fires and ashes were part of daily life.

The inside of our house was wallpapered by my mother. I will never forget how she wallpapered the stairwell. Her method was ingenious, but I was always afraid she would fall. Wallpaper was hand-fringed, and sizing was made from flour and water. When re-papering, the old paper was always stripped. What a job! The ceilings were normally white washed.

On top of the mantlepiece were brass candlesticks, ornaments, a tea-caddie, matches and other articles of trivia. In the back kitchen stood a huge mangle, with rollers eight-inches in diameter and a huge ring handle. There was also a back-kitchen table with a large mat on the floor. Through the back kitchen was the pantry. Always cool, it was shelved on both sides, and contained left-overs, jams, food, pastry and cooking utensils. I remember we usually got our groceries via the Co-op. The store man came every second Monday to take Mum's order, and we would get the groceries by horse-drawn lorry two weeks later. I recollect the sacks of flour, the sides of bacon, the lard, butter, cheese, tea, jam, sugar and various other staples. Green groceries came separately once a week and might consist of apples, fruits, potatoes, turnips, and sometimes a chocolate bar. The butcher also came weekly, using a horse-drawn cart. He would let the tail gate down and use it as a chopping block. He wore a *steel* by his side, and a blue striped apron. We often got big roasts, liver, sausages, and pork. This butcher did not carry game such as rabbits or poultry.

There were never enough bedrooms for us all. Two beds were in the large bedroom, and one was in the other. I remember that I and my two brothers slept in the same bed, often rotating places so that we each had a turn sleeping in the middle. Needless to say, we had some bustling about before we settled in.

Our move to Number 8 Middlefield Terrace made the walk to school much longer. With only an hour-and-a-half for dinner, we had to hustle in order to get home, eat and get back again in time for lessons. I don't recollect anyone ever taking food to school. My brother Ernest and I went to school together. There were other children on our street who went to the same school. In number Five lived the Moorelands. Billy Mooreland was my age and we chummed together. Billy and I were in the same class in standard one proper.

As the years progressed, we knew everyone in the class and going to school was pleasant. The hours were 9:00 a.m. to noon and 1:30 to 3:30 p.m., Monday through Friday. At 8:55 a.m., we formed into rows for inspection before we entered the school. Rules required that our shoes be cleaned and brushed. We all wore celluloid white collars, and our hair was groomed. The rules also required that we be scrubbed and clean. If one did not pass this scrutinizing, he would be sent to stand in the corridor by the head-masters office. Anyone who was careless about the school rules would be caned. At 10:30 a.m. and 2:00 p.m., there was a recess or playtime lasting for about ten minutes. During inclement weather we could play in a covered shed.

Our family were members of St. Luke's Protestant Church. Everyone was baptized there, and we attended church and Sunday school there. After a year I moved into standard two and my sister Amy enrolled in the Infant School. Amy went to school with one of the next-door neighbour girls. Her last name was Marley, and her father worked at the mine. The Marleys had two daughters, Edith and Evelyn. I remember how much we missed them when they moved to Dubois, Pennsylvania, a coal-mining area.

The next year I was in Mrs. Pearce's class three when my Uncle Jack died. He had never been really well. My Uncle *Big Ernest*, who had developed *galloping consumption*, a lung disease, also died. This was my uncle who had worked at the Station Hotel where the German specialists who had come to set up the new coking plant stayed, as it was a gathering place for them in the evenings. Uncle Ernest had often related to us how rough and gruff they were, always in arguments and causing trouble. This was a period of great anxiety for him because he used to carry trays of beer mugs to various rooms. He said that one night there were knives used in a fight where a man pinned another man to the table with a knife through his hand. This event was an anxious time for him since he was expected to deal with these characters and he had only the one arm to do it.

Uncle Bennett was my mother's youngest brother, and I greatly admired him, along with Uncle Thomas. They both played on the local football teams, and I often went to their games. I especially liked Bennett's team, The Heros. These young men soon became my heros. There were Batey, Hope, Walker, and Briggs. Batey was so good that a big-league team took him to play for them. Every Saturday afternoon I would go to cheer them on. I was very proud of Bennett, and would sometimes go home with him for tea. He was working at the mines and was very strong.

Soon a bakery shop opened in the Station Road. It was called Cawthornes. Bennett would buy pastry tarts for tea. Life was really good. It seemed that Mum was always there. Her life was her family. Dad never seemed to be concerned about us as long as we were growing up, except when we were causing trouble for anyone, especially at school. I loved my parents dearly, especially my mother, who cared for us so selflessly and lovingly. We had lots of fun.

After Rob, we got another baby sister, Jenny. We often gathered around when Mum was washing, changing and feeding the baby. She would send us into peals of laughter, picking up the baby and kissing her bum, *after it had been cleaned!* Sometimes after she fed her, she would squeeze her breast and squirt a spray of her milk at us. We had a rocking cradle, and often I had the job of rocking baby to sleep. As I remember, Mum's outings occurred mostly once a year when the dividends came from the co-op store. Our account for purchases was 1050, and it earned a dividend of about two pence on every pound spent during a year. Upon collecting the dividend, Mum would walk to Langley Park and outfit us with new suits, new boots, and caps.

It was a long walk through the woods and fields to Langley Park, and my mother's clothes were not the best for walking. Her skirt bottom was down to the soles of her *high shoes,* and the bottom of her skirt at the back trailed on the ground. She wore a big hat with hair pins sticking right through her hair. Langley Park was approximately five miles from our Ushaw Moor home, and a walk there and back consumed an entire, tiring day. I remember that Langley Park was situated in a valley, and the Co-op store was right at the bottom, so to get down from the Ushaw College was a very steep descent. If one didn't want to go down a winding road, a short cut was available, known as the *silly steps*, which I recollect were three-hundred-and-fifty steps down a quarter-mile drop. It was always a joke that we school kids would go there to *bowl Easter eggs*, a north county custom.

In class four, Miss Davis, our teacher, was very nice. She was also left-handed, and she caned with vigour. Some of the boys, now ten-year-olds, teased her, and when being caned would hold their hand out to arms length, then quickly withdraw it when she came down with the cane, causing her to hit her own leg. This resulted in snickers among the class members. Each desk had two tip-up seats, and on the desk was an inkwell. Underneath was a shelf for books and papers. By now, everyone knew every other person in the class. There was Dickinson, Hogg, Hudson, Shaw, Briggs, Jolly Longstaff, Mooreland, Nelson, Syd Rhodes, and Fatty Levin, who was the fun boy, full of tricks. One day after having excused himself to leave the room, someone played a trick on him. When he came into class and sat, he jumped almost to the ceiling in terrific agony. Someone had bent a pin so that when placed on the seat its point stuck upwards. This caused a terrific uproar in the classroom and it hurt Fatty Levin.

CHAPTER TWO

The Middle School Years

ONE DAY AFTER SCHOOL Billy Mooreland and I got into a dispute during a game of marbles. It was a bitter fight. As I recollect, this was my only fight during my school days. But we got over it quickly. We both played football. Billy played goalie.

At the bottom of Station Road was the north eastern railway station. Trains ran from Durham Station quite regularly to Ushaw Moor and on to Esh-Arid Waterhouses, which was the terminal of this branch line. In the evenings, Billy and I used to meet the incoming trains and carry bags or parcels for passengers. Our aim was to make some pennies, or maybe a sixpence, money for the *Big Meetings* and *Miners Gala*. Sometimes we would get a portmanteau, which we could hardly lift.

When I went into Mr. John Spiers, class five, this was my first class with a male teacher. He was a nice man, but sometimes he got very angry and would tear a composition page right out of the books. He was most severe on grammar. I was passing my school exams, but only with average marks, rarely getting more than six out of fifteen. I grew to like reading in his class because Mr. Spiers made it attractive. I liked his reading and explaining books to us. He had a library and encouraged his pupils to take books home to read. I always remember his saying that class five was *pons assinorum*. We never ask him what that meant, but he volunteered quickly that it meant the *donkey bridge*. He used to say to us, "If you can pass class five, you are over the *donkey bridge* and can go the rest of the way without trouble." He made it hard to get over, though. But he was a good man and a good teacher.

Mr. Spiers travelled from Durham via train three-and-a-half miles each way. Going home, the train left at 5:00 p.m., so to fill one hour he started a shorthand class for any one who cared to stay. I took in some Pitman's shorthand, but didn't retain a great deal. He also loved to read Shakespeare, and I remember almost living *The Merchant of Venice.* I used to sit next to Arthur Cunliffe, who was always top of the class. He was an excellent boy, and I respected him greatly. Since he was studious, I played more than he did, but I got through class five quite comfortably. Quite a few did not. I remember how Mr. Spiers would have all the *bad* readers stand up in the aisle. We didn't think any worse of them as I recall, only that they didn't read as well as the teacher thought they should. As the railway station was on my way home, sometimes I would walk down the road with Mr. Spiers. I liked that.

In 1914, at age twelve, I entered class six. Mr. Carr was the teacher. Mr. Carr and Mr. Ray came to Ushaw Moor School at the same time. They were great friends. They were great for sports: football, cricket, rounders and later tennis. Practically all the same girls and boys were in my class: Annie Rowe, Bella Raine, Elsie Chappel, Linda Brown, Dorothy Taylor, Elna Underwood, Marian Wilson and the boys previously mentioned. The routine of the classroom was 9:00 a.m. call of class register, then scriptures, arithmetic, composition, geography, history, spelling, singing, drawing for the boys, and sewing for the girls. I liked drawing. In fact, I loved school and all connected with it. Getting to school was troublesome in the mornings, though. Mum insisted that I wait so that younger brother Rob could go with me. None too eager to go, he pulled out every delaying trick he could think of. Consequently, I was often late and got the cane. I would be hurrying him up, almost dragging him, and we would shortcut behind the Empire Theatre. But every time we got there he would want to *go,* saying that he needed to relieve himself. This meant I had to help him with his clothing, and I would become horribly angry about these delays, knowing I would be late and would get a caning.

While in class six I was accepted into the Boy Scouts, Ushaw Moor Troop. Mr. Marchand was Scoutmaster. The scout room was an old empty house near the Ushaw Moor colliery, and was colliery property near the *Lop*, a games-room of repute. I loved scouting. I found lifelong friends and enjoyed the whole programme, both in the club room and especially the outdoors. How I admired Tommy Gill, who was assistant Scout Master with his two arms full of efficiency badges, and patrol leader Billy Martenson for his astonishing know-how of so many things. I was growing up, learning to tie the six knots, the Scouts Law of helping others and the motto: *be prepared*. It took me a very long time to acquire a uniform, which consisted of a blue shirt and shorts, a scout hat and belt, and tenderfoot badges. I learned so many things in those beautiful times; badges for first aid, flowers, morse code, and semaphore. Then there were the jamborees, meeting other scouts, hauling the *trek* cart, and singing while en route and around the campfire, along with paper chases and comradeship. Two of my scouting friends were Tommy Gamble and Jack Walker. I attended club night every week, looked forward to scout-life, and began to become interested in football. Ray and Carr, our class seven and six teachers were real football enthusiasts. I was in class six and played football with anything that could be kicked. At recess, our teacher would take one team's side, and the other teacher would take another. We would have a game every day, mostly with a small ball that the teachers brought.

Our school football teams played in a regional school league. I remember on Friday afternoons the teachers would have us choose the team for Saturday morning games. I was at some disadvantage inasmuch as I was not robust. I was small and thin, perhaps skinny. As a seven-year-old, my parents were worried about my health. At the suggestion of our village doctor, they got an appointment for me to visit a specialist. This meant a trip to the big city of Newcastle. I can vividly recall how I was stripped and laid upon an examining table, and how the doctor, with a small-handled rubber hammer sounded me up and down, front and back, chest and stomach. I was never in pain, only puny. The only thing that came out of the diagnosis was that I was to have a tablespoonful of Wincarnis Wine twice a day. I remember how the doctor patted me on the head and said, "We'll make a man out of you yet, son!"

Anyway, there I was waiting excitedly to see who was going to be on the school team. It seems that I was mostly first reserve, but I had gotten physically stronger, although wispy. Mr. Potts, the headmaster, was an impressive man. He went to watch the school team play. Often there would be a few parents at these matches, but few other spectators. Mr. Potts was nearly always present, though.

I often thought how odd it was that Mr. Potts could be so nice at the football pitch and yet so stern and angry in the classrooms. When he came before a class to ask questions about our school work, most of us just sat terrified that he would throw a question at us and we might not know the answer. The situation was somewhat like the petrification of chickens when a hawk is hovering overhead. There was just cause for this because his anger was vicious and he was so big and strong. His physical stance was over six feet, and he was wonderfully proportioned.

About this time the dress style of some golfers was apparel called *plus fours*. This kind of dress was really suitable for Mr. Pott's manner. The trousers came down to the knee when it bagged out, and his well-shaped legs and calf showed admirably. He really was of magnificent build. Fearfully so, for us kids. He caned viciously when he was angry, and it didn't take much to make him so. When he asked a question, those who knew the answer were to raise their hands. I never knew whether to put up my hand or not. I was afraid he might pick me if I had my hand up. But if I kept it down, he might pick on me because I didn't raise it.

One time I remember he was holding forth in fourth class and he asked the class a question. Of course, nearly everyone put up his or her hand, and unfortunately for Marian Wilson, she was asked and could not answer correctly. He got so mad that he kept on asking her easier questions, which she also failed to answer correctly. She was petrified even to speak. Marian occupied a desk second from the front, and she was a red-haired girl with hair more than halfway down her back. The drama became intense. Finally, she was asked, "How many farthings in a penny?" She could not answer, so the schoolmaster reached over the first row desk and hauled Marian out of her desk by the hair of her head. She howled and shrieked and he sent her to the Infant school where she was to ask them the answer to that question. It was an incident that I will never forget.

Mr. Potts called me "Mr. Proctor," and said "well done" at times. He treated me very kindly, and asked me to do things for him outside of the school. I used to cut his little lawn in front of his house. Outside of school, he seemed like another man, but inside the school he was an iron rod. I remember one situation involving the two Nichol brothers, Joe and Fatty. Our classrooms were partitioned off by a glass folding divider. Fatty was in class five and Joe was in class six. The rooms were next to each other. Mr. Potts was *leathering* Fatty and Fatty was hollering. Potts always *laid it on heavy*. Joe knew who was getting it, so he fled to Fatty's aid. Soon there was a real fight going on. It was mayhem. The outcome of it all was that next morning Mrs. Nichol came down to the school to see Mr. Potts. She had come prepared for a fray, wearing her husband's clogs, iron-shod footwear. They became engaged in a great shouting match, but the story does not end here. Later, there was a court case in Durham and Fatty had to appear to display the weals on his back.

There was once a saying, sort of rough rhyme:

Wilson Potts is a very good man
He goes to church on Sundays
He prays to God to give him strength
To whack the kids on Mondays.

Everyone in the school knew this chant. I have often wondered what discipline means? Keeping others in line or keeping self in line?

The two male teachers, Mr. Carr, class six, and Mr. Ray, class seven, were well respected, and I liked them both very much. Mr. Carr was my teacher when I was twelve years old. He was of small stature but good build, quick of movement and tough. Not in the classroom but in the schoolyard at play or at soccer he could take a kick on the shins and kick shins too. He scrambled for the ball, but he was clean, a nice person. While I have mentioned a rough occasion with the headmaster, Mr. Potts, I cannot recall any others except this one which occurred one afternoon in the class six classroom.

We were the same lads who as we got older moved through school class after class. One such lad was called Shaw, a nice fair-haired lad, tallest in the class, quite tall for his age. He wasn't really an aggressive sort, but being bigger not many fell afoul of him. He had a natural advantage, and he was at times cheeky with Mr. Carr. Maybe it was because Mr. Carr was small for a man. One could say it had to happen, a big lad a bit cheeky and a small man confident of himself. The two hit head-on. It was getting near the time for being let out of school. Shaw was acting up more than he should, and Mr. Carr asked him to desist. Shaw gave back some cheek so Mr. Carr called him out from his desk to come to the front of the class. There was bantering going on, and Shaw wasn't about to stop so Mr. Carr was going to cane him. Shaw refused to be caned, and when the teacher tried to give him the stick, Shaw responded with a fist. Then the battle was on. They squared off at each other as do boxers in a boxing ring. But there were no *Marquess of Queensbury* rules for this fight. It was really a rough-and-tumble blow and a wrestle-type, fast and furious. Well, Shaw might have thought of his chance, or fancied himself lording over his teacher, but the redoubtable little Mr. Carr proved his maturity. There was no bloodshed, but Shaw was surely *bested* and made to cry "off" and say "sugar." They shook hands afterwards, both respected. It seemed inevitable that Mr.

Carr would have to face circumstances of boys bigger than him in the classroom. Mr. Carr was a good sort and a good sport. It was exciting to say the least that afternoon, but I felt a bit sad that it happened.

In class seven, Mr. Ray was much taller and more sinuous than Mr. Carr. He also could join in with his pupils very well. He lived in a place called Cornsay, a colliery village also. I remember that he used to cycle the eight miles or so to Ushaw Moor School, and as I had never seen a bicycle with a motor affixed to the rear wheel, it was most fascinating. There were no busses or cars in Ushaw Moor in those days. It was horse conveyances or walk. Even the hospital ambulance was horse-drawn. I was into Mr. Ray's class seven at thirteen years old, and I could not leave school until I was fourteen. In the school system at that time there was no way that I could go to further education, so I was in class seven for two years. The last year was spent going to school as a requirement, doing any necessary job, such as making props and scenery for school plays, reaching, fetching, carrying. I was not the only one in that situation. There were several.

One Friday Mr. Ray had seven of us lads go to Esh Winning, five miles away, to fetch a long wooden ladder. It must have been a twenty feet. I wasn't very tall, and when we hoisted the ladder onto our shoulders and were headed on our way back, I found that the ladder only touched *my* shoulder now and again, depending on how even the ground was. It amuses me every time I think of it, getting a five-mile ride. After all, I would have looked silly walking on my toes just to reach the ladder.

World War I was on now and the classroom acquired a map of Europe. Each morning we assembled around the map and moved pins to denote the advances and retreats of the opposing armies. An exam was held at a Langley Moor School for boys who, if they passed, could leave school to go to the coal mine to work. A lot of miners had gone to war and help was needed to keep up the supply of coal. I failed to pass. However, the war was still on as I left school in 1916 at age fourteen. I remember arriving home and sobbing at my mother's knee with all my school books on the floor. I left school on a Friday at 3:30 p.m. and started to work at the mine at 11:00 a.m. the next Monday. Father took me to Sleetburn colliery and I signed on for work at the Pit Head, not below ground. I recall that I went to work at 11:00 a.m. and returned home at 9:00 p.m., as black as I could ever be. My family all laughed, accusing me of purposely blackening my face so that I might impress them about how hard I had worked.

The reason I was so black was that my work was at the Pit Head, i.e., the place where the *cage* goes up and down the mine shaft. Sometimes it drew four tubs of coal, and sometimes it brought up workers or took them down. It was always very dusty when drawing coal because the full tubs were pulled out of the cage and taken to a *tip* that discharged the contents into a *jigger* that shook the coals onto the *belts*. The belts were a conveyor squeaking and screeching endlessly all day long. They tipped the coals into railway coal wagons. Every time coals were *tipped* there was so much dust one could hardly see through it. We breathed it in for ten hours less a half hour for lunch, when we went to the *bait* cabin to eat. When I coughed and spat, the phlegm was always black. The dust penetrated nostrils, mouth, eyes and ears, throat, lungs and stomach. They said that it was harmless; just part of the occupation.

I have vivid recollections of German air-raids at that time. From the Mine-head we had a high spot, and each night the display of searchlights kept guard, trying to spot Zeppelin airships. When they found one, all the search lights would focus on it so that in the inkiness of the night sky it shone brilliantly. The ack-ack of anti-aircraft guns would feverishly try to get a hit and down it. During these times it was most exciting but not without fear, for they were dropping bombs onto areas that didn't stop working, although all lighting was cut off. It was eerie watching the cage going up and down drawing out coal in the dark. We would run to the open window hoping to see a hit, but hoping also that they were not getting any nearer to us, although we could hear the detonations of their bombs. Someone was getting it, perhaps Newcastle. They were always trying for the high level bridges of the Tyne and any ships on the coast. During the air-raids the pits worked on, but I remember at night how many of the neighbours would pack some belongings and go into the fields. They were afraid of being buried.

When World War I had been on for two-and-a-half years I was still in the Boy Scouts, when my boy scout troop was changed into *Sea Scouts*. We became involved in helping and watching in any way that we were needed as I was too young to be in the armed forces.

As mentioned earlier, my father worked at the patent coking ovens. He was a master mason by trade. My father didn't tell us much about himself, but my mother told us he was one of the builders of the seventy-five-foot stone chimney stack at Ushaw colliery. He worked at the ovens then, but before that he had worked underground in the mine building *stoppings*, walls built as airways to channel compressed air for breathing underground.

In our house at Middlefield Terrace we were about two-hundred yards away from the Albion House Working Men's club. My father was on the club committee and spent much time there. He worked at the ovens every third week. He would work a double shift on Sunday, 6:00 a.m. until 2:00 p.m. and 2:00 p.m. until 10:00 p.m.. On these days, my mother would put Dad's Sunday dinner into a large basin and sling it in a big red-and-white handkerchief, and she would make a big can of tea. I do so remember taking this dinner to these patent huge ovens. We could get right up to where he worked. He used to be so glad to see us and would show us how they worked.

The ovens were built like a row of low, oblong houses open at both ends, but with movable big iron doors. Wagons filled with finely-ground coal travelled atop the ovens, feeding the furnace from the top. There was a terrific heat in the furnace to coke the coal. When it became coke, a great big ramrod on wheels would be drawn into place and the iron door would be raised by a hoist. Then the ramrod would push the coke out the other side in a huge tray on wheels, via rail, and great water sprinklers would cool it off. The tray was hot to walk on so the men all wore shoes with iron cleats to protect their feet.

Dad worked at the New Brancepeth colliery for a long time. At the workmen's club, my father was an adept billiard player. He possessed a huge medal, worn on his watch chain, for being the first working-man to defeat the Borough and Watt's professional champion located in the city of Newcastle. In his younger days he was a competent runner, and could run a hundred yards in eleven seconds. But I remember him most in the garden. We had an allotment in the Allotment Association, at the top of Whitehouse lane, Ushaw Moor. There were forty or fifty of these allotments and we used to go with Dad to dig, plant and reap the harvest of this fifty-foot by fifty-foot lot. It was a mile from where we lived but I was with Dad more in the garden than anywhere. I remember one year that we had a lovely big cabbage. Dad was taking great care of it to put it in the annual Garden Produce and Leek Show. Unfortunately, the night before the show someone stole it. I remember his disbelief at not being able to show this lovely vegetable, but he was patient and disguised his feelings.

Earlier I mentioned my little sister, Jenny. She was a most beautiful and adorable child. The neighbours used to say she was too beautiful to live and one day she became ill, never recovered, and died. I remember the day. Dad was at work and was returning after 2:00 p.m.. I went to meet him. When we met he said, "She's gone hasn't she?" and we cried together. We loved her so.

In 1916, my dad applied for the job of club steward at the Albion Club. We knew the previous people, the Kirkups. Tom Kirkup was a very large man. They had a parrot which fascinated me whenever I was in their home. It could say many words. It would say "Hello Tom, Hello Tom," and then it would say "Go to hell, Tom." So we moved into the Albion House Club, Dad the Steward and Mum the Stewardess. World War I was still on and I was fourteen years old.

As the war continued, we were aware the Americans were likely to join the Allies. Rationing was in effect. The odd time there would be news of the stores having extra jams, sugar, margarine and such. I remember how we would walk to Durham and queue up for hours before the store doors were opened, and how disappointing it was when they were sold out just when getting close to the counter. Eggs were very scarce. There was much distress day by day.

My father died while we occupied the club. He was ill for some time, got a little better and had six weeks at a recuperation centre at *Sleetburn*, but he never really got well and remained bed-ridden for some months at home in the upstairs bedroom before he died. It was a great blow to us all. He was only forty-nine years old and we didn't know what would happen next. However, the Albion club committee appointed Mum to carry on as the Stewardess and see how things went. I used to help behind the bar. The club opened from 10:00 a.m. to 2:00 p.m., close, then open from 6:00 p.m. till 10:00 p.m.. However, there was a scarcity of beer and spirits in wartime, so that we could only open for beer when it was available. Some of the beer came from Newcastle.

There were a lot of things to do in the operation of the club. Mother used to get help from a Mr. Jim Jolly from the London North Eastern Railway who lived in the house next to the station. They had eleven girls and one boy, Jimmy. Living just a short distance from the railway station, Mr. Jolly would come and put the *hogsheads* and barrels of beer into the club cellar. It was fascinating to watch this job being done. At the big club, halfway up the Station Road, the dray-men from the brewery used to do it. The method was the same. At the place in the pavement where the cellar doors were, there were two halves to a very heavy door. When these were raised, which only happened for the lowering of the barrels into the cellar, there were always kids and bystanders to watch. When the covers were open one could see a *skid* like a wooden railway in place from the pavement to the cellar floor. These full barrels were of tremendous weight, yet one man, Jim Jolly, would sort of roll the barrel to the head of the skid descent and with the aid of a very stout rope looped into an iron ring cemented into the top of the cellar for the purpose, would loop the rope over each end of the barrel, then ease the barrel with his knees to start the sharp descent. Then he would take the weight with a firm hold and with the rope through the ring, control the drop and slowly ease the barrel onto the cellar floor. Then he rolled it onto the *gantry*, a raised platform, where it was blocked for storage. After two weeks it would be tapped ready for drawing and consumption.

The barrel was tapped to *lead* piping connected to the bar. The familiar pump handles allowed a smooth drawing of the beer or ale. After Dad died, Mr. Jolly would help us tap the barrels, which became my job eventually. The cellar was connected by a tunnel to the part of the basement where the heating installation for the whole club was situated. It was fueled by coke, a superior heating product refined from pulverized coal. It fell upon me to look after the heating and cleaning out of ashes. I also helped my mother behind the bar, washed glasses and served.

I was between fifteen and sixteen years old now and we were still at the club. There was a scarcity of beer, but we did get beer from various breweries. There was much grumbling about the quality of Burton Charington's and McEwan's Scottish. The place needed a lot of cleaning. Mum had a woman come in to help. There was sawdust on the bar floor and spittoons. There were seats around the wall and tables where one might sit, but it was a man's club and they would stand at the bar. There was a foot rail. If one preferred to sit and have drinks, there was a *snug*, a billiard room or games room, where tables were provided. Things were quiet. The miners worked hard every day, and the nation needed coal. In the evening the village was blacked out as the war entered its third year.

Uncle Thomas, Uncle Bennett and brother Ernest were away. Bennett and Ernest were in the Navy. Bennett was on the St. Vincent and Ernest on HMS Birmingham, which was the first British ship to sink a German submarine in the war. Thomas was in the army transport division, serving in France and Italy. It was always an occasion when any of them came home on leave. I was proud of them in their uniforms. In the evenings after the club was closed, Mum and us family at home, Amy, Rob, Harry and I would sit around the kitchen fire and wonder where our loved ones were. I remember one Christmas Eve, we were all around the kitchen fire sitting in the glow and wondering what kind of a Christmas they might be having, when a thud was heard on the front door. Someone was coming in without knocking, and when the inner door to the kitchen opened, to our amazement it was Uncle Thomas home from Italy. We hadn't heard from him for weeks and we never got his letter saying he was coming. What a reunion it was! We all cried happily. What tales he had to tell about the war. He drove horses to transport the necessities of war in front-line areas such as the river Po area of Italy.

We were still in the Albion House club at the end of the 1914-18 war. I vividly remember the day the Armistice was signed. Everyone was so happy the war was over. Celebrations were carried on with such a gusto that one would think people had gone mad. They had, too, with joy! I saw a crowd make an effigy of *Kaiser Bill*, string it with wire across the street in Station Road and then set fire to it. While it was burning, people went berserk with their out-pouring of pent up feelings about their kith and kin. The Tommys and the Sailor boys were coming home again. The war was over! The club had reserved some hog's heads of beer for this occasion, and they had a hurried meeting of executives and declared *free beer* for *all* while the celebration and beer lasted. The club was a mad house of jubilation. We had extra help behind the bar, six of us, but there were only two sets of pumps. We fairly spilled it out, running short of pints, pots and glasses. They simply held on to them, those that had them, and came for refills, all free!

I remember a man named Jim Howarth. He was a village character. He raised heck because he didn't have a pot and no one was about to give any up, so angrily he went home and got his wife's *laving tin* which held about half a gallon. It was reported, and I believe it, that he drank ten times the contents of that tin. I remember filling it four times myself.

The funny part about it was that the next day he came back to the club, telling everyone that the beer was rotten. Phew! What a guzzler! It was a lovely feeling to have the war over and the lights on again, but it took quite a while for things to get back to some form of normalcy.

Ernest came back from the Navy and began to work underground at the Ushaw Moor colliery. He was a rare and skilled miner. He always was hard-working and had little *shrift* for anyone who didn't give their best. So hard-working during the week, he didn't have much input into the workings of the club. The club was closed daily from 2:30 p.m. until 6:00 p.m.. On occasions when the chores had been done, Ernest and I would have fun around the billiard table, even when my dad was alive. When he could, he would give us pointers and acquaint us with the games of billiards and snooker. Over the years, we improved at these games, and even at eighteen years of age I played for the club billiards team of four in the district league. I have come to believe that this experience sharpened my perception of affiliated games such as bowling, curling, and quoits. Quoits were always available at the club and members would invariably take them out onto the grassy area behind the club premises and play.

Quoits weighed two pounds and were made of iron. They were round and about six inches in diameter. The game consisted of an iron orb, or pin, set at a distance of thirty feet. Usually two players, two quoits each, pitched alternately. Scoring was two points for a *ringer*, or circling the pin, and one point if no ringers, for the one closest. There were some expert players who could play ringers with great regularity, and great competition existed among club members. Ernest and I spent many happy hours together at this time in our lives playing each other at these games of quoits.

I became a regular behind the bar helping Mum, and open to all the talk and chatter that goes on in such a place. It had a congenial atmosphere of banter, thick smoke, sometimes fun and enjoyable, but at odd times unruly. It was always an astonishment to me how one could stand at the bar hour after hour, drinking pint after pint of beer, and still be able to stand. Most were miners and their club was where they spent most of their leisure time. They all knew each other and worked at the same mine. They had much in common about the *pit*, the *whippets*, or racing dogs, the football coupons, betting and the newspaper horse races. Their talk also included the local football and cricket teams. Many of the miners did not stay around their houses with wife and family. The house was the wife's, the family was mostly her concern and the house work was left to them. The father went to the mine in whatever shift it was, 3:00 a.m. to 11:00 a.m., 8:00 p.m. to 5:00 p.m., or 4:00 p.m. to 11:00 p.m.. When he got home, he washed, rested, then got dressed and went out to the club. Wives did not go to the clubs. There were always exceptions, of course.

From time to time there were shows like the Leek Show, Rose Show, and brass band competitions. Miners had interests in gardens. These things provided a social base for the family living. Most people of the village, especially mothers and children, went to one place of worship or another. There were Roman Catholic, Church of England, Methodist, Salvation Army, Baptist, and Wesleyan Churches. It was the thing to do. The club opened from noon to 2:30 p.m., then from 6:00 to 10:00 p.m.. Sunday afternoon was always our *quiet day*.

Syd Rhodes and I had been constant friends and companions since school days. The Rhodes family had moved down from Station Road, and since the Moorelands had moved away and Billy had gone with them, Syd and I became very devoted pals. So on Sunday afternoon we would go out for walks. We did enjoy these times. There were many places to go for walks, around the Ushaw College Park, around the *Pot and Jug* at Bearpark and the Esh Common and Broadgate Wood, especially the Esh. Hundreds of people would enjoy being in this quiet surrounding which was a very large area, and free to walking anywhere. Syd was a great *adonis* for the girls. He could gabble all day to girls and was well known and liked. He was also a very talented footballer and played for the local club. When at work he was employed as a rope guider. This involved seeing that the steel rope hauling the *sets* underground stayed even when the hauling was taking place. From this job he finally became Winding Engineer, even to hauling the cages up and down the pit shafts. However, at this time we were two happy lads. I remember the first time that I wore long pants. I was afraid to walk out in them. We had up to this time worn knee pants and stockings which turned down at the knees. I was very bashful, even self conscious about wearing a pair of tawny red shoes. Honestly, I was afraid that everyone would look at me. I never shared the outward aplomb that Syd possessed. I accompanied him when he would tease and entertain the girls, but I never could chatter and banter with them like he could. But we had fun in these teenage years.

Some Saturday afternoons Syd would accompany George Davidson of the Bottom House Pub to Tow Law, where George played football for this northern league club. It never occurred to me that I might go, and only once was I asked. I think it was the first time I'd ever been in a privately owned car. Syd lived with his widowed mother. When she passed away, he moved to High Field Terrace. During the years of our companionship, Syd became friendly with a girl named Bella Inglesworth. Her family was associated with the small Methodist Church on Durham Road. They went together steady. When Syd's Mother died, Mr. and Mrs. Swainston of Number One Highfield Terrace, who operated a fish-and-chip shop, adopted Syd. He and I were there often. They had an organ and Syd could play it well from memory. Many evenings we sang to his playing. The Swainstons were also of the Methodist Church. They were nice people, very generous, and we congregated at their place frequently.

Mr. Swainston had been a cricketer of some talent when he was young, and he used to umpire for the local club. One summer evening during a cricket game at which he was an umpire, Mr. Swainston was in his position at *square leg* when a bowled *leg ball* was caught by the batsman with a good hit. The ball, unseen by Mr. Swainston, hit him on the side of his forehead. He went down like a log! Everyone thought he was dead. It really was touch and go with him, but he recovered.

It was at their home where I first became acquainted with a brand new element in life: radio. Jos, as he was called, tampered with a thing called a *cats-whisker*. He fiddled with this apparatus continually and with ear phones on he would be able to pick up programmes, especially band music. One day he told me to come to his house to hear the Derby being run on his one-tube radio. It was marvelous. Radios changed quickly and soon became firmly established in homes and social life.

Sister Amy was beginning to work as a domestic. She was in the employ of the Bishop of Jarrow. His home was in the Lake district of Cumberland. After a year or two she found employment as a nurse trainee in Shincliffe Isolation Hospital. She went to the hospital on Monday morning and would have to be there by 8:00 a.m.. Shincliffe is about five miles from Ushaw and I would take her in on the bicycle. She would stand on the back step with her hands on my shoulders. It was quite a go! I don't know how she could hang on so well only on one foot.

I recall Shincliffe quite vividly. The staff was composed of the caretaker and his wife who lived in the adjoining house. There were also a Matron and three nurses. Amy was one, and there were Lottie and Georgina. The two wings of the hospital and the property were walled in. The grounds were treed and there was a large lawn. I didn't know much about any aspect of the hospital operations until an epidemic of the Black Smallpox broke out in Durham Prison, a maximum security prison. There was a real scare as there were over five hundred inmates in the jail. As it happened, nineteen patients were taken from the prison to Shincliffe, eighteen men and one woman. Amy came home and said that the Matron was looking for someone to be on guard in the ward, 8:00 p.m. to 8:00 a.m..

Work at the pits was slack, so I went to see about the job. It didn't call for any experience and there were no qualifications, just somebody to be there and watch to see that the inmates didn't get away. I took the job. One reason I got the job was that I was vaccinated. So there I was with these unfortunate people stricken with smallpox. They were covered with black scabs over their bodies and faces. They were all in one ward, and they were very sick. There were great windows that could be opened onto the lawns. The windows had curtains to draw in the night. There was a large heater at the end of the ward nearest the door and nurses' lab. The nurses went home when off shift; only one remained in the building. The Matron had accommodation at the caretaker's lodge on the grounds near the entrance to the hospital grounds.

Before I went on shift, they wanted me to have a revolver. I said I wouldn't know what to do with it, as I'd never had or tried a real weapon. However, the sick were too ill to present a threat of escaping. Even if they wanted to, they couldn't just walk out of the place. So there they were, each in their own hospital bed, eighteen men and one woman, and they looked awful. Unsightly, is the word. It was wearisome. There were toilets and a bath on one side of the ward. The only time they were out of bed at night was when they went to the toilet. It was all a temporary situation until the time that other accommodations could be found, or until the epidemic was over.

There were no incidents of trying to escape from the hospital, but there were two separate occasions of attempts of suicide, both in the toilet and bathroom, but they were averted. It was difficult to try things like that when they were all using the one utility. One was the woman. She attempted to drown herself in the bathtub, poor soul. She was an awful sight, even to see herself in the mirror was a most distressing sight for her, covered as she was all over her face with black scabs. It all seemed so hopeless. There were occasions when the pillow covers had to be changed several times a night because of the discharge from their hideous sores on their faces. The beds were side by side, so of course they conversed with each other, usually about prison life and what they had done. I never heard any other topic all the time I was there. It seemed to be a world of their own, which possessed them. One was a youngish man. Many times he would talk in his sleep. He must have been in love for he used to continually call "Myra! Myra!" out loud in his dreams. It sadly occurred to me how imprisoned they were, not only in this building, but in outlook. There wasn't any light in their daily life; a brightness of expectation was hardly evident. It seemed to me that if one wasn't criminal-minded before going to jail, that having heard all of what appeared to be a sort of trade, then he would be criminal-minded when his prison term expired. Jail environment certainly promotes a way of life for those caught in its snare.

Throughout my school years my class standings were average or a little above. I always had enough marks to proceed to the next class. I was pretty fair at geography and history, average at sums, only fair at composition, a good speller and reader. The one thing where I did excel and definitely the thing I liked to do best was drawing. I was always with a pencil in my hand. Whether it was drawing black and whites, or painting, or pastel, my work would be selected. When I was between twelve and thirteen years of age, I joined two others and went to a painting class held at Esh Winning every Wednesday evening during the winter months. It cost one pence each time I went and three pence each way for the train ride there and back. This is where I started to oil paint. I took lessons for three years and did some work at home. I still have my starter box of paints. I was always reading about painters and looking at art work and galleries. My interest in nature is a joy to me, fascinating. I remember how we would be asked to take nature things to draw, like an ivy spray, a sprig of blackberry, flowers, cowslips and marigolds, or still-life objects like a shoe, kettles, a hat, or a cup and saucer. I would also copy out of the Graphic Magazine to help me with colour. So basically throughout my life I have found joy in nature and painting. I even took my box of paints through World War II, but being an infantryman it didn't allow me a chance to get anything done. I often wished I'd had time, though.

I still kept on painting when I got to Canada. It is something I've always been thankful for. I've never had a time when there was nothing to do; I would simply go and paint. It isn't work! Time gets lost. I think I paint landscapes just to evangelize the beauty of creation, the things we take so much for granted and rarely stop to see, let alone ponder. My philosophy is that we, me, mountains, rocks, rivers, trees, grass, soil, sky, clouds, are all the same, or at least related. All these things are more durable and constant than I, yet I understand insects, birds, fowl, fish and animals.

Uncle Thomas in Italy in WWI.

Sister Amy.

Mum in 1930.

Our football club. I'm front row centre.

CHAPTER THREE

The In-Between Years

After the war of 1914-18, as servicemen and women came home, the village began to become alive. In the club, all was well and Mother managed nicely until about 1921. In the club's operation was a club committee chairman, secretary, treasurer and a committee of fourteen. There were elections every year at the appointed time and qualified members could be nominated to stand for election. Up to this time the Secretary, Harry Holcombe, and John Hardman and a crew of committee men were all friendly and got along well. It was a happy situation. The odd time there would be trouble when a member would imbibe too freely. In these cases, unpleasant decisions had to be made. Mother, as manager, would have to say to an offender, "No more to drink!" So he wouldn't be served and most times would go home, or his pals would take him out. If a man had to be put out for the sake of the business, the committee men would be called to help. There was no great threat in this. Usually a member would be back to apologize next day or so. However, there were those who thought that a man steward would be preferable to a woman.

Nothing was brought up about replacing my mother until one Sunday evening a *returned* man was drinking at the bar. I was behind the bar helping Mum to serve drinks when this man, Rothman by name, seemed to get unruly for no apparent reason. Quite a few people were present. Then for some reason, best known only to himself, he began tossing pint pots at the club clock high on the east wall of the bar. There were some awful crashes and commotion and scattering of customers. It was believed sometime later that he was aiming at the German eagle atop the clock. Possibly the war and the reminder of it by the German eagle, along with a few too many beers, sent him temporarily berserk. I believe this was the beginning of a search for a man to run the club. It was difficult for Mum or me to do anything under such circumstances, or anyone else for that matter. But, nevertheless a new committee was nice but sorry, and on the pretext they wanted a change, my mother was given her termination as stewardess of the Albion club at Ushaw Moor.

In due time we moved from the Albion House and could only find upstairs rooms in a house at Broompark, two miles from Ushaw Moor. For my mother, this became a most unhappy time as she was in surroundings devoid of her usual life style. It was cramped quarters for Ernest and me. Amy was *at place* with the Bishop of Jarrow and was away most of the time in the Lakes District, and she came home only at intervals. Rob did not stay with the family at Broompark. He was very friendly with another boy, Norman Wright, whose parents lived at Ushaw colliery. Mr. Wright was a deputy overman at Ushaw pit. They persuaded my mother to let him stay with them, and he did. Rob and Norman played on the school football team, and Ushaw school boys had an excellent team at that time and won many trophies. Ernest rarely stayed at the place except for his meals. Mother, with Harry, was bottled up, upstairs. The woman downstairs was very uncooperative in many ways, mostly about using the facilities, such as washing. It was impossible to live around the house. I remember it nearly broke my heart to see Mum so unhappy. I hated the place! But we were there for two years.

Ernest played football for the Broompark local team. We would go on Saturday afternoons to watch them play in a farmer's field behind Love's Inn, the Pub. At this place there was also a handball court where many match contest games were played. Durham champions, the Mordue brothers who played for Sunderland Football Team found diversity, often playing in this court. I walked to Ushaw Moor practically every day. There was no work, only *dole*, which was eighteen pence a week.

Mum used to walk to Langley Moor, four miles away to draw a little social assistance. *Relief* she called it. This really hurt her pride as Mum was by nature a cheerful woman. We had a laugh one time when she was half a mile away from the house and discovered that she didn't have her skirt on. She always got a laugh out of that. Eventually we moved back to Station Road, Ushaw Moor Number 26, Amy was back to Durham, and Rob came home again.

In this house a new phase of life began for my mother, Jenny and the family. We were under one roof as it were, and Mum was like a broody hen caring for her chickens. Watson's Shop neighbours were on one side, and the Lewis's, who had an electric and appliance shop at the top of Station Road, were on the other side. At home were myself, Rob, Harry, and Amy, who was either away in domestic work, or at Langley Park Hospital. Ernest married Hilda Wood. Bennett, Mum's brother, married Mary Elsden and lived at New Brancepeth, Prince Place, with children Molly, Jacky, Bernard, Thomas and another little sister Jean. Thomas, Mum's brother lived at New Brancepeth, Unthank Terrace, with wife, Lizzie, and one son, Arthur, and an adopted girl, Joy. This was between 1921 and 1928.

I worked at Ushaw Moor colliery now in a job underground as a *datal* worker, that is, hourly pay, rather than *piece work*, which was typical for the miners. Brother Rob also worked at Ushaw. We both did shift work, so sometimes we would go to the mine at 4:00 a.m., *fore-shift*, or go at 9:00 a.m., *back-shift*, or 3:00 p.m. to 11:00 p.m., *night-shift*. And so five and a half days a week we worked in the mine. Harry was still going to school. Rob had been a good football player in his school days. He was *capped* and played for the Durham County Schoolboy Team, against Yorkshire. Harry also played for the Ushaw Moor Schoolboy Team and was an excellent player. After his school days he signed to be a professional member of the Hartlepool United Third Divisional Club in the English football league. I remember how proud I was of them, and went everywhere to see them play.

Our house at 26 Station Road was sort of a halfway house for the McEleavey family, there being no picture house like the Empire Theatre at Ushaw in Sleetburn. Consequently, there was a lot of walking traffic and every time the members of the McEleavey family came to Ushaw they called in to our house both coming and going. Though Bennett and Mary's family were like beautiful little urchins, we loved them. Arthur McEleavey, Thomas and Lizzie's boy was often at our house too. He was a cheerful funny lad, always the life of the party. We had a Master's Voice Gramophone. He loved to dance and we went to dances frequently with Sister Amy. I remember every Friday night at the Ushaw Memorial Hall there were whist drives and dances. There were one-steps, two-steps, waltzes, barn dances and other sequence dances. Just about that time, the *Tango* became very popular. He would tango to *Sunny Havanna, California Here I Come* and *What'll I Do*. The Strauss Waltzes were always favorites.

Sometimes we'd go to the Globe Theatre in Durham to see the picture show. One Saturday evening when we were watching a black-and-white picture there was a strong smell of burning. Of course, smoking was allowed anywhere, but this strong smell of smoke was not from a cigarette or pipe. And it wasn't kipper this night, as was often a student prank. However, we thought it was some joker having fun and it was near the end anyway, so we came out, and when we got outside, Arthur's pants were smouldering. He had on these Oxford Bags, and when one sat down they caused folds. Somehow a cigarette end had gotten into the fold and Arthur's pants had a large hole in them between the knee and the hip. The smell was like a burning blanket. He was a great talker about recent movies which were always popular in those times.

Some famous movies of those days, like *Way Down East* with the Pish

Sisters, had terrific runs. I remember queuing up for them. Doug Fairbanks Sr. was an outstanding star, with Mary Pickford and also Rudy Valentino in *The Sheik of Araby*. Bing Crosby, was becoming popular, as was Bob Hope. Girls' hair was *bobbed* or shingled. Men were always clean shaven with short hair. Arthur had beautiful curly hair, and was so popular with the girls. On the busses coming home, he was a riot; everyone knew him. He was part of our daily life.

About this time a village recreation area was laid out in the area where we lived behind Station Road. It became a football field, a soccer field, one bowling green, two tennis courts and a cricket pitch. These were the same fields where we used to fly kites and look for mushrooms. Sometimes it was called Benny Beach field because he was a fruiterer and fielded horses there. Now it was the Recreation Grounds, and I remember its many pleasantries, particularly the tennis courts. There was a private tennis court down at the old football ground, but it had a closed membership. I remember watching them play many times when we went to see football games. I would always go to watch them play tennis in their white flannels and dress. It seemed to be lots of fun, so when the new recreation ground tennis opened to the public, I, along with Syd Rhodes, John Nelson and others, got to play. School teachers Ray and Carr also joined until there were quite a lot to form a new club, so that we could play matches and in tournaments. I remember it was proper to wear white flannels when playing tennis. For us pit lads it was as difficult to get tennis garb as it had been to get boy scout uniforms. The first item I needed was a pair of white shoes, for these got me onto the court once I'd saved up to buy a racket.

Mum kept me cleanly dressed for whatever games we did have. We lads were enthusiastic and played for fun or in matches. The one great thrill that remains with me was when a match was arranged to play against a team from the old closed club. It had existed for years and the members had much experience. It was men's doubles and mixed doubles to maximize participation. What we upstarts lacked in finesse we made up for by enthusiasm and sweat. For doubles, one member played the net and one played back. There seemed to be a lot of stops in this match. I don't know whether they thought of showing us how to play or us showing them that we could play; but it was exciting. We were definitely the underdogs who barely knew the etiquette of the game. But we toppled the pros, sort of. However, a good relationship resulted. After a year or so the old club folded and all tennis at Ushaw was played at the *Rec*. In the pavilion was a large central area where table tennis was played. This became a great favourite pastime. The recreation ground provided me involvement in several sports and I became acquainted with how to play, to win, and to lose in sports, for which I've always been thankful. The *Rec* really broadened the concept of community.

School teachers, Mr. Ray and Mr. Carr, gave prestige to the new recreation club and organized much fellowship for us lads. In those days, after recreation games, there used to be a lot of gatherings at the Station Hotel in Davidson's billiard room. There was not much drinking there, but it was a popular place because of the snooker, billiards, keen competition and really good matches. The camaraderie was great; everyone knew everyone and sometimes four or five of us would go for walks along Broompark Road to Browning and back via Bearpark or around the Ushaw College park. One particular walk was along Durham Road, past Broompark Village to Hill's Farm house. Here the road crossed over the main north and south railway system. We would stand for hours on this bridge with its commanding view of the express trains and goods traffic. We made special note of the famous Pullman coaches travelling from London to Edinburgh through Durham and Newcastle. Syd Rhodes was particularly interested in all railway engines and had a great collection of them on cards. It was natural for him, being engineer-minded. He finally became a winding engineer at Holton colliery.

Life was casual during 1921 through 1926. Work was spasmodic. The government of Lloyd George was in power. Unemployment was rampant, and was so bad that the government brought in an unemployment insurance plan. Contributions were imposed upon employer and worker to finance the scheme, but unemployment was so rife that there were practically no funds and the country fell into huge debt. The unemployment plan became known as the *Dole*. To us, and miners in general, it was little to get by on. At slack times one went *on the dole*. One lined up in huge queues as the mine owners got tougher at keeping expenses down. To get the *dole*, one had to produce names of six potential firms or employers, with signed statements saying the claim was authentic, before receiving the eighteen pence. This became an awful burden for a dole recipient because after a few weeks the circle of potential employers widened into miles of walking, and there was no money for shoes. So it seemed natural to be inventive when putting together new lists as it just was not practical and caused cheating. Bad laws inevitably are conducive to bad things for people. This was a weekly nightmare. Work was not possible and completely unavailable. The pits were down and there was no other employment, Durham being a coal field. However, human nature being what it is, like all other living things, will struggle to live by any means. So one scrimped by, growing one's own stuff on allotment, raising a chicken or two, living hand-to-mouth. It cost two pence for a picture show, a half pence for a paper packet of five woodbine cigarettes, and three pence for a haircut.

I recollect that in those days getting married as a teenager was very rare. Young people courted and went out together, but weddings didn't happen early. One had to be in late teens to be old enough to go to dances. We used to have a tennis dance annually. We played tennis or danced, then walked home together. We were not old enough to enter a place where beer or alcohol was served until reaching the age of twenty-one. Then it was time to leave home, find a wife and make a home for oneself. In the teenage activities there was a lot of mixing. Young people coupled themselves off, going together, getting friendly and enjoying life, all from home. I remember quite a lot of my acquaintances, Syd

Rhodes, Bella, Billy Simpson, Dorothy Ward, John Willis, Annie Rowe, Norman Young, Bella Raines, Jim Hogg, Fred Hogg, Fred Parkinson, Ray and Carr and their wives.

At about this time, St. Luke's Church got a new vicar, Vicar Welby. He used to go to all parishioners' homes to see how they were faring and to say a little prayer. He was a quiet, refined man and people liked him. I know I did. He was so educated and seemed to know something about anything one would like to talk about. He knew eleven languages, including Latin and Greek. Since he was educated at Oxford University, we wondered why he came to a coal mining village. He was a devout man of the cloth. He also had spent three years on the river Orinoco in South America. Although single at first, he later married the church organist, Jennie Brown. He started a reading class at his library at the Vicarage, Ladysmith Terrace. Jim Hogg, Tommy Clarke, Jack Walker, Tom Hudson and others joined. We would go once a week on Mondays and study a book. One was The Yellow Peril, about China. His place was full of wonderful books. He let us go there whenever we wanted to read. He undoubtedly changed me. He put some purpose into my life, which I was thinking was sort of aimless, although Syd Rhodes and I used to talk often about going abroad. I think he changed all our lives. Tommy Clarke later became a bishop.

We also had a young men's club at the church under the leadership of Harry Kipling. I spent hours there. It was like an exercise club, with horizontal bars, rings, parallel bars, Indian clubs, soccer, cricket, table tennis and gymnastics. I remember that I used to be on an exhibition team for *swinging clubs*, and on the football team. One night I had a mishap while swinging on the rings to the horizontal bar. I missed and fell to the floor on my head. There was no mat and I was stunned for an hour before I came to, but I was dazed for a couple of hours. I remember how concerned they were about it. Forged friendships resulted out of all these associations. Being baptized when I was a baby, I was as yet not confirmed, so I went to the Reverend Welby's confirmation class. He was nice to be with. Years after this event, even after I came to Canada, he sent me a yearly remembrance card of my confirmation. He remained at Ushaw Moor until his death.

I loved the village and I loved the miners, but I was never happy with pit work. I did not have the physical make up and never accepted or felt happy going down the mine, but I didn't have much choice. A person must work, of course, but I couldn't be a miner as a miner should be. Oftentimes on our walks around the beautiful countryside, Syd Rhodes and I would romance about going abroad to some far off country. Even so, it was hardly realistic, as we had no other trade and working as a pit man wasn't a trade as such.

Prior to 1926 there was union trouble, about wages mostly, but other conditions too, especially concerning safety and health. Work was always precarious in those days. Politics were entering into the economy and labour was organized into a Trade Union Council, (T.U.C.), a nationwide effort of workers. The politicians, conservative and liberal, were opposed to labour organizing into a political body. There were accusations that the new labour party was backed by Russian Communism. There was, as I remember, a famous or infamous letter called the Zinovive letter, which was said by opposition parties to be some sort of proof of connection with communistic ideals. I was too young in politics to know what it was all about. But this much I do know, there was a conflict arising in the workers' world of my time, and it surfaced in 1926, when a general strike came about, shutting down all T.U.C. members. Coal-miners, Transport, just about everything the country depended upon was shut down. It was uncanny. There began to be trouble where some non-union workers would clash, but as I recall it was not widespread.

So the mine fields were on strike, the pits shut down, and I was one of those affected. The miners had a slogan, "Not a penny off the pay and not a minute on the day." I didn't know much about objectives, concepts or what it was all about except what the slogan said. Anyhow, after three weeks of uncanny calm, the general strike ended. All other factions of the T.U.C. went back to work, except the coal miners. They stayed out on strike, and it lasted thirteen months. A year and a month the pits were shut down. It was weird in a sense. There was a lot of belt tightening. I cannot recollect that there were many confrontations, but there was a lot being done.

Soup kitchens were started for miners' children under fourteen years. Each day their mothers would go with them over to New Brancepeth where the centre was set up. There was no strike pay, no social welfare. Everyone did as best they could to survive. To keep the home-fires burning, the men mostly went to the slag heaps at the mines to find coal from waste from the mine called the *pit heap*. They would take their sacks and little hammers to separate coal from stone. There would be scores of fathers, sons and wives helping to get these precious bags of coal. Sometimes if they found a good spot they would leave a person there to hold possession of it as if it were gold. The heap of course was a giant mound of colliery *tippings* throughout the life period of the mine. Incidently, these pit heaps were the blight of the landscape at every mine shaft. Wherever one saw a mine one saw a *pit heap* where the whole coal field became a source of supply in times of a strike. In a mild way, the authorities tried to discourage these gleanings from their property, but never were able to stop them. There had been some enterprising individuals who would gather sacks to sell. That was frowned upon by authorities and others who only wanted coal for their own needs. It seems a truth about people that there will always be those who take advantage for self and spoil for others. But again there were those who would give away a sack to widowed households. Sometimes we would get up early in the morning and seek for mushrooms in the farmers fields before he got around, and pick the hedges for blackberries. Turnip fields got raided near the roadside.

It was common to scrape up horse droppings from the road with a little shovel and pail. Whenever there was a prolonged stoppage at the mines, they would bring the pit ponies to *bank* (surface). This was the only time they ever saw daylight after entering the mine. So there was a pit field where scores of pit ponies ran free. The authorities did not mind the men and boys exercising these animals. I remember one especially, he was so small that when one sat on his back one's feet dragged on the ground. But there was plenty of activity. Races or gallops were organized. It was a real field day to be at old Ushaw to see the fun they had with these horses. Some had gone blind from being down in the pit so long. There used to be a saying when one asked a pit lad what he did when down in the coal mines. One might get a smart answer such as, "washing the stable windows!" Underground were a stable and a horse keeper. Ponies had to be allocated to their various boys and places of work. This job fell mostly to the boys just beginning their mining career. The horse keeper was responsible for the horses and stables. Horses are unique in that they have a particular sense of danger. I remember a young driver down the Victoria Seam where I worked who, while going to and fro pulling full tubs out to the landing and taking empty ones back, had his little pony stop with his two tubs hitched on. There didn't seem to be any reason why the little animal could not go. The lad thought the pony had gotten obstinate and wouldn't move in spite of all urging. He was about to use some force on the blighter when a few yards down the track, the roof caved in. Had the pony not stopped, he would have been right underneath the falling stone and perhaps would have been killed. This pony had sensed danger, which was why he stopped and refused to move.

The strike was a really long, drawn-out experience of having nothing. Why such things have to be beats me, except that without protest there doesn't seem to be any progress. Certainly, mine owners did what they wanted to do within their own mines, for it was a business and they employed people to make a profit. They would seek coal that was the most profitable and not mine coal that couldn't show a profit. So the mine was not properly mined for its full resources. Private ownership went for instant and easy profit, leaving the hard-to-get coal as a wasted resource. Mining was somewhat like raiding an apple tree and going only for the juicy ones. Primitive or early logging firms did this with forests, cutting away little and medium trees just to get the big ones. *Plundering* is a good word for this kind of working of a national resource.

Ushaw Moor was a Peace and Partner's mine. They owned eleven coal mines but only nine of them made a profit. The two borderline operations were to be closed and when they closed the pit gates at Ushaw Moor, they wrote on them "No Work Today." Nobody asked what you were going to do now. You walked back home with your bite and bottle. This threw you *on the dole*. At that time I became a labour follower politically. There had to be some protection from the whims of people who used you for profit. So after the strike, the pits became worse off than when the strike started. It was apparently all for naught, but not exactly. A labour government of Ramsey McDonald was elected and changes came, however slowly. So life picked up where it had left off. In the meantime, I had written to some mining people in Brazil, South America for a job, but unsuccessfully. I tried for Australia, too, but had no references. So an opportunity for some change in my life came when reading the local paper one day in July 1928. This evening paper had in it a little advertisement, "Harvest Help Wanted, Now. In Canada." The ad gave all the conditions, and appeared an exciting adventure. The first impression from my friends was "WOW! Let's go!" Although Englishmen are always dubious about leaving their country, the idea of a good jaunt made a positive response in me and a few others.

I recall a group of us lads used to hover around the Top Shop. This was a temperance bar in a convenient place opposite to the Empire Theatre, almost at the cross-roads of the Durham Road and the Bearpark, New Brancepeth Road, a busy corner. It was a sort of haunt or meeting place, to hang around watching, fooling and waiting for something to happen. It was kept by the Lowerys. There were Joe, Billy and Jacky and Jacky's wife, Lizzy. They were very nice people and popular with the younger people.

At home, I discussed this adventure with my family. I was very interested in going. It seemed like a chance for something other than the pits, even if just for a time. My mother was against my going, fearing she wouldn't see me again. However, I was determined to try my luck, so I went and got the papers and signed my willingness to go. Eventually there were four of us committed to going: myself, Buller, Lightfoot Ralph Rowlands and Teasdale. All four of us would leave from Durham Railway Station after getting there by bus from Ushaw Moor. There were hundreds to see the bus off. I had said goodbye to my family. Mum was very upset and crying, but the crowd was in a jovial frame of mind and made much of us. Lizzy Lowery gave me a box of goodies. My belongings were all in my portmanteau. Mother had thought of everything that I might need, even to needle and thread. There were all kinds of "don't go." It was a wild country they said, with wild Indians. And it was so cold that people froze to death. It was like I was preparing to leave the world. I was really, their world of the pits. Vicar Welby knew better. He told me of times he had been in Canada and other countries and as he spoke of the wonders of the world it was reassuring to me. I recollect he gave me a Canadian one-dollar bill which I kept for a long time before I had to use it. But I have often wished that I'd never parted with it. It was an early confederation, new condition large specimen. I didn't know the value of antiquities then.

We left Durham Railway Station at 11:40 p.m.. The station was packed. It was like the leaving of an army. I suppose it was, really. We took a special harvester train, and the goodbyes were heartbreaking to some; to others, this was the start of an adventure. I had never seen anything like it. The aim was to have ten thousand harvesters and there were that many going. The four of us from Ushaw were supposed to sail from Liverpool on the Franconia, but a last-minute switch changed us to Southampton to the fourteen-thousand-ton ship, Auronia. This hurried change turned into something else when we faced those who signed us up. We were told gruffly that we might need blankets, that we would never get beyond Winnipeg, wherever that was; that our contract was only for them to get us to the designated place, work thirty days in the harvest field, and to get the farmer's signature on the form provided for validation, and that would enable one to return to England. This was the contract and it was a must. Fair enough, I thought: taken out free, brought back free, if fulfilling the conditions. So we had all the signed forms for emigration authorities and identification. It was still dark, 5:30 a.m., when we arrived in London. I had never been away from home before, and had never been to the south of England. Everything was new to me and I was green.

My worldly possessions were in my portmanteau, along with one pound, four shillings and a few pennies. We would be fed on the ship, and allowed vouchers for train food in Canada. That was good; my money wouldn't have gotten me far. The journey down to Southampton on a packed train was a raucous experience. People yelled, shouted, played cards, and gambled. I got a seat and stayed put. It was all so different for me and I was timid, at least not so sure of myself in anything.

We detrained at Waterloo at 6:30 a.m., and had to wait for the boat train at 10:00 a.m.. This gave us a fair chance to see a bit of London. We viewed the Houses of Parliament from Waterloo Bridge, a most magnificent view. We saw Trafalgar Square and the Strand, the Thames River and London Bridge, plus various other places. We left Waterloo for Southampton, which was a pleasant journey, and arrived at 12:30. After an hour and a half of tedious handling of passports, we boarded the Auronia. From her decks we saw three wonderful ships: the Majestic, the Leviathan and the Mauritania.

Auronia weighed anchor at 4:10 p.m. on August 13, 1928. It was a wonderful sight as we sailed down the channel past the Isle of Wight and the Needles, then branched off for Cherbourgh, landing at 11:00 p.m.. There we took on seventy-eight Frenchmen.

Reverend John Welby, became rector of Saint Luke's Church, Ushaw Moor, Durham, England in the 1920s

The four Harvesters from England and Scotland in 1928. I'm second from the right.

CHAPTER FOUR
Life as a Canadian Harvester

MY FIRST MIXING WITH THE STRANGE FRATERNITY of harvesters convinced me they were a rough bunch, but I soon learned that they were generally of good humour. Along with the others, Buller and I were allotted a small berth containing two bunks on one side, with the other side being only the curved frame of the ship. Close to the bunks was a small cabinet with a wash stand. There were also two life belts. After loading our baggage, one grip each, we decided to have a look around the ship. The berth next to ours was occupied by a quartet of Londoners who we were soon to learn were a raucous gang. Next, we discovered that the after part of the ship below decks was in a most disturbed state. Baggage, grips and men were in general confusion. Even when in one's own berth, boisterous singing or vulgar swearing over improvised card tables prevented any attempt at peacefulness.

Since there were four of us from one locality, naturally that tie bound us together as companions. Buller, being a wild type of character, confided in me that he held about thirty shillings, but his fever for card playing, particularly pontoon, rendered his total financial possessions somewhat unstable. My own credits amounted to twenty-five shillings. Our other confederates, Ralph Teasdale and A. Rowland, two small but stocky fellows, made up our party.

The first sitting for a meal was a somewhat exciting affair. The nature of the unruly passengers, combined with crying stomachs, inclined to worry the harassed stewards. These stewards had my deepest sympathy. I don't expect they ever had such a bunch to deal with before. I don't say the fellows were bad, only unreasonable, and the great demand for various things brought forward all their animal instincts. Yet, a full stomach generally made them amiable, sometimes even charming.

We sometimes had community singing, which in my opinion was remarkable for its spiritual value. We sang songs and hymns of every description. These sittings were required to pacify and serve these healthy appetites. My own emotions were far from peaceful, for the effort of leaving home, departing from the ones I loved, and the things that meant everything in the world to me and really tore at my heart-strings. But I was too busy to think of much except my own immediate affairs as the land that I loved had faded out of my sight, perhaps forever. I was conscious again of what England, home, mother, and a hundred-and-one different little things had meant to me. Leaving them shook my very soul.

The soothing of my soul came only after pondering the actions of the last day or two. I realized, with a startling stab of joy, the beautiful scene before my eyes, and from the ship's deck I was reassured and uplifted. I rejoiced as I gazed with a sense of peace at the glorious blue of the sea, the beauty of old Mother Earth, the small and large ships all around, and the soar of silver gulls. I saw the King in this beauty and was filled with contentedness. I rolled into my bunk that night, wondering what the future held, but entirely unafraid of the possibilities.

On the second day out, *mal-de-mer* became acute, both in me and many others. The first symptom of this malady was amusing. After breakfast, we decided to adjourn to the *well*, or the card room. It also served as a liquor counter. Things were always confusing in this room because of gambling and drinking. However, after first visiting the well for various commodities, we settled down to our would-be quiet corner for a game of whist. The first hand was just being lifted, and we three,

Buller, Teasdale and I, having arranged our cards, were watching Rowland, waiting for him to bid. But Rowland's mind was far away from cards. He turned quite pale, his eyes became dull, he laid his cards down quietly but uncertainly, and staggered toward the deck-rail. This incident provoked much laughter amongst us, but alas, we, also in turn found it wasn't a laughing matter, for the next day we same four sat on deck for sixteen hours in a very sorry plight.

Aside from the seasickness, our voyage was most interesting. We saw many icebergs and other remarkable scenery. Our first glimpse of Belle-Isle was awe inspiring. The beautiful cruise of two days up the St. Lawrence river to Quebec lulled my brain and lifted my being with a soothing feeling of happiness. I was on a ship, but felt as if I were soaring up in fairy land. Heaven is within, but thank God for the window through which we catch relationships with each other. Senses are gifts by which the soul understands; consciousness is the critic of the soul. The soul is at the mercy of consciousness. Only the wonderful mystery of what I am is shouting to the Lord. God is all! Leaving the Heavens and sea behind again, we come to Earth. I cannot imagine Columbus being any happier than I was when my feet touched down on good old *terra ferma* at Quebec.

We were denied a survey of Quebec, which was very disappointing considering it was one of the most historic places in direct touch with our own people. The most notable thing for us first-time visitors was the eternal and infernal clanging of bells. It struck me that the churches must have their services early, as it was only 4:00 p.m., but later I found that their railway engines also had bells attached, tolling their warnings.

There was great confusion in Quebec station. The demand for provisions for the forthcoming train journey was more like a panic. Harvesters cudgelled their brains and pockets for any supply of money. However, the wily French held the day for *made-up parcels*, which they sold for one dollar. They were very mysterious about their contents. We, however, made a bill of such commodities as we thought would be sufficient, then pooled our efforts for a price. The price was one dollar and fifty cents each, but the supplies were justified.

Puffing out from Quebec at 4:30 p.m. on the train, we were enroute for what proved to be a most arduous journey. We rolled through the province of Quebec and viewed it as a series of woods and lakes with such persistency as to make the land seem drab and cheerless. We had lots of company and noise en route. The train stopped at every little station. Immediately all of us would alight to stretch our legs, even if only for ten minutes. We made twenty miles per hour, which was remarkable for the rough state of the railway.

After two days and nights, we reached Winnipeg. The arrangements for these 1928 harvesters were actually quite good. Winnipeg, being the spot of gravitation for nomadic, would-be farmers, was alive with officials and officialdom. I had often watched sheepdog trials back home and marvelled at the skill and tact of the Collies, but in Winnipeg the officials outdid them. They worked with exceedingly great skill and patience. We were next transferred to the C.P.R. depot after receiving our allotted destination. Mine was a place called Kincaid, Saskatchewan. I might state here that those back home who were handling this trip were not very well versed with what would be happening. One of the answers they gave the harvesters was that they probably would not get beyond Winnipeg. Canada is a bigger country than even they were aware of.

My destination was seven-hundred miles west of Winnipeg. Buller and I were to stay in Winnipeg overnight. The station floor was a little hard, but preferable to the unclean immigration places. We had a little spare time in Winnipeg and decided to have a look around. After travelling so far along the street, a car pulled up alongside and an old country fellow and his *missus* invited us into the car and showed us around town. Such friendliness bucked us to no end; it was great. Then it was back to the railway station, settling in to sleep on the floors. Later, the weather became very dull with thunder and lightening. Then came a frightening rain storm the like of which I had never experienced. Anyway, we survived and next morning we boarded a westbound train for Kincaid, all four of us still together. This in itself was a consolation. We had our doubts and fears about what was going to happen to us. However, we agreed to stick together as far as possible as we only had our lives to lose.

The great wheat belt went on around us, miles and miles of seas of wheat. We had many advisors who could see that we were just in and looking particularly green. Some praised Canada, some otherwise. Our own opinion wasn't very optimistic, although we were spurned by the industrial chaos we had left behind. I had lots of time for meditation and often thought of the funniest subjects. It was a very long train ride to Kincaid. We stopped for change and had to spend the night in Weyburn. It was 8:00 p.m. and we wandered around this village for a while. Finally we decided to see a show. They called it Pantages, a sort of turns and variety show. The four of us sat midway down, with me on the outside end. The performance didn't seem very interesting, so I turned to remark to some of my pals. All were leaning forward, heads down on their arms, fast asleep. I dwelled on the question of why we should come six thousand miles to find work. It seemed so important and here we were blown away like chaff on the wind, to where we knew not, except the name Kincaid.

Every station saw a few more wayfarers step from the train into space, just away, never more for us to see. It seemed providence must take care of us all. As they went up the platform out of sight, my heart went to them. I seemed to understand that providence was our mainstay and relied absolutely on God's mercy. The country at this time of the year was inspiring for its wonderful sunsets over the golden fields. We rumbled into Kincaid at 3:00 p.m., weary and fatigued, thirteen of us in all.

So this was Kincaid. At least I believed that was what we were all thinking, judging by our inquisitive glances and stock-taking of our surroundings, which were not by any means inspiring. Still, Kincaid was our destination. It had so filled our minds in the past forty-eight hours that we were relieved at being there. Our spirit of adventure had been mostly spent, long before we reached the place. As we sauntered from the Kincaid station, we must have looked a fantastic lot, for we were the targets of all who had gathered at the station. These people were so isolated that the arrival of a train was an event. I guess our melancholy expressions, strange apparel, and green English appearance hung around us like a shroud and struck them as gapingly interesting. However, advice was asked for and given, and we were steered to the municipal office where we trusted our fortunes were to be cast.

Kincaid was a small village of four hundred people, surrounded by farms and farmers that we were to help. The clerk in charge was soon on the telephone with the outlying farmers and our services were engaged at remarkable swiftness. Courtesy and kindness were bestowed upon us. We were helped in every possible way to be placed and transferred to our various destinations. This was the first parting of the ways for us four harvesters. Rowland was placed to the east, Buller, Ralph and me, to the north. The farm allocated to Buller and me was fourteen miles north of Kincaid and Ralph's was twelve miles north. It was impossible for the farmer to come for us that night, and no transport was leaving, so the municipal authorities found us a kind lady who provided bed and breakfast. Now relieved of the awful suspense, we breathed in the air of adventure and hope. Rowland left for his destination, taking his leave stoically, and we all felt the parting. Then we had our first opportunity to look over the little town.

Kincaid was a town covering an area of about one quarter of a square mile. All buildings were wooden structures, the residences being scattered about. The main street ran east and west and was approximately two-hundred yards, or two city blocks, long. This was the business section which contained two chinese cafes, a general store, a drug store, a picture show and five grain elevators which distinguish a town because they can be seen at a considerable distance. After such observances we located the shack which was to be our shelter for the night. The lady made a fuss about us, literally storming us with questions about the Old Country, being Welsh herself. She was definitely the more dominant of a happily married couple. It seemed that the husband had long ago been reduced to a reconcilable silence. He was the postman, officially, and the odd-job man about town. Generally his mode of conveyance was an automobile, although whether it was an antediluvian Rolls Royce or a prehistoric Ford, I never did know. Its signs and symptoms, both of a traction engine and a steam engine, snorted like a fiery beast, quivered and convulsed like a sick dog, although it went okay. I had to admire these people; they made do. Thankful for a good night's rest, and heartened by an appetizing breakfast, all attempts at remuneration thwarted, we were eventually aboard a truck for a fourteen-mile, bumpy ride to Mr. Haist's Farm.

The vast extensiveness of the countryside was breathtaking and amazing to us strangers. The landscape was dotted with farmsteads. The roads, like all the roads except the main highways, were graded wagon tracks, rough in dry weather, and almost impassable when wet. Wheat was ripened and unending, miles upon miles of golden heads. The golden wheat, the light blue of the cloudless sky, and the burning sun all made it seem as if we were nothing in ourselves. I think we wished that we were back home.

After a series of exciting episodes and heroic attempts to hold on to our grips, we reached the man who was to be our host farmer. Coming up the side of a field, or half-section, was a tractor engine drawing behind it a *binder*; it was far distant and we saw it before we heard it. It was a pretty sight to see them crawling along, the flashing of the binder as it cut and bound, and then threw out a golden bundle of wheat. I thought it worthy of a brush. We stopped, awaiting their arrival. The man who had driven us up yelled to the farmer, "Hello! Hello! these are the two Englishmen that you said you could do with."

"All right, come on, jump on here," he said, meaning the tractor. So we descended from the truck and scrambled aboard the tractor, grip, overcoat and all. We must have cut an interesting figure with our blue suits, our cricket white shirts, our caps, and an overcoat over our arms. An English cap is a *brand* in Canada. Anyway, there we were aboard a John Deere tractor, sitting on the fender, holding on as best we could. I hardly had time to see how Buller was faring as we set in motion. I soon became very apprehensive. The terrific vibration unseated me frequently and the large teeth on the massive wheels came uncomfortably near. Glancing again at Buller, I noticed he was in no better position and was hanging on for dear life. After a dangerous half mile in which conversation was impossible, the farmer finally stopped the tractor and told us to jump down.

By now, the sun was extremely hot, far hotter than we had ever experienced. In fact, our calling in England as coal miners made us more or less accustomed to being shut off from the sun. Consequently, we felt the burning rays awfully uncomfortable. And these endless bundles of cut and tied wheat were laying, it seemed to us, eternal. They stretched as far as the eye could see. To the farmer, it was usual. Finally, he asked us if we had ever done any *stooking*. Of course, we replied in the negative. So Mr. Haist, the farmer, who by the way had one arm paralysed, and his binder man named Allan, proceeded to demonstrate how to *stook*. After taking particular notice, we had to try. Then he pointed out his farm buildings, which seemed a few miles away, and left us to the *stooking*. That word I shall *never* forget, but it should have been *stooping*.

This seemed a strange period in our lives, at least in mine. There we were after six thousand miles of travel, left on a prairie amid a sea of wheat sheaves, with our coats and grips, the sun almost unbearable. The temperature was eighty-five to ninety degrees, and our mouths soon became parched. However, we set to with bare hands to build *stooks*. We worked conscientiously, although thoroughly inadequately equipped for the binder twine that reddened and almost cut our hands. Thistles tortured us, the sun was most unmerciful, and the immense quantity to be *stooked* saddened our hearts. Each of us at that moment undoubtedly rued our adventure.

Mr. Haist proved to be a gentleman, although rough, unshaven, ragged, and almost at poverty's door. Nevertheless, he was a gentleman, in the good sense of the word. Allan, his helper, did all that he could for us, too. Eventually, midday arrived and we walked together to a ramshackle building which served as the home of these seemingly primitive people. What had struck me most was the kindness by which we had been received. We were treated with every possible courtesy. We noted that the people were of one class. It was refreshing to find oneself treated as a person, regardless of worth or wealth. Master-servant did not exist in Canada where Democratics or Socialists didn't matter. So we *stooked* for a trying week, having acquired protection for hands and from the sun.

This is where I found a step in life. One needs such circumstances to prove oneself. We were among strangers, far away from loved ones, far from the accustomed conditions of moderate climate, and in a burning prairie. We were also away from a set time schedule of working hours in a land where people worked from sunup to sundown. We were away from a land of sporting recreations to a land of essential work, and we were homesick, wishing we were back in England. We yearned for our friends and customs. The things that we left behind now became lovely, and for the first time in my life the once "hell hole" of our town of upbringing seemed a little bit of heaven. And to think, I had to come six thousand miles to find that out. In my quiet moments, thoughts of Vicar Welby would come to me. I am sure that my association with the Vicar and the church and the Christian way of life prepared me for the things that befell me during this undertaking.

After ten days, we managed to obtain a newspaper and read of the large number of 1928 harvesters wanting to be returned home. They stormed the immigration authorities, and stole rides on freight trains. A crowd, with some of whom I was acquainted, actually started to walk from Moose Jaw to Montreal, a distance of two thousand miles. They were panic stricken; the country and conditions frightened them. They were, I believe, more afraid of themselves. I think some of their trouble was in being unprepared, both for the job and also with inner strength.

The next most interesting experience in store for us was threshing. For two days following *stooking*, Mr. Haist acquired a crew, consisting of four teamsters, two field pitchers, one separator man, one person to haul grain, and himself on the power engine. This is where I found the extreme cosmopolitan nature of the province of Saskatchewan. I discovered that apart from our own place and the immediate neighbour, we were the only ones of British descent. People amongst the adjacent farms were a gathering of Russian, Polish, Czechs, Slavs, Yugoslavs, German, French, Norwegians, Swedes, Serbians and Americans. Our particular crew, drawn from neighbours, was made up of German, Czech, Yugoslav, French, two Canadians and we two Englishmen, along with Mr. Haist, a German-born Canadian. Strange as it seems, after a week, we harmonized and worked in a perfectly happy state, against the odds that four languages were spoken at the same table. Although we could only speak English, the Yugoslav knew only Yugoslavian, the German spoke Yugoslavian, Mr. Haist spoke German and English, the Frenchman spoke some English, so that each had one another and interpreted their conversations. Each at first was silent and dubious. There was a veil and a constraint which only the meal table broke down. The Breaking of Bread around the table, whether the various differences are racial, economical, or religious, provided sincere *give-and-take*. A round table and a broad mind could be a salvation for hosts of estrangements.

The first week of threshing was a severe test for me. We worked from 4:00 a.m. until 7:00 or 8:00 p.m., with blistered hands and skin and sunburned faces. Alkaline water, of which I drank gallons, raised havoc on one's internal organs. And the mosquitoes! I lay for nights on end without sleep. I cried and prayed, and soon became soothed. My hands toughened, with my determination, or inner strength. Now was my time of probation. We grow in adversity. Never would this country defeat me.

Never would I fail my country. When in the boy scouts at home, we had a motto which read, "Grin and Bear It." That helped me now. To those who know it not, an Englishman didn't have an auspicious bearing in Canada. In some places, opinion is extremely anti-English and *Green Englishman* was a by-word, spoken sometimes with venom.

But we stuck it out. Buller seemed not to have as bad a time as me, physically. He was stronger, more fresh, although I believed that he was fighting a losing battle spiritually. Many a time he would say to me, "I wish I had my sixty dollars." That was the return fare. We had to fulfill thirty days to gain fare home. Buller was a great fellow. He often thought of his wife and family, his parents too. My people were also in my mind. Naturally we were lonesome, homesick and weary. There was one consolation; we had each other for the time being. This again emphasizes the need for spiritual training in emigration. One battles within oneself. No one trains people how to deal with these elements, but they are far more real than any outward struggle. It is better that one conquer oneself, with self discipline. I found the teachings of Vicar Welby and the belief in Jesus Christ within my heart to be of great support, especially in these lonely times. Jesus is a faithful companion who not only soothes one's troubles but reveals happiness. He sort of opens the windows of one's being and lifts us above the earth, causing us to look down on it with wonderment, and sometimes with sadness. Jesus knows the whys and wherefores. There is only one life, regardless of where that may be. There is no weakness in Christ. There is no strength in a person without Him. He shows Himself in greatness everywhere. These were the thoughts I lived by.

The routine became less arduous as we got used to it. To some, it was a matter of putting in hours. The day became to them a dull, tedious affair. To me, the world was becoming more wonderful. I was beginning to live, even to enjoy and look forward to the next dawn. My days were full of life. The divergence of the strange countrymen with whom we were mixing; the wheat; the horses; the machines; the coyotes at night;

the bath every week; the wonderment on the faces of the central Europeans when they congregated to see us have a *cold tub*, stripped to the waist. We were harvesting a part of the world's bread.

The trip to town every Saturday night, bumping, racing, flying, scorching across the prairie, with no fences, was fascinating. What amazing greatness! One seems as nothing in the vastness, then one can see further. The mind broadens, the eternal wind and zephyrs are electrifying, blowing a sense of unshakable freedom. One seems to have shaken off shackles. When breathing the fresh air the world becomes or is seen from a different angle. I don't know, nor can I put into words an adequate expression of a thrilling sense of something which one breathes; it is in the very atmosphere. Jump in an old Ford and off everywhere, no one minds; all is taken for granted in this great country.

After one month, Ralph Teasdale and Rowland, who came from Ushaw Moor, took their leave for the homeland. They had fulfilled their thirty days. They had worked for a farmer a few miles from where we were. Their departure affected and weakened Buller. Then one day, after having received a letter from home, he broke the news to me that he was going home. His father was sick. He must go to see him before the worst happened. I sympathized and condoled to the best of my ability, but it seemed he had to go. I tried to reason with him. His father had been a very sick man when the letter was posted two weeks before. If it took a few days preparing and two weeks for the return journey, by that time the crisis would be over. What good could he do? His father would be either dead or well by the time he got back, and he would be powerless to aid. However, he was headstrong, and I could not say whether he was better off to return or not. It was difficult, but I think his mind was made up. He wanted to go home and he had strong reason to do so. This was a trying moment for me, also. My only pal within six-thousand miles, and he was leaving. This bore into my inner self. I was again on trial. It pulled at my heartstrings. My eyes were dim with tears, my world felt empty. I prayed. Jesus was my life-belt. Had I been without

Him, certainly I should have packed my grips, but the arm of Christ is most reliable. He bore me up, he was my reason, my courage, my healer and my friend.

Buller went. I was saddened and my tears welled at his receding form. I thought of where he was going, what he was going to see, his home, his loved ones. Oh, that sinking feeling! But finally a soothing feeling came to me as resolution stirred within. I was in His hands. I could not take any harm. This was when I first thought of going to Regina, the capital city of Saskatchewan. But I had no qualms for I was with Christ and perfectly happy.

CHAPTER FIVE
The Green Englishman

WHEN SOMEONE GOES TO STRANGE SURROUNDINGS and engages in different types of employment, this could be called *green to the job*. This was how it was with me. I was green, all right, to unfamiliar farming procedures, as may be witnessed by the following two incidents.

The *stooking* at Mr. Haist's farm had taken two weeks. In Saskatchewan, way out there in the stubble of Kincaid, there was no shelter from the sun except behind a *stook*, but then the miles of *stooking* to be done left little time for shady rest anyway. The Haist family did their best to accommodate a couple of greenhorns. They got us horsehide gloves for our sore hands. These were of little help because it was so hard to work with gloves on. As an English miner, I didn't usually wear gloves at work because the gloves were roughly stitched and could be as painful as twine around a sheaf. Englishmen traditionally work in shirt sleeves, and that is the way we tackled the *stooking*. But soon the butt end of the sheaves wore the skin raw on our bare arms, and for the first few days of *stooking*, we were the objects of pity. At one time I counted seventeen blisters on each hand. However, with lotions, improved technique, becoming used to the environment, and with the Haist's encouragement, we survived. We were especially thankful for the Haists' tolerance, for we must have been the slowest *stookers* on the prairies.

Another thing that retarded our progress was *thirst*; stooking was a thirsty business. We took a gallon stone jar of water to the field with us and parked it behind a *stook* for shade to keep it cool. We continually moved it along with us to keep from having to go back too far. This soon developed into our seeking it after every windrow, and then after almost every *stook*. The Haists warned us that their water was alkaline and that we should drink it sparingly because of its laxative qualities, but we were unable to resist our thirst, and soon we were suffering from intense diarrhea. At times it became an exercise in futility to fasten one's pants, and it even got to a point when it was not a laughing matter. As the days wore on, Mrs. Haist's cooking became more delightful, Mr. Haist's humour cheerful and assuring, and somehow our *stooking* improved.

The sun is often portrayed with a smiling face, but to me it was merciless. Imagine coming from a coal mining community in the north of England. When working underground, sometimes I would never see daylight let alone the sun. On these Canadian prairies working hours were 8:00 a.m. to 4:00 p.m. and the sun stripped the skin from my face. Mosquitos were terrible.

On a Sunday morning I would typically walk across the stubble fields and have a talk with Mr. Haist; other Sundays I would help his two small children with their school homework. Mr. and Mrs. Haist generously offered us use of their home in the evenings after supper as they seemed to enjoy hearing us talk of worldly things.

Generally, the weather was hot, but there were days when it rained, and on these days Mr. Haist would have us help build a caboose. This was a wooden cabin used to provide sleeping quarters for four. It would be mounted on wheels so that harvest helpers could sleep closer to the job. So I became a *green* carpenter, too. Although I could not saw straight, I could drive nails and I helped as best I could. Once the caboose was completed, we moved into it and were to begin threshing. A threshing separator is difficult to describe. Its function is to separate the wheat kernels from its straw. The wheat was funnelled into a wagon and the straw was blown away clear of the machine. It works in ways unbeknown to me. There are wheels and belts galore connected by a long drive belt to a tractor. Mr. Haist was the tractor man and a separator man kept the thing going. His name was Rick. Allan was the hired man and his job was to haul away the grain and replace the wagon. There were two field pitchers, one from Yugoslavia, one from Czechoslovakia, and four teamsters, one of German descent and one French Canadian, and of course we two from England.

The Haist's separator was a twenty-two-inch model, which didn't mean much to me except that it could only be fed one sheaf at a time, with the heads of the sheaf going into the feeder first. The tractor was a John Deere, which was about as much as I knew about it, but it could chug along hour after hour. The two Slavs in the field had pitchforks and the teamsters had a pair of horses, the rack and a pitchfork.

Once we began threshing, our goal was a thousand bushels a day by using four teams of horses. Two of the four teams were borrowed from a neighbouring farm. It was now Sunday, and I was very interested in everything that was going on, but I hadn't seen any horses or racks and wasn't so sure I wanted to either. If I knew nothing of *stooking* or carpentry, I knew less about horses, never having been around any. Tomorrow, Monday, we were to start. This is when Mr. Haist called me from the caboose. I was to go with Allan to the neighbouring farm, approximately three miles away, to bring back two teams of horses.

After exchanging cheery salutations with the neighbour, we went to his barn to fetch two teams of horses. Allan knew I was green, so he harnessed the horses, with me earnestly observing what he did with the leather trappings he was placing on the horses. He finished hitching one team of horses to the rack, and I viewed my first horse-drawn vehicle with which I was to have an intimate relationship. When we had completed harnessing the second team and were about to take our leave for the Haist farm, Allan showed me which team I was to drive. Gosh! The horses looked formidable and unfriendly. It wasn't that I didn't like animals, it was just my strangeness, I suppose.

But if the horses presented a challenge, the *rack* terrified me. It was something the likes of which I had never beheld. In fact, it was nothing but slats on wheels. I climbed up onto this contraption and found there was no safe place for my feet. The floor of the rack was made of five twelve-inch wooden slats, one at each side, then a broad space and two more, plus one down the middle. The sides were slotted all around. In the front of the rack was a two-by-four, which ran right up the middle, about a foot higher than the slats. This way the driving lines from the horses could pass at each side and be tied.

I finally stood with the lines firmly in my hands and planted my feet as solidly as they could be, one foot on each slat from the centre one, which placed my head exactly behind the two-by-four in the middle of the front rack. While I'd been settling myself to start, Allan saw that I was as ready as I would ever be and he *giddy-upped* his team. I simply had to follow him out of the farm yard and onto the road. However, it wasn't that simple. Most people know that Saskatchewan roads are built by scooping earth from along each side and using it to build up to the top surface which is the road. Thus, to get onto a road a wagon must dip down into a hollow, then up onto the road. Allan didn't appear to have any difficulty with this situation, but then I could see things he never could see. So I *giddy-upped* my team and headed for the road. What I didn't foresee was that I should have moved my face from behind the two-by-four, because when the rack went into the hollow, the two-by-four sort of went forward and then whap! It came back, hitting me square on the forehead. It knocked me off balance, and my feet went down between the slats. The pin that fastened the horses' harnesses to the rack flew out and the horses bolted. I didn't see what happened for I was knocked out cold. I didn't know where my horses were going, but their harnesses were scattered along the road for some considerable way. However, Allan, good man that he was, corralled the horses, collected the harness, and we, yes *we*, I was still game, got them ready to go again. This time we made it back to the Haists' farm, but it was long after dark.

Allan and I unhitched the horses and led them into the barn. On our arrival, the other four horses were already in, munching hay, flaring their nostrils, pricking up their ears and whinnying. Horses are perhaps more friendly than most animals. Allan showed me the stall containing the horses I was to care for. I was copying Allan in his horse talk. "Hah! Up a bit, over, whoa now! Steady." The names of my horses were Ginger and Blackie. Ginger was ginger in colour and temperament. Blackie, the other horse, was quite a bit taller and much more docile and contented. Before I started taking the harness off the horses, Allan showed me some pegs at the end of each stall where the harness was to be hung. He was patient and slow of speech, something of the nature of Blackie, my horse, tall, dark and quiet. He took considerable time showing me how to dis-harness. After loosening the trapping, he took his position facing the flank of my horse, Blackie. He put his right hand over the horses back and grabbed part of the leather and with his left hand he took hold of another key strap of harness and lifted the whole harness. Then he carried it to the peg and hung it there. It seemed so easy! He did the same with my other horse, Ginger. I took careful notice as he repeated the performance. He advised me that when harnessing the horses I should just reverse the operation, grab the same two leather straps and throw them over the horse's back. I thanked him for the lesson and advice. The horses were watered, fed and bedded down and we related the day's events to the Haists while eating a late supper, then turned in to rest. Tomorrow was the first day of threshing.

The next thing I heard was "Twilight in the Swamp!" I hadn't been in bed five minutes when I heard those words. Twilight in the Swamp, time to get up. Gosh! It was black dark. I was groggy trying to put my half-damp clothes on in the oil lamp light. The first thing to do when dressed was to get to the barn as fast as possible, feed the horses, throw the harness on and then get into the house for breakfast. I heard monosyllables of the others in the crew grumbling about readying things in dim light. Then it seemed all at once that I was in the barn alone. I had gotten all things done around my horses except the harness on their backs. I went to the stall end where the harness was hanging and pondered Blackie. I favoured Blackie, because he was quiet, and I am sure Ginger knew this by her attitude toward me. Frankly, I'd forgotten the routine of the previous night so I figured out the straps I should grasp, lifted the harness, carried them to Blackie and threw them over his back, expecting everything would drop into place. Well, it did, but the place was on the floor, on the other side of Blackie. I don't remember what I said. I guess Blackie wondered what was going on, or not going on, as I hopelessly tried to sort out the bewildering rabble. When Mr. Haist came upon this scene, he nearly laughed his head off at what he saw. But he was a patient man. He didn't berate me, and even sorted things out with me and helped to harness the team. As I accompanied him back to the house for breakfast, the others of the crew were coming out to hitch. I didn't say much and ate fast. I guess they all wondered about me, but no more than I wondered about myself.

It was in the light of dawn when the outfit pulled out of Haist's yard for our first day of threshing. It was the most wonderful sight I ever witnessed to see the sun rise over the fallen wheat fields. It was enough to strengthen my sagging spirits and lift me up to renewed effort to stay with it.

The separator was set. Rick had all the belts on the pulleys except the long drive belt which was to go on the tractor drive wheel. Mr. Haist slowly backed the tractor to tighten the belt to its proper tautness. Allan was there with the half-ton truck to haul away the grain, the field pitchers were out, the Czech with the German and French Canadian, the Yugoslav with Buller and myself. I was *last* in the field with my team. The others were already loading down the wheat row.

I slowly began forking for the first time. There were usually nine to eleven sheaves to a *stook*. I pulled alongside one and commenced to work, loading my rack with the horses lines tied around the two-by-four that had knocked me out. After loading the *stook*, I led my team to the next one. I was terribly slow in getting my first load in. The others had all loaded and unloaded and I wasn't even ready with a full load, even working with the over six-foot-tall Yugoslav, who could lift one whole *stook* on one fork lift. Rick was hollering for me to come in. The French Canadian was supposed to be first, then my pal Buller, next the German, then me. The separator was running empty, so I was up on the load hurrying in. Approaching the separator, Rick got to the head of my horses and steered my rack to the place where it would be easiest to offload the sheaves onto the feeder conveyor. The nearness and noise of all the belts and wheels on the shimmering, great machine was enough to unnerve me. Truthfully, I was apprehensive of falling onto the feeder belt with its terrifying, clutching arms of steel cramming sheaves into the shaking monster's innards. The thought of being a sheaf horrified me! I began unloading warily while these things were going through my mind. An untrained *forker*, I gripped too hard, and was working torturously hard trying to keep the feeder fully occupied, impeding my progress by tugging at a sheaf upon which I was standing.

It was nigh impossible at first to keep the feeder going to capacity. Eventually, I got down to the floor slats and finally offloaded, once I had stopped the machine by throwing sheaves onto the feeder butt-first, which Rick cautioned me not to do. On driving away I noticed that the other three teams were all back at the separator, fully loaded. Only one rack could be unloaded at a time since too many sheaves at one time would choke the machine and stop the outfit. I urged the horses out and did my best to keep up, but was unable. My inaptitude and strangeness worked against my honest endeavour. I was always last! When the end of the first day in the field came I was almost dead.

Some interesting vignettes of the first day were that at noon, as the outfit was not far away from the house, a flag signal from the house denoted that dinner was ready. Mr. Haist shut the tractor's engine down and hollered, "Come and get it!" The Teamsters unhitched their horses, tied the lines around their own bodies and ran like hares to the farm. I followed suit, but it was fairly hair raising. I felt sure that I would fall flat on my face and be dragged. However, I survived and the others seemed to get some pleasure at my discomfort. One thing which awed me was to see that marvelous Yugoslav put his fork into a *stook* of nine sheaves and pitch it onto the rack. Lordy me! It took all my concentration just to get one sheaf on cleanly.

Racks were left in the field in various stages of being loaded and would be picked up where left off next day. I got my team unharnessed and had all the trappings hung up, horses fed and watered as I had been shown, and was last out of the barn to the house. There was a wash basin on a stand at the door and water in a barrel. The one towel was wet enough for the last one to use it. I often came in for ribaldry from the others, particularly one of the German boys. But the Haist family was kind. The blisters on my hands were many and raw. Supper was good and the camaraderie of the crew was cheerful. It was near dark, and as the crew headed for their own quarters, one of them jokingly asked if I would like to have a wrestle with him. I honestly believe if somebody breathed on me I would have fallen down, so I headed for my bunk, the day finally over.

Next day, or seven hours later, it was *Twilight in the Swamp* again. There was a scuffle to be first at the breakfast table. I was out in the barn doing chores with the rest of them, but I had more trouble with the harness. My horse, Ginger, resisted having the bit in her mouth. Since they missed me at the breakfast table, Mr. Haist came to see what was holding me up. What he saw was me, trying to get the bit into this crazy horse's mouth. Every time I'd get the bit to its teeth and push, the horse's head would go up in the air. It just wouldn't cooperate. Mr. Haist just laughed and laughed. However, he came over to me and showed me how to put my thumb into the horse's mouth at the same time as applying the bit, and it was so simple. I could almost feel Ginger's disdain for me. Again, the others were coming *out* when I was going *in* to eat. What a way to begin the second day.

However, as the morning wore on it wasn't any worse than day one. But my hands were horrible with blisters, and I must blame them as the cause for my being unable to extricate my fork from a sheaf when pitching and the fork went with the sheaf into the separating machine. Needless to say, it threw the belts for a loop and made a terrible grinding noise. The outfit came to a halt. Yes, for two hours. Rick wasn't very happy, although Mr. Haist took it philosophically. Other than this unfortunate accident, day two was much the same as day one. I was always *last*, and the separator was often waiting for me to get in with my load.

In the mid-afternoon, lunch was brought into the field for the crew. Mr. Haist's daughters drove out with it. It was my turn to be unloading, so one of the girls climbed up onto my load, took my fork and sent me to get my snack. It was a great break for me and she was a real professional, making it look so easy.

I was getting used to the early rising, and even though I was last in for breakfast, at least I was there before the meal was completed. Someone made a snide remark about my tardiness, which perhaps was legitimate to some extent, however, Mr. Haist took advantage of the situation while all were present to express something of his observations in the field. He went so far as to say, especially to the other two teamsters, the German and the French Canadian, that they were not putting a full load on their racks and that if they did, there wouldn't be so much waiting. The gist of what he said was that they were taking extreme advantage of me. Evidently, while I was fully-loading my rack, they were stacking up the sides and throwing a few in the middle. They would be out and back again, always waiting for me because it was taking me longer to load and unload. It was a revelation to me, because I was working my hardest, yet I was always behind. I thought they were so much better and experienced. Now it was exposed. They had been cheating in order to have maximum rests. What's more, he said that they were not looking after their horses properly. He said for them just to do their job better and not be sitting around so much. Needless to say, I felt much better and the situation in the fields was much more uniform and regulated. The blisters on my hands were healing and my skin was toughening. I was progressing, but still very green with the horses.

The outfit moved further afield and new locations always meant shorter hauls to the separator. However, the teamsters still ran with the horses to the house at lunch time. I was eating and sleeping healthily now and enjoying the days in the field. Mrs. Haist's cooking was really appetizing, especially the pie. The twenty-two-inch separator at times had minor breakages causing stoppage and a trip to town for parts. During times like these, we would stretch out in the shade of the wagon and enjoy the rest. I still had lots to learn, and was never really relaxed with the horses. I honestly believe Ginger had me figured out. We just didn't see eye-to-eye. I wasn't doing too badly with the harness, except one morning I couldn't get it all fastened. I couldn't figure out why for the longest time; then I realized the horse's collar was on upside down. I felt that Ginger was laughing at me all the time. Another day I had them all harnessed and was trying to make a left turn through the gate. I pulled and pulled on the line on Ginger's left side and the team just kept going on straight; they just would not turn. So with much chagrin I reined them to a stop, got off the rack and walked to the horses' heads, only to discover that I had the line snapped to the collar instead of to the bit. There were so many things the horses and I had in common, secretly.

We had been doing well for about six days and the machine was also behaving well. I was finally keeping up with the others now because of the things that I had learned; handling the pitch fork, picking the top sheaves when unloading, getting the team close to the *stooks*, and a pattern for loading. The harnessing was no longer a problem. The only thing was all this time Rick had been sort of leading my team into the separator when we came in for unloading. The other teamsters drove in by themselves. It was a tricky business driving alongside the feeder conveyor to get the rack in as close as possible, making it easier to unload. The end of the separator protruded out about six inches and one had just to miss this by the outside post of the rack to have the rack in the right position to offload. If one got wide, it made unloading much harder, consequently the teamsters tried to keep in very close. So Rick had been leading my team in, guiding me in carefully on occasion. It was a bit scary what with all the machinery going, creating such a noise of squeaking wheels, shakers and belts. The din was tremendous. The horses were nervous of it all, too.

It had to happen sooner or later. We were at work and a couple of racks had been unloaded as I approached the feeder conveyor with temerity. Rick was not present, so I stood up on top of the load for better vision. I cautioned the horses and tried to get in close. I don't quite know exactly what happened. I was watching the big sheaves snatching hook at the head of the conveyor with one eye and the corner of the rack and the protruding separator with the other, when suddenly I thought the world had come to an end. There was a jolt, followed by a grind and a crunch, simultaneously. The heavily loaded rack had come into sharp contact with the separator. The whole outfit became engulfed in a thick cloud of dust that totally obscured everything. Belts from every part of the separator flew in every direction. Mr. Haist shut the tractor engine off quickly and everything became ominously silent. The collision must have been heard from miles away and so could the swearing of the separator man, Rick. The separator had been knocked off base, but not only that, the grain-carrying auger had been broken, along with several other parts, which required closing down the whole outfit for the rest of the day. The damage had to be assessed and a journey made into town for spare parts. It was unfortunate, for delays were not only expensive with a bunch of people to be fed, but the time element was a factor. Apologies were not much help. Mr. Haist couldn't be pleased, but he was kind. He wistfully remarked that this wasn't the first time for this type of happening. It seemed everything had to happen to me. There has to be one in every pack. I felt dejected. The other guys were elated. An afternoon off!

Finally, Mr. Haist's crop was completely harvested. It was a bumper yield in 1928. Perhaps this was one reason why he kept me around. It was a happy June for western farmers. I was used to most of the procedures now, enjoying the clean fresh air, the hard work, good deep sleeps, the weather, the beauty of the largest sky in the world, and the miles and miles of golden grain and stubble straw. Mr. Haist had taken on a couple of neighbours, since he had the threshing outfit to cut the grain, which necessitated a move from the home farm, although the arrangement was that we would still go to Haists' for meals. The outfit was set up a couple of miles from the house now, and the teamsters were riding the horses in. I was still running in behind the team with the lines tied around my waist, but frankly it was too far now. They all had been encouraging me to ride the horses in, but I had never ridden a horse in my life and I delayed the ordeal for as long as I could. One day I felt it was too far, so I said I would ride. It seems the whole crew was waiting for this moment. They'd been wondering when I'd give up, so when I asked Rick for a leg up on Ginger, the whole bunch of them were there to watch the performance. I gathered the lines, as I had seen the others do, bent my lower leg backwards and Rick hoisted me onto Ginger. At the same time, all the others yelled and screamed as loudly as they could. Rick swooped his broad-brimmed hat off his head and walloped Ginger on her rear quarter; how those horses scattered! Things were happening so fast! The horses galloping, and I about to be pitched off, so I let go the lines and fell on Ginger's neck with my arms clasped desperately about her neck. She never had such an embrace! They knew the way home and I didn't have much time to see what happened to the harness, but the crew whooped it up behind me and brought the bits and pieces in and put them together again. My first horse ride was quite an experience, but even so I persevered without much option for it seemed like this might be the final test of being a teamster on a threshing outfit.

Life is experience and things happen to us all. One example was an incident with cows. Two holstein cows on the Haist farm had somehow gotten into a feed of wheat grain. When we got to the house, the cows were down on their sides with their tummies so swollen they looked like round balls. They would surely die if something wasn't done. It was perplexing. The big Yugoslav came forward and said he was a *Krava Doctor*. By hand signs he told us he had some Veterinarian knowledge so Mr. Haist let him try. He stripped off his shirt and put his arm way up into the cows' insides in an endeavour to save their lives, but to no avail as both animals died. I had never seen anything like this before.

One afternoon the outfit moved to a new location on a neighbouring farm and after Rick got his separator set, the teams were all loaded awaiting the start of the engine. As usual, I would be the last man to unload so Rick called to me to unhitch my horses, go back to the farm and bring the *Stone Boat* and a forty-five-gallon barrel of oil. A *Stone boat*? I hadn't the faintest idea of what he was talking about. As a matter of fact, I was leery that they were playing another trick on me, but they assured me there was such a thing as a *stone boat*, and told me where I would find it. So, suspiciously I went. My doubt was dispelled, however, when I got back to the farm and dubiously asked the boy, Eddie, about the *stone boat*. Immediately, he took me behind one of the many sheds and pointed to the thing. He even helped me get it over onto its right side and hitched. I just stood and stared at it. I don't know what I expected. It was sort of a huge sled or skid that could be pulled over the land on its broad runners. Once Eddie helped me hitch onto it, I proceeded to the field to load the oil drum. I found the drum and managed to get it up onto the sled. As one can stand on the *stone boat* and ride it, I thought this was a good idea, so I casually started back to the outfit. All was going well until a jack rabbit bounded out in front of the horses and scared them. They took off. I yelled at them to stop, but not them. We hit an uneven roll which flipped the sled, and the barrel of oil and I went flying. I sat and watched the *stone boat* twisting and turning after the horses. It was almost funny. The prairies are really not flat.

The harvesting came to an end after six weeks. I often wondered why Mr. Haist didn't fire me just to get me out of his life. Then I came to the conclusion that things would not be the same for him. He would miss me as the joker in the pack. In fact, I believe the whole crew couldn't find time for grumbling, simply because I was a distraction, contributing to their enjoyment.

In the six-weeks harvesting on the Haists' farm, I came to love the Canadian prairies, their great open spaces, vastness, silence, breezes, beauty, sunsets, dawns, and clean air. In the evening I would go outdoors and stare in awe at the starlit sky. During October nights I beheld the frightening aspect of the Northern Lights, their brilliance indescribable and compelling to behold. They seemed to be right amongst us, and fairly crackled, dancing radiant greenish-blue flames in perpetual motion. They were truly unforgettable above the far distant horizon, the place where earth and sky met in one straight line.

CHAPTER SIX
Sequence to the Harvesting

I WAS GENUINELY SORRY to leave the Haist family as they had been so good, so generous, and so tolerant. I had spent many happy times in the evenings talking with them and there was a warm empathy between us. On leaving the Haist farm at the end of the 1928 crop, with a hundred and sixty dollars in earnings, I decided to go to Regina, the capital city of Saskatchewan. The Haists knew the country and offered an arrangement that in the event I might not find work, I could come back and put in the winter doing chores for my keep. The advice given to me from people who had experienced the country's rigorous winters was to *get in somewhere*, even if just for room and board; to stay alive, as it were. However, I resolved to take a chance on work in Regina and arrived there in early November 1928.

I stayed my first night there at the Ottawa Rooms, operated by Chinese. The next day I started looking for board and room. There were quite a few harvesters in the city then who often congregated at the United Cigar Store, and it was from there that I found a place to stay. My new home was located in the 2100 block of Broad Street, in a big multi-roomed house run by a Mrs. Morgan. Board and room cost eight dollars a week. We chaps were always talking about things like work, digs, home, etc. As the days were getting cooler, and the nights colder, we invariably talked about our lodgings. Most of us were looking for something cheaper than eight dollars a week. Mrs. Morgan's place wasn't bad and she was nice enough to us, but frankly I detested the peanut butter sandwiches every day in my lunch pail, so I kept looking.

I finally got a job with a builder, Wilson Brothers, but I had to buy work clothes since the weather was getting colder. I equipped myself with moleskin work pants, gloves and a fur-lined helmet, with flaps to pull over the ears when it was cold. It seemed every workman wore one of these kinds of hats. My first job was digging a church basement foundation. Basements in Regina must be eight to nine feet deep because in the winter the earth freezes to that level and watermains must be placed below those levels. There must have been twenty men digging, spaced around the building of the hall around St. Paul's Church on McIntyre Street. There was a chap about ten feet in front of me, and another about the same distance behind. We didn't say much to each other because many languages were spoken in Regina. Finally, the fellow in front of me came up out of the ditch for a breather, as did I, and he came over to have a word with me. A lot of these men were from central Europe and were commonly called *Bohunks* (a contraction of Bohemian) by the Canadians in deference to their gypsy-like behaviour. This one said to me, "How long in country?" I told him I had been in the country for two months. He said, "You speak good for time you been here." This shook me for a minute, but I suddenly began to feel more like a Canadian.

This work didn't take long and so I was sent to a job where a new filling station was being built. It was located at the corner of Broad Street and Eleventh Avenue, near the Regina Police Station. When I started work there, they were laying foundations and had the cribbing castings all in place to receive concrete. I was a general handyman: carry, reach and fetch for most of the first shift. On the second day they were ready to pour the concrete. The gravel, the cement and the water were all ready. Two men were mixing the cement, and two men were to wheel the cement to the finisher. I was allocated to a wheelbarrow. There was a track of planks from the mixers to the finisher, which was a fair distance away, with the final ten-foot run going up a plank. From there I was to tip the barrow load to the finisher, who was German. The other chap, my mate, was from central Europe.

The weight of an empty wheelbarrow isn't bad, but when a wheelbarrow is full of wet cement it is darned heavy. The other lad went first. A strong lad, used to heavy work, he did okay, but I didn't do so well. I managed to get the barrow going, but rather uncertainly, then came the big push to get to the top of the last plank. I put all I had into it, but when I heaved to tip, I overdid it and the whole barrow and load went over. There was a terrible reaction from the German, who was badly splashed. I learned more Deutsche swear words in those five minutes than I have heard in a lifetime. I was sorry because it was unfortunate.

They didn't fire me, but I soon began to look for another job. It was still sunny and warm in the daytime, Indian Summer they called it, and it was nice. On the weekends we would go for walks around Wascana Lake to view the Parliament buildings where there was a pleasant walking area. The lake wasn't very big, but nevertheless we spent a lot of time there. In the evenings we might go to the Capitol theatre at the corner of Twelfth and Scarth Street. There were two other places of amusement: Rex Theatre and The Grand, both for stage plays.

Time was running out for the few harvesters still around. If we went back to England before December 31, 1928, and had a signed work order from the farmer stating that we had completed our contract, the return fare would be paid by the British Government. Another thing that concerned us was that construction work ceased at *freeze-up* and there might be no jobs until spring. Thus, while I was working, I scanned the newspapers frequently. I didn't want to go back to the coal mines. I had done better here already than I'd ever done back home. I had sent some money back to Mum, and thought I could help her better by working in Canada since the English pound was worth five Canadian dollars in those days.

On December 1, 1928, I found a job at the Kitchener Hotel downtown on Rose Street. The hotel was fairly large, with several rooms and a huge banquet hall. It was a two-story building with an elevator from the lobby to the second floor. My niche was night porter, which entailed working from 8:00 p.m. to 8:00 a.m., a twelve-hour shift, seven days a week. I cannot recall that I had a day off, nor did it occur to me to question it. I was so glad to *get in* for the winter.

I was to meet all trains coming into Regina. There were many trains, but only two railway companies, the Canadian Pacific Railway (C.P.R.) and the Canadian National Railway (C.N.R.). My job was to meet and greet any prospective customers looking for hotel accommodations, take care of their baggage, and see that it got to the hotel, a half block from the station. For this, I was provided with a luggage wagon, best described as a *hand cart*. It had large hotel signs painted on it. I was provided with a hotel jacket and a red *bell-hop* cap. What a sight! If Mum could only see me now, barking out "Kitchener Hotel here!" in a dignified manner in keeping with the profile of The Kitchener.

I began to see that everything one does in the process of daily living is a training for something else. The trial of harvesting had tempered me with confidence in myself, and helping Mum in the public bar had been a bit of training for me in this job. I was finding out that all things are relative, such as coal mining and harvesting grain. For instance, the blackness, the utter darkness of the underground coal mine versus the extreme brightness of the large prairie skies are relative opposites. In everything there is a top and bottom. The extremities are usually the most harsh. All seem to be one, though, as they are here and now. My own spirit was growing with each new exposure to life.

In between trains I was on duty at the hotel elevator and generally helped around the hotel, setting the hall and doing any necessary odd jobs. I got to know George, the day porter, and Pat, the girl in the office. There was a night clerk on duty, and I believed he knew everything. It was just as well he did, for I knew nothing. Mr. Lush, the manager, was sharp and looked efficient, but was brief and strict in manner. Mrs. Lush was kindly. The chef was a coloured man and it was he with whom I talked the most.

I lived and ate *in*. Working long hours and sleeping in the day allowed me little time to see much. I remember my greatest problem was staying awake. I really had trouble being up all night. Every night between 12:30 and 1:00 a.m. I would go into the kitchen and literally plunge my head and face into a tub of cold water.

I remember Christmas 1928. I was lonely and missed home terribly. With my odd working hours I ate alone, but the chef was very good to me and did me many favours. I think I must have cried all the tears I had for a couple of weeks, but gradually I got over my home-sickness. I believe something of the Reverend Welby encouraged me to carry on. We are never alone, if we are aware. The staff was very patient with me, which seemed the story of my life. I was being *broken in*, as it were.

Invariably, customers came into town off night trains. At these times the liquor stores were closed. There were no beer parlours or pubs, nor any other place to get a drink so drinking had to be done at home or in a hotel room, nowhere else. Consequently, customers coming to the hotel from night trains were hard pressed to obtain an alcoholic drink. So in the course of getting them and their baggage from the train to the hotel room, they would almost without exception ask me to sell them a bottle. They expected it! Me? New in the country, I knew nothing of the laws, and having no knowledge of bootlegging I was unable to be of any assistance in assuaging their craving, so I came in for much abuse.

One belligerent individual, driven to frustration I guess, said, "What in the hell kind of porter are you?" I said I wasn't quite sure, but providing a bottle wasn't one of the terms of reference for my job. However, I did discover in due course that the night clerk was an expert at bootlegging. In fact, he had taxis running bottles of liquor to residences, all very illegal. I stayed away from that stuff. The night clerk was indeed a character. Couples came into the hotel, booked a room and signed the register as man and wife. He would tell me to take them up to their room and when

I returned he would say, "I'll give them an hour." He seemed to know every character in Regina. I often wondered if Mr. Lush, the manager, knew about the night clerk. It was his job to awaken the early morning waitresses for their shift. He used to go into their bedroom area and fairly throw the bed clothes off them and slap their buttocks. I was amazed at the man's effrontery. It was brash fun, I suppose, but I was embarrassed.

At another time, an elderly lady coming off a late train had me take her luggage to the Kitchener. I had just come down with the elevator, and she had finished registering, so I put her luggage in the elevator and she got in. I closed the elevator door and swung the starting handle. When we were halfway up, she asked me if I could find her a clean old man! Well, that caught me with so much surprise that I forgot to switch the handle to stop and the elevator went through its pulley. It took more than half an hour to get the thing righted. Was I ever embarrassed! Hotel life had its moments, but all in all it was fairly routine and pleasant. Quite a few members of the Conservative Party at that time stayed there. The members, Anderson and McConell, were frequent visitors when the House was in session, and I remember the St. George's day banquet was a gala affair.

In the fall of 1928, General Motors Corporation began building a huge GM automobile assembly plant in Regina. The opening was anticipated to be January 1929. So after the new year some of the GM officers from Detroit, USA arrived in Regina in preparation for setting up the plant and hiring personnel. Quite a few of these key men booked into the Kitchener. Because of my work at the hotel, I occasionally talked with some of them. One such person, hearing me speak in *Geordie* vernacular became interested and probed a little further into my background. He was Scottish, but he knew of northeast England. He asked how long I had been away from the homeland, and we talked quite a bit. Soon he asked me if I would like to work at GMC. Of course I would and as I hadn't yet gotten around to asking him, it was nice of him to save me that. He wrote on a slip of paper a man's name I was to go see and I would be given a job. It was a little sad leaving the Kitchener, especially the coloured chef and also some others of the staff. My wages were fifty dollars a month plus board and room and some clothes, such as coat and cap.

Having now to move my lodgings, I found a place to live with board and room at Mr. and Mrs. Walter Barker's at 1321 Cornwall Street, off Seventh Avenue, on the north side of Regina. They were asking six dollars per week. Walter was the projectionist at the Rex theatre in Regina. They had three children: Gwen, Peter and Dolly. Gwen died of TB at the age of eleven. The area near 1321 Cornwall was pleasant. A few blocks along Seventh Avenue were the Timothy Eaton Store, the Broad Street big building of John Deere implements for farmers, and a block north was Simpson's great store, along with lots of warehouses. This was the north side of Regina. There were underpasses at Broad Street, Albert Street and Winnipeg Street, all of which often flooded when downpours occurred.

The GMC plant was located at Winnipeg and Fourth Avenue and it covered a half-mile square area. In it were testing grounds for finished automobiles under big glass warehouses. It was a huge place with assembly lines, storage, parts, huge machines, all used for the mass production of automobiles. At first I was a floor sweeper. I was content being paid six dollars and fifty cents a day for eight hours a day. There was also time-and-a-half for overtime, which was every Monday, Wednesday and Friday. I was able to send money home regularly during these times.

Sometime later I got a job on the production line doing piece-work, where I joined Bill Reid and Jack Hubbard who had also been harvesters. They were working on an assembly line in the molding section and I worked with them installing front moldings. The assembly line kept moving, with a car every fifteen feet. If one got behind, he got in the way of the other workers and their jobs. Once a lad had difficulty keeping up with the side moldings. There were holes in these moldings, with two screws to fasten them onto the car. When this lad got behind, he would miss tightening some screws. As there were inspections at the end of the line, before the cars went onto a painting line, several would be pulled off or rejected. But I believe many cars got by with work not as good as it should have been.

I now began to notice a great difference between jobs in Canada and ones in England. The job at GMC fooled a lot of us new Canadians. In England when one had a job it usually was stable and continuous, even passing from father to son, but that was not the way in auto plants. I found out that after they filled the orders for autos, they closed down until the fall of the year and the new change of model. So when the month of May came, work ended. There was not much one could do about it.

Bill Reid was a dapper little fellow from Birmingham, England, a real factory town, and he was a real factory worker. I learned a lot from him. He called his city Brum. Characteristically English, he was *straight John Bull*, forthright, blunt but humourous. We enjoyed each other as pals and often went on walks together to the train station. Regina is in about the middle of Canada, miles from anywhere. Seeing the great trains was always interesting, especially the steam trains with their constant bell ringing and huge wheels taller than I was. It was exciting to see these monstrous trains which traveled thousands of miles with a great variety of people from many lands. At any time, one could hear ten or eleven languages spoken on Eleventh Avenue. I believe I read that Regina was 46 per cent English speaking, 30 per cent German, with the rest made up of Ukrainians, Central Europeans, quite a few French Canadian and lots of Chinese, who incidentally played a large part in building the railway across Canada.

We would put time in going around to shops, and frequently ended up at the United Cigar Stores for chats with other cronies. We took in shows at the Capitol movie theatre. Ushers, mostly girls, were employed to take people to vacant seats. Bill and I went to one show once, and since it was dark an usher picked us up and we followed her, Bill first, then me. She was taking us up some stairs toward the back when Bill missed a step, stumbled and shouted loudly, "Shine the bloody light!" It surely disturbed the folks around us, and I felt like getting lost. Bill was like that. Another time we went to the Darke Hall, where Gilbert and Sullivan operettas often took place. We were there at one performance when some ladies sitting directly behind kept jabbering. This finally got too much for Bill, so he turned around, looked at them and said in a loud voice, "SHUT UP!" Bill was always to the point.

A couple of months went by and harvest time came around again. It was now fall of 1929. Bill and I decided we would go harvesting together since we were experienced. For several days we waited at the big Co-Op building at the corner of Albert Street and Eleventh Avenue, a place many farmers came to look for help. One morning, a small rotund man, unshaven, in old work overalls, came looking for two men. He certainly didn't look very impressive, but I don't suppose we looked all that impressive either. We said that we were available. He stated that he wanted one man for a *spike pitcher* and one for a *hound*. I thought I was back in the old *stone-boat* game again. This was a term neither of us had heard before, so we asked him to explain. Of course, that gave us away as still being green. He explained that his outfit had a *stook* loader, and in the process of loading racks, sometimes sheaves would fall to the ground and the *hound* would retrieve them. We took the job, Bill to be the *hound* and I to be a *spike pitcher*. The farmer said to follow him, and to our amazement he got into the biggest, most shiny black Buick, with a red interior. There was always something to learn in Canada; never underestimate a man by his looks. It turned out that he was the father of three sons who also had farms, with one outfit just for their own. We spent eleven days with them.

A note about *spike pitching*. There were four racks, four teams of horses, and two field pitchers to help load. The spike pitcher gets off the unloaded, emptied rack, and climbs up onto the back of the incoming rack and begins pitching before the horses stop. One does this for twelve hours. It was exhausting. One evening while talking about the day, Bill told me that the separator man had bet him a dollar that I wouldn't last. Bill won, since I had stuck it out, but I really was drained. Even so, it was a good place, the people were nice, and we enjoyed harvesting together. I received seven dollars a day for the eleven-days work.

After this, we came back to Regina and I went to room with the Barkers. The GMC plant opened up again and we reported for work. But in 1929 there were not a great number of cars to be made, so the plant closed early. All in all, 1929 was a pretty good year for me, but towards the end of the year the economy failed. The world seemed to go into a tailspin. Suddenly there was nothing, no money in the banks, and businesses went *kaput*. Stock exchanges went mad, as did people. People in queues half a mile long waited to get their money from the banks, but there was none. Suicides were common among those who were once rich and now were flat broke.

What happened? I really didn't know, but I wasn't severely affected financially. I hadn't any money in the bank, but it was worse than just the collapse of stock markets and banks and lost possessions. Everything went dead; no work, no jobs, no money, no purchasing power. Nothing except relief, a government handout for children. The government was unable to rectify the situation which paralysed industry, stifled life, and to worsen everything a drought began on the Canadian prairies. As the land dried up, year after year the soil yielded no crops. In southern Saskatchewan, the situation from these two calamities was hard to describe. To live through those barren, dust-filled wind storms was something that had to be experienced to be believed.

In the Barker home in 1930 there were Mr. and Mrs. Barker, their three children, two other boarders, and myself. Walter Barker was still employed at the Rex theatre as a projectionist. I remember a Mr. Willits, one of the boarders, saying that he had lost all his money in the grain market. He came from Ontario every year to join the harvest and play the wheat market. In 1930, the bottom fell out of the wheat market and the price of wheat kept going down every day. As the price of wheat fluctuated day by day, if one wished he could buy by phone whatever grain he decided upon, and somehow it was on a margin basis. If you had money, for example in number one northern wheat, and the price went up, of course your money was gaining, but if the price went down to the margin, you had to pump in more money to keep it up, or lose the lot, so you kept putting more money in to keep your margin up. The more often the price went down, the more money you had to put in to try to hold in, hoping it would stabilize. Poor Mr. Willits. Every morning at 8:00 a.m. he would be on the phone enquiring about the price of wheat, and when it started to go down it just kept on dropping, from a dollar eighty a bushel down to below a dollar. Down and down it went and he went flat broke. He *lost his shirt*, as he said. But that didn't stop the price from going down, until it finally stopped at an all-time low of twenty-six cents per bushel.

I remember Mr. Paul, who had a water-softener business in Regina. He lost two hundred thousand dollars when land values dropped. Mr. Paul employed an Irishman named Paddy Dumingham to install the water-softeners. Bill Reid knew him and that's how I became acquainted with him. I used to earn a few bucks now and then helping Paddy. He suffered from chronic bronchitis and after a month or so returned to Ireland. Also Bill Reid returned to England when it was evident there wouldn't be work, and that the GMC plant would never open again. But before he left, he and I went to the Sons of England Society Hall on Retallack Street, off Dewdney Avenue in Regina. Every Saturday night they held a whist drive and afterwards a dance. There was usually a nice crowd who frequented these occasions. Bill and I went to play whist, which was from 7:30 to 9:00 p.m., and then we stayed a little while for the dance. It was always good for a laugh to hear Mr. Harper, an oldtimer from some county in England where they dropped their

"H's." He would holler out, "'arts 's trumps," and in his endeavour to spread goodwill he would remind us to keep "'appy."

I was sorry to lose Bill from my life at that time but the depression was settling in and the outlook was grim. Thousands lost all their possessions. They that had most, lost most, and all were razed to the same level in a material sense. I knew and spoke with a Mr. Harry Wade, who was a driver on the street cars over a long period of time in Regina. He had done well over the years. He told me that he owned six houses but had lost them all in a short span of time because of his inability to pay their taxes when his tenants couldn't pay their rent. It seemed everyone was reduced to nothing. I wasn't affected in the same way; not having anything, I lost nothing. My only problem was raising six dollars a week to pay for board and room. Some of these people who said they had lost the lot still had much more than I did. I had over a hundred dollars, more than usual for me, but work was going to be a problem. I meditated often about returning to England but now I didn't have the fare. It was just a passing thought, though, since I really didn't yearn for the coal mines again.

Mr. Haist from Kincaid was now at Froude, on the Stoughton line. It was a barren area. He asked me in a letter to come and help him and since I was doing nothing then, I left Regina to join him. Froude was a dejected and depressed area where dust storms were enough to drive a person out of his mind. The relentless howling whine of winds never ceased and the air was vaguely brown as top soil was blown away. Great balls of Russian thistle rolled along until they blew into piles against the fences. What a dreary sight to behold. Inside the house, in spite of nailing blankets around crevices, windows and doors, the dust was inches thick. The wind blew dust into absolutely everything, everywhere. It was really a nightmare.

Mr. Haist really had no crop. It was estimated at five-bushels an acre, but in fact there was no crop at all in southern Saskatchewan. There was not enough to pay even for the harvesting. The whole area was so short of the necessities of life that the population qualified for relief. Relief was a dirty word in western Canada, having a connotation that went against the grain of independence and self worth. This sort of relief was from government agencies set up to direct other local agencies to receive boxcar loads of food and other necessities to keep life together. This help was coming from eastern Canada. There was also a vast movement of cattle from the drought areas in Saskatchewan to the eastern part of the country to save them from starvation.

Life was sad at the Haist farm. There was only one sort of general store in Froude. The owner couldn't let things out on *strap*, and there being no money and no income from crops, they were truly left to the good Lord and were at the end of their tether. The farmers lived this way: they bought gas for machinery, food, everything on the strength of the income from the harvest, and it worked well until crop failure. I left Froude after two weeks of helping them with what little they had.

So with no money I returned to Regina, to the Barker's. Regina was in the middle of a stricken area and it was difficult for even a single person to live, work was so scarce. I remember vividly how one was forever looking for a few hours' work. At the Barker's, things had changed while I was at Froude. Mr. Willits and Mr. Stultz had gone. There were only two boarders now, a younger woman, Dolly Graham, who worked in the nearby Timothy Eaton store, and a young fellow named Tommy Bowers, who worked at number two powerhouse on Winnipeg Street. They were both of English descent, so now the whole lot at Barker's were *Old Country*, and we had much in common. Dolly came from northeast England, and Tommy from the Midlands. He was a boiler pipefitter by trade and earned fairly good pay. We frequently went places together.

Walter Barker belonged to a fraternal order, commonly called the *Buffs*. The real name was the R.A.O.B., or Royal Antediluvian Order of Brotherhood. At home in England there was one of these chapters that used to meet in St. Luke's Church Hall. Walter invited me to join; they met once a month. There were about forty who used to attend. It was a secret sort of deal, locked door with a peep hole. "Who's there?" "Brother So-so."

Anyhow, I stayed with the Barkers and went with Walter to the R.A.O.B. and got to know more people. One was a pianist named Winters, who was Dolly's friend. But really the R.A.O.B. wasn't for me. I preferred to be with Tommy Bowers, and he and I used to frequent the Sons of England Hall. This was always fun and there was always someone different, mostly old-country people. There was nothing like their dances for mixing. So Tommy and I would go and have a good time. One was always looking for work and Tommy and I kept our eye open for each other. During the hard winter there was always lots of snow, and after much snowfall there would be a need for snow shovelling on certain streets and areas. I would arrive early at the streetcar barns to get a few hours shovelling snow off the sidewalks at forty cents an hour. Boy, was it cold.

Once, the old coloured chef from the Kitchener Hotel got in touch with me to see if I would like a small job fixing up an old shed building on a property in the east end. Every little job helped. I remember one incident. I was locking the door to go home, and it was very cold, twenty below. In messing around getting the key out of my pocket, I dropped my mitt. I had the key in my hand and put it to my mouth while I picked up the mitt and the key froze onto my lips the second it touched. I promised myself that I'd never do that again. Come to think of it, I saw a dog make a similar mistake. It went to lick something off a streetcar railway line and its tongue froze onto the iron rail. A druggist brought some oil to release it, poor thing.

Finally, it was springtime, 1931. The winters in Regina are from November to April or May. Tommy Bowers bought himself a pretty fair coupe which he used for work and pleasure, so we would drive to the S.O.E. dances in his car. These social times fostered acquaintances and friends, and it was at one of these occasions that I first met Anne. We had seen the sisters, Anne and Gladys Tindall, a time or two, and as always someone had to ask someone for a dance. And so it was, Tommy and I used to go on Saturday nights and ask Gladys and Anne to dance.

I recall one time Anne and I had a good laugh. Tommy and I had been going to the S.O.E. hall for quite a while, and had gotten to know most of the people who attended regularly. Anne was dancing with a smaller chap who fairly rushed her around the rim of the dance floor like he was in a marathon. I scarcely got a chance, and I did so want to get to know her better. Since this other lad was giving her so much attention, it didn't seem I had much chance. However, Anne and I did dance together. At least my cheap ballroom dancing lessons at home in England had taught me how to one-step, two-step, pivot, waltz and reverse, and Anne was a beginner. So we began to enjoy each other and would sit together with Gladys and Tommy between dances.

I think I loved Anne from the first time I saw her. Tommy and I continued to go to Saturday S.O.E. dances and we soon began to take the girls home afterwards, Tommy and Gladys in the front seat of the coupe and Anne and I in the back. We really had fun. Anne was nineteen and I was twenty-eight. Gladys was a little older than Anne and Tommy was a little younger than I. Both Gladys and Anne were in domestic service in Regina. Their parents lived at Bethune, Saskatchewan, about forty miles northeast of Regina. Their brother, Norman, also lived in Regina and operated a butcher shop on Fifth Avenue between Retallack Street and Robinson Street, called The Grand Meat Market. At home, Arthur and Mary Tindall, their parents, lived with their third daughter, Joyce, and two younger sons, Victor John and Arthur Thomas. They had all emigrated from England the same year as I, 1928, and had come as a family to settle at Bethune. The girls had found places in Regina, either boarded or lived in, and Norman boarded at Mrs. West's on 9 Block Robinson. They went to St. Peter's Church.

I also went to St. Peter's at the corner of Seventh and Garnet Streets, and soon began to teach a Sunday school class. The Reverend Howard

Creal was the Rector. Anne and I became members of the A.Y.P.A., Anglican Young Peoples Association. At that time the age group was older, late teens and early twenties. They were a grand lot to be associated with. So time went on, sometimes a bit of work, sometimes none at all. Still, people in general, like me, hung in and somehow hung on.

I was the only boarder at the Barkers now. Tommy Bowers had left to marry Mona. Dolly left to live with a friend. Mr. Paul died, and Mrs. Paul was trying to carry on the water softener business. Business everywhere was slow, but there were bits of work. Having no car, I used street cars or walked. The water softener materials that had to be transported were too heavy to carry and would be delivered by the *Dime Delivery,* a new delivery system started by a man I knew, Tommy Atkinson. Often, after a job was done, bits and pieces were left over and thrown in the garbage. Over the years there were bits of mineral, pipe etc. and I would bring them back to my place as the Paul's basement was miles away.

One day I was helping Walter Barker clean out his basement and there were several bits of leftovers of this mineral. The Barkers didn't have a water softener and there were, when added up, about forty pounds of this mineral. So I thought we could use it. It could be washed and put into a little container, which could have a tap on the bottom, like an urn, so soft water could be had by simply pouring water in the top and drawing it off at the bottom. At least it would provide soft water for washing hair, for a bath or for washing clothes. It would be a crude thing, but useful. This got me into trouble with Mrs. Paul, who worried about everything. I don't know how she learned about it, perhaps through the plumbing shop which supplied the pipe fittings. What worried her most was the mineral. She seemed to think that I had stolen it. She was very upset and made a big issue out of it, that perhaps I had taken tons of it.

There was a lawyer in the next office to Mrs. Paul's, and she took the matter up with him. So I was called to see him, while Mrs. Paul was present. Good gosh, the thing took on horrendous dimensions. Fifty pounds of mineral at forty cents a pound amounted to twenty dollars. She would have the lawyer believe that I had walked away with the Taj Mahal! However, as the lawyer pointed out, it legally was her mineral that was used, even though it was bits of leftover from other peoples' softeners that had been washed out. So I admitted, apologized and agreed to make restitution. I really was sorry to see Mrs. Paul so upset. Maybe it wasn't so much the value of the mineral as it was one of the things among many that prevented her from seeing any future in a business so inactive and her so incapable of understanding it. Needless to say, it was the end of my participation. It would probably have been better for everyone had I chucked the stuff. It was one of the sad things in my association with the Pauls.

The water softener repair service calls had helped me manage to keep up the cost of my board and room. In the winter pre-Christmas rush, R.H. Williams would sometimes hire extra help. So did the post office, but I never made that. However, I did get on at R.H. Williams, through an R.A.O.B. association. Len Arkingstall worked on the fourth floor in the glass packing and window dressing department. He tipped me off, so I got into the toys and books department and made appearances twice a day, two hours afternoons and two hours evenings being Santa Claus: hat, whiskers, leggings, the whole red and white outfit. I did this for three years during the depression period. Ho-ho! In a way, it was a great experience. I will always remember the look on some of the children's faces, especially the younger ones. I can also think of some of the older ones trying to play tricks on old Santa.

When I wasn't playing Santa, I was a salesman. The Arkinstalls knew the Barkers, and Winters, who knew Dolly, worked for Yarnton who had a painting business. He took me on as a helper for a while. They were painting sign-boards and I was taken along with three other fellows, all in overalls. They were supposed to be painters getting sixty cents an hour. I had never painted except when I helped cousin Arthur in England, but they didn't know or do any better than I did. It was so different; Arthur was so expert and thorough. In Canada, it was *get it on, slap it on*. I recall another job at Imperial oil houses, California-style roofs and design. I and another chap were to stain the shingles on the roof, so they handed me an eight-inch brush. Of course, you really had to work hard because there was always a crowd waiting for a job, watching for someone to get fired.

At one time I tried to count how many jobs I had. One job I had was to repair roofing on a huge warehouse north of the railway. It was high and I was thankful to be done. In some of these warehouses, the ice company used to store huge cubes of ice that had been taken from Wascana Lake when it froze to four feet thick. The pieces were sawn to fit ice boxes, which most people had in their homes in the hot summers for food preservation. Having lots of time on our hands, it was always fascinating to watch them saw large chunks with huge special saws, and load them onto lorries on the ice. It was quite a business. The ice man was a regular caller at houses, just like the milkman and postman. In the winter, the milkman's horse-drawn wagon was equipped with a heater stove. It was common to see the milk protrude three-to-four inches out the top of the bottle when it froze. The hair on the horses was covered with frost, and usually a long icicle formed from their bottom lips.

Through St. Peter's Church we became friendly with the Loving family, Mr. and Mrs. Loving, two daughters, Gwen and Ethel, and a son, Lesley. Mrs. Loving was president of St. Peter's Church Altar Guild. Mr. Loving worked for the wholesale firm of Tees and Persse. The more people one knew, the better the chance of work. The Lovings knew that the neighbour across the street wanted a wallpapering job done. As a boy I had helped to hold the paper for my mother while she pasted it and that was the extent of my knowledge, but they thought I could do it, so I tried. It wasn't easy, especially the ceiling. Mrs. Dunn was glad to get it done, though, and so was I. But she was kind in spite of my uncertainty.

Mr. Loving sometimes needed someone to unload boxcars for his firm, especially to escape *demurrage*. And so it went on. My life revolved around this circle of people. I would see Anne if she could get off her domestic job long enough to come to church. She had changed jobs. She first worked at Hamiltons as a domestic, but Mr. Hamilton who was manager of Barrie's Furs got her a job at the store where she became a furrier. She learned the trade and did well. The Hamiltons were good to Anne. After she left the Hamiltons, she moved to board and room at Mrs. West's where her brother Norman lived. Also boarding there was Ethel, one of Anne's previous roommates. Anne and I sometimes went on dates. We would go to shows, and we kept company regularly and we were happy.

I still saw Tommy Bowers. One day coming home from his job at the power house, Tommy told me they intended to build a new boiler, a Foster-Wheeler turbine boiler. So I went every day on the chance I might get work. There were more than forty others with the same idea. Of course in times like this one said one could do anything. One morning after three weeks vigil, there was a flatcar of steel to be offloaded, huge girders. I remember the foreman pointing his finger at me.

"Me?"

"Yes, you!" Guess he had noticed me there often. He said, "Can you climb?"

"Of course," I said. "SURE!"

"Well," he says, "go on that sled gang and help unload those girders." By golly! I now had a job at fifty cents per hour. Labouring was normally thirty-five cents an hour. Things worked out well. I rode to and from work with Tommy. Installation of this new type turbine boiler was a huge job, with the steel rising to seventy feet. I adapted fairly well to climbing. It put a better outlook on life for me, and Anne was pleased for my sake. Ever since I had met Anne, I had felt some more meaning to my life.

Anne and I, along with Tommy and Gladys, had acquired tennis rackets and played on the Scott Collegiate courts. Quite a few used to be there and we decided to form a tennis club. We continued to play frequently and had much fun. Having a job made so much difference. We worked mostly five and one-half days a week. A few incidents come to mind during that employment. One was seeing a workman named Duke Sullivan freeze. He was such a big man that the foreman called him *Fatso*. One day Fatso was on a second story girder when a fear of falling seized him and he embraced the steel girder and would not or could not let go. It was some considerable time before his hands could be pried from the girder. However, they retained him, but never again did he climb on the job. I had never worked on a steel erection outfit in my life so I was naturally ignorant of the language and names of things used in the industry: block and tackle, drift-pins, I-beams, rivets and riveting, *bucking-up* on those red-hot rivets. The beams were shaped like an I. Steel workers climbed up these beams like going up a ladder. It took me a while to accomplish this finesse. I went the slower, longer route up the real ladders, and down them afterwards, although I finally mastered climbing the I-beams and slid down them for lunch breaks. Nothing teaches like doing.

As the job progressed there were accidents. It wasn't unusual that workmen's tools, or other building material would fall. "Look out below" was a common exclamation. Our friend, Fatso, was maimed by a falling drift-pin, an iron tool for bringing girders together for rivetting. When rivetting was taking place, the red-hot rivets would be tossed from the forge to the riveter, often a few feet away. The helper would catch the hot rivet in a funnel-like metal basket. The riveter would pick up the hot rivet out of the funnel with pincers and insert it in holes where two beams come together and were temporarily held together by a drift-pin. The rivet was shaped, head and stem. The riveter covered the head with his automatic hammering machine and the bucker-up would be on the other side, with a tool to hold against the rivet. With the riveter on one side and the bucker-up holding, one would hear the "RRRRRRRRRRRRR." This burring, repetitive sound reverberated all day long as beams were set in place and riveted. It was incredible how the structure grew and the girders became smaller as the job went higher from the ground. I remember one time I was on the thirty-foot level and there were workers on the forty-foot and fifty-foot levels. I heard a yell, "Look out below," so I hugged in close to my girder where I was working and had I not, a drift-pin would have hit me. I could hear it banging off one thing and another.

There is one occasion that I will never forget. On the sixty-foot level the girder was only six inches wide. I was at one side of the structure and the foreman at the other, about fifteen feet away. He wanted a rope from my side, so he told me to bring it to him. I put the rope over my shoulder and was going to sit on the girder and sort of *frog* my way across. He told me that was dangerous and that I should walk. A fifteen-foot walk on a six-inch girder, sixty feet high! I stood up where the girders met, and started gingerly, one step and then hesitatingly another, and I was four feet along when I wanted to turn back. It looked like a mile down there. My confidence was leaving me as I glanced down into what seemed an abyss. The foreman was watching and noticed that I was fearful of falling so he yelled, "Come on, Red." I really believe he brought me out of a stupor and I got across safely. It would have been difficult to try to get back. It really was a miserable experience for me, I was thankful I made it over.

I liked the foreman who was an expert at building this type of boiler. He was from the USA. He seemed to like me and helped me a lot to negotiate my job, for which I was thankful. I was the last of the unskilled workers on this job. The huge complicated, modern boiler was put into operation after nine months work.

The dances we attended took on a *hard-time* look. One went in old clothes, the more patches the better. One also took his own lunch then swapped it. It was hilarious. One of the A.Y.P.A.'s favourite activities was sleigh rides in the deep snow of winter. St. Peter's parish was on the north side, St. Mary's south side, St. Paul's downtown, and St. Matthew's, Reverend Adcock's church, southeast. There were other, smaller Anglican churches, but these were the four principal ones. They all had A.Y.P.AS and there was a central committee elected from the churches. Each church had its own programme. At St. Peter's we had dances, visits, plays and helped the church in its programme, teaching Sunday school, singing in the choir, putting on plays, and visiting. The central committee decided to have debates with the main churches and there was strong competition in these debating contests. The chosen subjects were often controversial. They usually had prominent citizens for judges. Anne was on the St. Peter's debate team. I recall meetings with the team and the correlation that went on because I went with her and discussed the whole subject. It surely kept us thinking. Debates can be enlightening and exciting. St. Peter's had good success and won the inter-church trophy one year. I think Anne kept some of these papers for keepsakes. She and I talked frequently in those debating days about philosophy and the purpose of life.

Another job I was fortunate to obtain was at the Regina General Hospital as a male orderly. When smallpox broke out in Durham maximum security jail, they took me on as a security guard. Since I had that experience in a hospital, I wasn't entirely green when I went to the Regina General Hospital. I was with another person who had worked there for ten years and I did more or less what he prompted. This job lasted eleven months before a lay-off, which one had to get used to in Canada. To get laid-off wasn't like getting fired. It meant things changed, like closing one wing of the hospital. One got laid-off or taken on routinely. It was the way of life.

One of my work mates, a chap named Blakey, was quite a case-hardened individual. A patient at one time was hollering in pain. It seemed to be his tummy. I helped Blakey give him enemas. Blakey got mad at him and treated him roughly. After six days they found out that the man had typhoid fever and was in the wrong ward altogether. I saw a man expire for the first time in my life. It was serious for me to witness such a thing. Within ten minutes, the patient was hardly cold yet, and there was Blakey saying, "Come on, old fellow, turn over," and patting him on his buttocks as he was preparing to remove the poor chap. I suppose in his long experience it was just one more incident where a bed had to be made up for someone else.

On summer evenings Anne and I would go to her place after playing tennis. Her brother's place was on the way and at times Norman would be in his store preparing for the next day. This was how I got to know Norman as I often went into his shop. Norman's butcher shop was really something. When Norman acquired the Grand Meat Market, it was from an older chap. Although I didn't get to know him, I remember that he and Norman were in the store together for a day or two during the hand-over of the business. I remember the fellow's work outfit, bowler hat, striped apron, and butcher's steel hanging by his side. It was an antiquated but interesting sight. I never saw Norman like that; he was always dressed in white. There was the store front plus a back room where hamburger was made.

Now Norman and Anne were boarding at Mrs. West's, one block from the store. I went to the house with Anne and met with Mrs. West for the first time. I saw her often over the years at St. Peter's Church where she was in charge of infant church school. I had a class of boys twelve to thirteen years old. So I was beginning more than ever to feel acclimatized with a sense of purpose taking hold inside me. I used to have long talks with Reverend Creal who was the superintendent. The Creals were a nice family, three boys and one girl. I had all their children in Sunday school at one time or another.

Anne and I were still together and enjoying each other's company. Times were really good for us. We used to join other couples at A.Y.P.A. There was George Todd and Mae Hanson, Norman and his girlfriend, Gert Aldon, Tommy and Mona, and Gwen Loving and her boyfriend,

Bill Andrews and Molly. After church on Sunday evenings we would all assemble around the piano and Mr. Loving would play while we sang.

The congregation at St. Peter's, and indeed the whole community of the north side, enjoyed The Music Hall Memories. This was a real Music Hall show in character and in audience participation, complete with heckling and catcalls. It was a very entertaining two and one half hours and once I had a part in it. I painted some scenery for the sets and was also the curtain man. George was a star. The audience would never let him off the stage until he had rendered "Albert and the Lion." In fact he could do any of those series by memory. Mrs. Walker was the pianist and had all the music and songs of the 1900s. St. Peter's had a good choir and singers with Albert Yates and Mr. Teelman and their families. Mr. Calcott always sang *On the Road to Mandalay*. Skits were usually lively. Mr. Loving delighted himself by positioning himself at the rear of the hall and hollering back at the performers.

Music Hall Memories lasted many years. The whole church was involved, A.Y.P.A., choir, men's club, ladies' auxiliary. Anne and I were right in there with it all. I recall Anne and I did something new at the A.Y.P.A.. We held a pick-up-sticks drive. We played it as a whist drive, with four at a table, and kept count of scores. We had fun with that but it didn't catch on. The church also raffled one of my paintings. I recall that I sold some small ones, five by nine, for two dollars and fifty cents each.

Norman Tindall sometimes got me to help at the butcher shop on Saturday mornings. It was always busy. Norman and his helpers would always be working late on Friday nights, getting ready for the Saturday morning rush. Often he would tell me just to answer the phone as orders by phone were steady. I got caught one morning by a lady who was well known to Norman and Ernie Ireland, his henchman. I answered the phone, "Grand Meat Market!"

A lady said, "Yes!" in very cultivated English, "I would like to order a beef'art."

My *Geordie* ears couldn't quite comprehend what she said, so I repeated out loud. "A beef fart?" She repeated that she would like a *beef'art*. I made frantic motions to Norman to come to the phone, but he couldn't for laughing. Neither could Ernie, who was doubled over with laughter, as were some of the customers at the counter. Was my face red! Mrs. Stephenson and her beef'art. Some people never do pronounce their "H's." Anyhow, it was good for a laugh.

It was now 1933, Christmas was coming, and winter was upon the land. Anne asked me if I would like to go with her to her family home at Bethune. Norman and Joyce were planning to go, and Norman was borrowing his friend's car. I was working in R.H. Williams toy department and playing Santa Claus. The store would be closing at 9:00 p.m.. Anne would be off at five o'clock, but Norman's store would be busy until 9:00 p.m., so they wouldn't pick me up until ten o'clock. It was wintry, very cold with blowing snow. We wondered about the trip in this weather, but decided to try it anyway. The journey to Bethune was forty miles. The ground was already covered with snow. Chains had been put on the car tires before we snuggled into the old car. It wasn't snowing too hard when we started out but when we got clear of the city, it got worse and we were soon into a blizzard. The snow was drifting so badly that it filled in all the car ruts that previous cars had made. Norman kept on driving as best he could, but we often got stuck. I would get out of the car and push; it was exhausting. When we were near Lumsden we became lost, stuck, and couldn't see the road. Norman left us in the car while he went to a farmhouse to ask if the farmer could help to get us out. The farmer came with a team of horses and pulled us onto the road. He wanted us to stay at the farm until morning, but Norman thought we could drive on, so we did. I really believe had it not been for a small mickey of brandy that Norman had brought, we would have frozen to death. We had blankets in the car, but no heater. So we would go, then stop, push and go again. Finally we saw a light and thought it must be Lumsden. It was now 2:00 A.M. The lights showed in the sky, so we headed for them. Alas! We were back in Regina. Thank the Lord we were somewhere. We went home to sleep, but Norman was determined we could get there in daylight, so off we went again at 7:00 a.m. It had stopped snowing for a while and this time we got to Lumsden and on to Bethune, but it was slow going and took us seven hours.

Anne's parents were so glad to see us. They had worried themselves sick, but now they all were home. Mr. and Mrs. Tindall, their three boys, their three girls, and me. The Tindall family was the best thing that ever happened to me. They made me feel so happy and they were all so good to me. I remember Christmas dinner and the family joy. The house was on high ground and it was cold as the wind whined like it always does on the prairie. There was a ladder to go into the attic space where I slept. My, it was cold! I was glad when morning came. Norman had to be back in Regina, so we didn't have much time together, but experiences like this cemented friendships and welded hearts together. I really got to love the Tindall family as if they were my own.

The time came to take our leave and start back for the city, leaving at 1:30 p.m., just after lunch. We should be in Regina, even on a slow journey, by four or five o'clock, but no, we were in Lumsden at three o'clock, twenty miles from Regina. It snowed again, the snow drifted in the tracks, and I pushed the car the whole twenty miles. We arrived, thankful but utterly exhausted, at ten o'clock that night. I never had been so tired in my whole life, but it was all worth it. I think I would hesitate to have another such journey when the temperatures drop to forty degrees below zero.

A family moved into Regina and lived near the Lovings. Their name was Mellor and they attended St. Peter's Church. The man was employed as an accountant by the Adanac Brewery. Anne and I got to know them through the Lovings. The Adanac employees were mostly of German descent, although the office staff was not. He put in a word for me and I got taken on to work on the bottling line. The brewery was bottling three days per week. There were several men on the line; two feeding the bottles into the machine; one man on the soaker; two examining the full bottles for *oysters*; two putting on the wrap; two putting the bottles into cartons; one taking them away. I was packing. When the brewery bottled it was similar to the automobile lines. It was so many cases for the day's work, then go home. Sometimes there would be extra work correcting rejects and cleaning and washing down the machinery. At other times there would be extra work revarnishing the insides of the huge storage vats. This was an experience hard to forget. The vats, six of them, were located in the cold cellar. They were ten feet high, with a radius of nine feet, and were sealed tightly except for the crawl hole used to get inside for cleaning and revarnishing. There was no circulating air inside and a heater was used to dry the wood before the varnish could be applied. The temperature was kept high for the best job of varnishing. Consequently, it was hot and with no circulated air there was a very strong smell of varnish. I recall how I would gasp to get my head outside the hole. It made my head spin. The heat was like being in a Turkish bath.

Outside the vat, but still in the cellar, it was freezing. But there were others to do the work if you complained. It was a custom that at lunch one could have a free bottle of beer, and two bottles at the end of work before going home, if consumed on the premises. There was a lunch room that the workers used and it was interesting to me to see how the others lunched. The Germans used to have a lump of bread and cheese and they would just cut chunks off the cheese with anything that came to hand. I also remember how the Germans used to argue heatedly about politics in Germany. Frequently, the name *Hitler* would be the centre of big rows. I got to know some of the men quite well. Two of them that I knew, Anne also knew since their wives worked with her at the Queen City cleaners.

Anne and I used to go quite frequently to the German Canadian Hall where music and dancing were enjoyable. We loved the Strauss Waltzes and the Polkas. As we walked home from these dances, the vastness of the prairie skies gave us a humbling feeling. We loved walking and often walked north on Fourth Avenue along the railway tracks to the terminal. These were memorable times for us, courting, just being together, and talking about everything one could think about.

The Regina public libraries were great consolation during this time because they provided books, papers and magazines from other locales. I frequently used the main branch downtown near Twelfth Avenue, at McIntyre Street for newspapers, and the one near where Anne boarded, at Seventh Avenue and Robinson Street. I walked from the Barkers, who lived just off Seventh Avenue, so it was an eight-block walk, and the sidewalk was *duck-boards* all the way. I read mostly the classics and the arts, bringing two books home at a time. I recall one time walking back with two books under my arm with my hands in my pockets. Some of these boards in the sidewalk became loose, and I stood on one of these loose ones, then fell flat on my face, with my hands in my pockets. It wasn't funny, but it must have looked funny. When I had a date with Anne, I would walk this same route so I'll always remember how happy I was, knowing I was going to be with her. I recall a little verse I used to hum. It went like this:

I am stepping out to see my sweetheart
I'm stepping out to see my girl
I'm stepping out to see my sweetheart
For I know that she is swell.
The boards on the sidewalk spring
As my heart and my voice, join in, and sing.
I'm stepping out to see my sweetheart
I'm stepping out to see my girl.

It really was lighthearted.

By now Anne boarded at the Cochranes. They were good people and thought a lot of Anne. I would call for her there when we went to play tennis, and proceed, still on Seventh Avenue, to McTavish Street. The courts were on Scott Collegiate grounds. We were well acquainted with the group and had a very nice tennis dance every year.

As the depression years wore on the drought continued and grasshopper plagues began. Farmers' crops were ruined in a single day when clouds of grasshoppers descended to feed. On weekends, I had been going to Bethune where Anne's parents lived. Norman had a car now and I would ride with him. They lived on a scanty piece of land and hardly ever was there much growth as it was too dry and stony. Also living at Bethune were Uncle George and Aunt Mary, Anne's dad's sister, Uncle Will and Martha, and also Uncle Fred and Grace. They had better times in earlier years. Uncle Will held a good acreage of land and he and Fred had been there for many years as homesteaders. Uncle Will was also Reeve of the Municipality, an elected civic job, so they were all well known. Anne's mother and father were newcomers, and it was tough to make a go of it. I met all the relatives. Anne told me at one time that Aunt Martha wasn't impressed with me as Anne's choice. Uncle Will was a big man but quiet in his speech. What he lacked in volume Aunt Martha easily made up for. Uncle Fred was a serene, easy going farmer. He told me that in his early days he had spent one whole winter in a small cabin on his land and never saw another person until spring. Uncle George Lord was also a war veteran. The only water pump, the village pump, was on his land in the town of Bethune. Norman used to go to Bethune to hunt. I remember a time one of his guns was laying in the bottom of the democrat wagon and went off, blowing a hole in the tail gate. It surely gave us a scare.

The whole family knew now that sometime when economics improved, Anne and I would get married, but things didn't improve for Anne's family. In Regina, Norman was doing okay and Gladys and Anne both worked in the city. But the outlook on the farm was glum, and after family talks, they came to a conclusion that there was no future on the farm, so they made a family decision to move into Regina and rent a house at 550 Scarth Street. It had a fair-sized garden, a large barn, and a shed. Now the family could live under one roof. The house was situated in north Regina, about a mile from the big Simpson's Store, on Broad Street, north.

The girls used to cross the field in order to catch the streetcar for downtown. The fare at that time was a nickel. There were not many cars in those days so streetcars were frequently used. One could buy a ticket and transfer if necessary to connecting lines. Anne told me of one amusing event. She bought a ticket and boarded the streetcar, getting a transfer, but she didn't use it that day. A few days later she got on a streetcar and gave the conductor that same transfer. A little later he called her and asked her about the transfer. Anne said she'd had it for a couple of days. He said, "Did you read the writing?"

"No," said Anne.

"Well, it says this transfer is good only for fifteen minutes after issue!"

Ah well! We all have to learn.

When they moved, the whole family went to plant the garden and generally get settled in. They had brought a couple of horses with them from the farm: a grey named Lucy and a sway back, quite old, named Dolly. I recall how Joyce loved to ride Lucy. They also brought with them their lovable collie dog, Blackie. After a week or so the dog was missing and could not be found. Three weeks later they heard from people at Bethune that the dog had returned to their old home place.

In 1934 there was great unrest in Canada, particularly on the prairies and especially in Regina and Winnipeg. Unemployment was rampant. The government in *Saskatchewan* had single men sent to camps where they were paid twenty-five cents a day. It was dismal, so much so that a trek of protest workers was organized in Vancouver. Their aim was to board a train in Vancouver, pick up adherents at every station enroute to Ottawa, and there confront the Prime Minister. Daily the media and papers kept track of these protesters.

By the time their train reached Regina, the mood of the protesters was heated. About two thousand got off the train. They lived in railway sidings, or anywhere that they could find. We had read of skirmishes occurring between marchers and police previous to the mob reaching Regina, and now they were in Regina waiting for word from a delegation enroute to Ottawa. Regina was a likely place to halt this march because Regina was the headquarters of the R.C.M.P., the Royal Canadian Mounted Police.

The government, headed by Prime Minister R.B. Bennett, sent out an order that the trek had to be stopped at Regina. The marchers were many and were organizing to continue their move on to Ottawa. On July 1, they were confronted by lines of Mounties on Eleventh Avenue, when rioting broke out. I remember the noise of that encounter. I was at Tindall's home. Everyone wondered what on earth was going on. There was roaring, gunfire and smoke. We were about a half mile away from the fighting and destruction. A cemetery and dump separated us from the melee. The noise of battle, shooting and screaming went on for hours. It had spread out onto Broad Street at Eleventh, all the way down Eleventh Street, Rae Street, Scarth Street, and the whole downtown area.

Apparently the leaders of the trek to Ottawa were getting the crowd assembled, ready to move, when the Mounties and the city police moved in to halt the whole thing. It was awful! I heard someone was killed. The marchers' leaders were arrested and hundreds were hurt by rocks, clubs and guns. Every store window on Eleventh Avenue was broken and some stores were burned. It was days afterwards before anyone could get around. I remember how awful Eleventh Avenue looked as I ventured out to see the damage. The trek was stopped, although some of the marchers did go on to Winnipeg and there was some trouble there.

Every city had soup kitchens and there was no work, no money, and no hope. The prairies were dust bowls. One weekend as I was going to

Qu'Appelle with Walter Barker, the wind was blowing a bit when we started out, but when we got out of the city the wind got stronger and the dust was making the air brown. It was so bad that we could not see the road, and the ditches at both sides of the road were dust filled so there was great difficulty keeping on the road. We had to get out to get the car turned around, covering our faces with handkerchiefs because the dust and wind were like being sand-blasted. Worse even than in the snow, the headlights just reflected everything in the same colour back at you! We were extremely lucky to make it back to the city without injury. I was so thankful to be out of that unforgettable prairie dust-storm. One of the most distressing sights was the telephone poles all askew, wires hanging down and barren nothingness, only howling wind and blinding dust. Even when the wind died down, the sight of farmhouses and sheds, barns and outhouses was appalling. The soil was literally blown off the farms.

I remember a cartoonist who had drawn a farmer in his best old Ford car trying to keep up with his farm as it was being blown down the road. What causes disasters like this? It was true that too much of the earth's crust had been taken off the land, exposing the loose soil to be blown. These dust storms occurred every time there was a strong wind. It was correctly named the Dust Bowl. In later years, farmers resorted to *strip* farming to correct all the land being bare at the same time.

I was in a home atmosphere again and it was good. Anne's mum and dad were really good to me and welcomed my visiting with them. I had somewhere to go now. I loved Anne's mum and dad, they were the salt of the earth. Dad was quite a humourist, especially his witty sayings. Anne often said, "My Dad used to say . . . ." We regularly had fun in the evenings, especially in the fall and winter nights, playing cards, crib and whist and rummy. Norman had his store, Anne worked at Rose's cleaning plant, Gladys worked at Simpson's, Joyce worked for Norman, and the two boys, Vic and Arthur, lived at home and went to school.

The Tindall's eventually bought a home at 350 St. John Street. It was much more spacious with a basement and a second storey with three bedrooms, a nice kitchen facing west and a large living room. There was a large garden area, a fair-sized shed, and an outside toilet. There was also a large soft-water tank in the basement.

Mr. Tindall at various times worked for Canada Packers, plucking chickens, earning a nickel per bird. I also got some work at Canada Packers, making twenty-five cents an hour. Since I only worked by the hour, some days I would be at the building all day and have only three hours work. Mr. Tindall sometimes helped Norman at the butcher shop making hamburger meat. Norman and Ernie Ireland did the boning. Joyce also worked at Norman's store, making Melton Mowbray pork pies. The Grand Meat Market was a busy place and in a way supported the entire household. The girls, Gladys and Anne contributed to the home also, and all in all it was a very happy place. I have always had great admiration for the family. Victor and Arthur were great fun, playing pranks on their dad as boys would. There was a table tennis set up in the outside shed and it was fun. Mr. Tindall played a good game, as did Vic and Arthur. Young Arthur also played hockey. His dad and I used to travel around watching games on open-air ice. Arthur also had a paper route. I recall during the winter how he would go on his rounds on horse back and frequently his cheek bones would be frozen white by the time he returned home. Dad Tindall was an excellent gardener and grew most of the family's vegetables; potatoes, carrots, spinach. He was self supporting in garden produce. Norman usually provided the meats. I remember always the lovely meals at Thanksgiving, Christmas and New Years and what joyous times they were. The family attended church regularly at a little church in north Regina.

Mr. Tindall's family lived in Lincolnshire. His parents are buried at Market Rasen. They were farmers. Mr. Tindall (Arthur) and his wife Mary moved to Derbyshire where he worked at the coal-mine. Before that he worked on the Duke of Portland's estate. Mary worked as a domestic in Nottingham Castle.

Mr. Tindall was a real family man who took his responsibilities seriously. He was very even-tempered and I never saw him in a rage; quite the opposite, he was always cheerful and humourous. He put his family first, both in word and deed. Mary was the same. Devoted to her children, she baked, washed, and canned for the home with such dedication. One couldn't help but love them as they were honest and kind people. They became my surrogate mum and dad, too. I thank the good Lord so often for leading me to them. The Tindall family provided ideal examples of love at home. They had their share of trials to contend with, of course, but they had a faith in God and themselves, always doing what they thought was right. I couldn't have found a better family anywhere. They became brothers and sisters to me and I shall always be grateful and humble to be one of them.

At that time so much of the recession's politics entered nearly every aspect of life. R.B. Bennett was still Prime Minister and unemployment was rife. Truly the country was in difficult times. There were two main parties, Conservative and Liberal, with a new labour party coming on, called the C.C.F. or Co-operative Commonwealth Federation. I remember it so well because Anne's dad used to talk about the political situation. There was an individual who called on him and his every second sentence was, "The System's got to be changed." That became a byword. The system had to be changed, and so it was. In Saskatchewan, the men at the head were Coldwell, a schoolteacher, Douglas, a church minister, and Fines, a school teacher. These men became nationally famous later on when the C.C.F. party became the N.D.P., or New Democratic Party.

CHAPTER SEVEN
The Wedding

THROUGH MY WORK WITH THE Bird Construction Company, I was able to get on to their painting crew when they won a big contract to do maintenance and painting at the Imperial Oil Plant in Regina. This was a big break for me. The crew was composed of Charley Varley, the foreman and six of us painters. Our work was mostly in a big barn of a building where we repainted and did upkeep on rolling stock, such as tank cars. Our job was to sandblast all the old paint from these great *oil tanks on wheels*, then spray paint them with red oxide paint, followed by another coat of black spray. After these coats had been completed and were dry, we painted names and numbers on both sides of the tanks. My mate was Arnold Harrison. We stencilled and cut-in the large letters. There were three of these rolling railway stock tanks in the shed at one time. This work continued steadily and I was paid sixty cents an hour.

When there was a lack of tank cars, we would work in the yard, repainting the very large storage tanks which held four million gallons of oil. We painted them with aluminum paint first, then spray painted them, working from an aerial platform called a *sailor's chair*. We also painted the seventy-foot high smoke stacks using these chairs. Here my experience with the steel gang on the power house boiler helped me tremendously in working at so great a height from the ground. I remember how I would sit on a sailor's chair, a large pot of paint hanging at each side of the seat, and I would be hauled up by workmen on the ground. Then at the top, seventy feet up, I snubbed the rope and got on with the painting. I would hardly notice it, but there was a six-foot sway at the top of those stacks. When you moved downward, the snub was slackened and the descent was controlled in that manner. It was all in a day's work and I was glad to get it. I recall one member of our crew falling sixty feet, but fortunately he only got burnt hands from the rope. It was amazing that he was not killed.

Working regularly now, I was feeling better about myself. Anne was still with Art Rose's cleaning plant, repairing furs. We were together as much as possible. We really loved each other and had great joy planning our wedding. Deciding to buy an engagement ring was exciting. Anne shopped for a few days, then led me to a jewelry shop on Twelfth Avenue, McKenzie Jewellers. We were in the store for about a half hour and Anne had her engagement ring. Thirty-two dollars, it cost! This was a week and a half's pay. We intended to go to the show at the Capitol Theatre, but then decided this was too joyous a moment in our lives to sit watching pictures, so we went walking. We talked and laughed and were walking on air, feeling buoyant. We never forgot that Saturday evening. We were so elated. We looked forward to the day we would be married.

There was plenty to live for in those days. The world puts on its best face for those who find a zest for living. Then there were lots of things to be done. George Todd, my best friend, was to be my best man, and Anne had decided to ask sisters Gladys and Joyce to be her bridesmaids. Anne's mum and dad were very happy, and the whole family accepted me graciously. The wedding feast would be at 350 St. John Street. All arrangements were being made with Reverend Creal at St. Peter's Church. So the days and weeks went by with great anticipation and preparation. This was the first marriage of a daughter for the Tindall family and in that sense it was special. My own family in England was unable to be present, although we received many well wishes from them.

It has been said that preparation and anticipation are the best parts of an event. I could hardly say that as I look back. Certainly everything leading up to the wedding was fantastic, looking for new clothes, making the bride's and bridesmaid's dresses, ordering the wedding cake, inviting the guests, and arranging the church. We were all into the spirit of the occasion. But love is all this and more, so much more knowing we are to share our lives together, to be with one another, giving the best of what we are in the joy of each other's company. We had courted all those years during the depression of the thirties, tying our hearts into one knot, never to be undone. We were confident in each other. God had blessed us. During the time previous to our marriage, we had many gatherings with those involved, George and Mae Todd, Norman and the family and all those around the circle of our day-to-day living.

George Todd and Mae Hanson were going together. George was from England, and his family was all in England, so he was forever at the Hansons as I was at the Tindalls. Mrs. Hanson was a widow, and at home there was one son, Bob, and two girls, Mae and her sister. We were often together at one place or another. Mae and Anne were real pals and along with several of the other members of St. Peter's, they formed a group: Evelyn Baldwin, the Champion sisters, Norman's wife Addie Madden and her sisters. They were a goodly number and met for decades.

Other neighbours and friends were the Skillicorn family. Mr. Skillicorn worked at Imperial Oil as a carpenter. Mrs. Skillicorn kept the home. They were involved in the little Anglican church. Mr. Skillicorn was church warden and looked after the building. There were two daughters, Carrie and Ruth. Carrie played the church organ and Ruth was quite a dancer. She married a fellow named Melanchuk. They had two boys, Wayne and Rick. Other friends, the Kerleys, had a daughter, Kay, who was to sing at our wedding.

Christmas and New Year of 1937 passed and at long last our big day was at hand. Winter was receding but I don't think we ever gave the weather a thought. Finally it was April and everything was in place, especially the girls' wedding dresses, fitted with flowers, posies and boutonnieres. I bought a new suit at Tip Top Tailors on Scarth Street. It cost twenty-five dollars.

So we gathered at St. Peter's Church on April 20, 1938, at 3:00 p.m.. I with George, waiting, waiting, waiting. Finally the Reverend Creal came. It was he who was late. The organ played "Here comes the bride," and sure enough there was Anne with her dad. Life stood still in the sheer ecstasy of the moment as we held hands. After seven years of waiting in times of great uncertainty, we had forged an understanding of the values that make for joy and happiness. We were truly happy, praise God. The wedding was memorable. Kay sang "Because God Made You Mine" for both of us. She sang beautifully and everyone was so sweet. The bridesmaids were lovely in their long dresses.

We finally got out of the church after the ceremony. We were smothered with confetti at St. Peter's main door and went off noisily in Norman's car with the tin cans rattling. We were with the photographers for quite a while and then on to 350 St. John Street for the reception, just the family and those partaking in the wedding and Mr. and Mrs. Creal. It really was a feast and fun that night. About 10:00 p.m. we were to go to a house on Dewdney in the car, but someone had inadvertently (most likely, on purpose) let the air out of the tires, so we fled across the fields. Oh! it was joy, so cool in fresh air, and we were alone in utter bliss. Nothing would ever take this from us.

The years of the depression held great trials and much worry, but I remember it with great joy and thankfulness. After all, it gave me Anne, a partner in life, bound by a love that no trials could sever.

The Tindall family at 350 St. John's. From L to R: Anne, Victor, Gladys, Arthur and Mary, Joyce, Arthur, Norman.

Our courting days.

Anne and I on our wedding day, April 20, 1938.

CHAPTER EIGHT
Prelude to War

UPON RETURNING FROM OUR HONEYMOON, we accepted the loan of a furnished house at the corner of Robinson Street and Dewdney Avenue while the owner was away. I had been friendly with a chap named Jack Hempson, who was also a harvester. He stayed in Canada for a while before going back home to England, residing at Mrs. Corson's, which was the house next door to St. Paul's Church. Thus, I met Mrs. Corson while in her home calling on Jack. She therefore knew I was getting married. As she was planning a six-months holiday in England, she offered us the use of her furnished home. All we had to do was look after the house, along with her dog, a big German Shepherd. So Anne and I had a rendezvous with Mrs. Corson, saw the house and the dog, and we accepted her offer. She intended to be gone for the whole summer.

I was working at Imperial Oil, but Anne did not go back to work at the dry cleaners. When we moved to Mrs. Corson's, I had to take the street car to work. It was June when Mrs. Corson left on her holiday. She was kind and left us well informed about her house and dog, which was a large gentle animal. I found time to complete a painting of its head in profile, and we still have that painting. It was fun settling into married life in our own quarters. There was the house to look after as well as the garden. I worked at my job from 8:00 a.m. until 4:30 p.m., with half an hour for lunch. We kept up our church activities and church school.

One day a circus came to town. We heard it was worth seeing, so we went. It was no big deal, other than being out together now as man and wife, but the circus was really enjoyable. It was set up in the Regina Armouries, a great hall. The circus fitted in comfortably and left one end for small concessions. The show started at 7:00 p.m., and after an interesting first half, there was an intermission. So out of our seats we went, down to the concession to see what was being offered. We elected to have a soft drink, so we approached a stall and a rather husky chap waited on us. We ordered soft drinks and snacks and I bought a package of Players cigarettes. I smoked a little those days. So I said, "How much?" paid the man and we walked away.

Anne said, "He charged you too much!"

"Oh," I said, "they always charge more at concessions."

Anne insisted that I had been charged too much and said, "Why don't you go back and protest?" I was reluctant and tried to pass it off. I didn't want to go back. Anne teased me, laughingly saying I was lacking in intestinal fortitude. We had our refreshments and took our place to see the second half of the circus. The first item was a comedy act. Then it was announced that the feature act was a strong man. So this fellow came out in scant apparel, showing bulging muscles with legs like a billiard table, a nineteen-inch neck and a forty-six-inch chest, and, alas, he was the same guy who had served our refreshments at the concession! Anne and I both shook with laughter. It must have been my lucky day not to go back and start an argument with him.

The first thing the strong man did was to put iron bar in his mouth. Then he took hold of each end and bent it into the letter "Q." "My Gosh!" I said to Anne, "Can you imagine what he'd have done to me?" Then he asked for two men out of the audience to go up and help him in his next feat of strength. He wanted two men who could wield a sledge hammer. I thought I heard Anne say, "Now's your chance." The man lay down on his back on stage and his assistant brought in a blacksmith's anvil and placed it on his chest. The two fellows out of the audience were to pound on the anvil. I chafed Anne about the kind of characters she picked for me. We laughed so many times about that night at the circus that over the years we really did get value for our money. It was great fun.

There was a little corner store a block from the Corson home, quite handy for household commodities and snacks. Anne and I would use this small place for an ice cream cone or soft drink when sauntering out after working in the garden. It was downtown and Anne loved to walk along Eleventh Avenue and window shop. The backyard was next to the United Church yard. By being out in the garden we became friendly with the Baldwins. Mr. Baldwin was a caretaker at the United Church. They lived in the basement suite. Anne used to visit Mrs. Baldwin at times when I was at work. Their son Billy Baldwin was an excellent tennis player and he and I got to the finals in the civil service tournament. We took it without much trouble. I think that was the highest point I ever got in my tennis career.

Wascana Park was on College Avenue about four blocks away. We would go there often to view Wascana Lake and the Parliament Buildings. The grasshoppers were taking full advantage of the heat and dry land. The soil was dust, with no moisture to hold it together. The garden was a struggle to grow, and stunted. I kept the carragana hedge around the back yard trimmed, althought it wasn't growing as it should. Some of the things we had planted and watered were growing weakly, but the horrible grasshoppers took their toll. In the Imperial Oil yard all the large storage tanks were surrounded by built up earth, which acted as a dam should the tank burst or spill. When we, the paint crew, were within those confines, we got a real opportunity to watch these grasshoppers. We could shade our eyes in the shade of the tank and see millions of these creatures in flight, just like it was snowing. When they came down to feed, your crop would be gone. One day they came down in Regina. When I got home, Anne told me to look at the garden. It was unbelievable! The carragana hedge looked like a tree in winter, not a leaf was left on it, and the carrots and other vegetables in the garden were also stripped bare.

In August it was time for the Regina Exhibition. Every year great preparations were made by the whole city to put on a good show. It was always colourful with its booths displaying products. There were cattle, Indians in native garb with teepees, and shows and barkers of every variety. There were horse races every day for the whole two-week period. I recall how busy Anne's brother, Norman, was supplying the fair people and booths with meats. Nearly everyone had a day at the exhibition. Anne and I certainly enjoyed going each year. I remember one of the nights in particular, the hour was getting on to 8:00 p.m. when a very dark cloud appeared on the horizon. People began to scatter, knowing what to expect. A storm could be seen coming and when it struck it was with great force. In spite of the warning and battening down, there was always a lot of damage with high winds and blowing rain. We got home before the brunt, but preceding the storm was a terrific wind creating much dust.

There was expectation and then great excitement in another direction now. It was confirmed that Anne was pregnant. One can hardly describe what this meant to us; we didn't know whether to laugh or cry, we were so excited! It seemed like the baby-to-be took over all our activities. It was something new, of course, the first baby. What care we must take in everything we do. Anne was a naturally practical person and therefore remained calm. I was scared, and didn't want to leave her, even when I went to work. The family was as joyous as we were, their first grandchild on the way. We tried to remain sophisticated and went around as if nothing were happening. But the baby showed anyway. I remember Anne and her morning sickness at first. It was a worry for me to see her in distress. I recall one night at almost midnight when Anne had me go down to the little snack shop for a hamburger. She said she was famished for a hamburger. So I got her one. She would get fancies for incredible tastes.

Mrs. Corson would be returning soon now, so we did everything to have the house as nice as when we had moved in. Everything was okay and the dog was fine, for which we were thankful. And so another chapter ended for us when Mrs. Corson came back home from England. She had enjoyed her holiday and was glad to be back in her own home. It was very satisfactory to her and us, for which we were also thankful, both to her and to the good Lord.

When Mrs. Corson returned to her home, Anne and I moved back to Mum and Dad's at 350 St. John Street. Anne would have the care and company of her mother and dad while I was at work. Christmas was not so far off. Anne was able to go to the doctor's as frequently as necessary and all was well. It was always nice at the Tindall home. There was always fun with the lads, Vic and Arthur. Anne kept busy, usually reading about care of babies. The weather was getting cold. Anne sewed a lot, and I remember that she made her own fur coat and hat. She looked stunning when dressed up. Her morning sickness and other consequences of her condition had run their course and at least she was now more comfortable.

Day by day we did the things we would ordinarily do, working during the day, homemaking, cooking, house cleaning, washing. In the evenings we would sit around, talking and listening to the radio. In those days, Sunday evenings featured the Jack Benny show and the Charley McCarthy show. In the afternoons, we heard the Orphan Annie serial, and the two black clowns, Amos and Andy. The bands were usually Benny Goodman and Nelson Eddy. Joyce at that time had a boyfriend named Charley, a local boy. He was always laughing. When he came to the house, it seemed he had the answer to everything. His response was: "It don't matter." After a few months, the affair didn't work out. I guess it didn't matter! Perhaps one is the way one thinks.

When Anne's time came to have the baby, she was taken to Grey Nuns, the Roman Catholic Hospital at Dewdney Avenue and Pasqua Street, Regina. The date was March 10, 1939. Our baby was born March 12, 1939. We were all so happy. Everything went well, and Anne was fine. I was at the hospital at every opportunity. We had previously decided on a name. Anne liked the name Pamela, her mother's name was Mary, and my mum's name was Mary Jane. So praise the Lord we had a wee bairn named Pamela Mary! Anne's philosophy of life leaned to the importance of family and family life. She was always concerned with children, not only her own, but all children. To have her own child was an experience she looked forward to with great zeal. She now had her own lab, as it were, in which to bend the things dear to her feelings of love.

It seemed to me that the hospital kept mother and baby for ten days. Going to see Anne and baby after work every night seemed a long time, so we were happy when we got Anne and the wee one home to 350 St. John Street. It was a different situation at home now, with a wee person in a way calling the shots: feeding time, cries and getting all the attention.

In the spring of 1939, newspapers carried news of an upheaval occurring in Europe. There were great disturbances, especially in Germany. The country was torn by the ravings of a bloke named Hitler. I remembered this name from when I had worked in the Adanac Brewery. I recall that more than half the employees were of German descent. Many times during lunch break the Germans would enter heated arguments about what was going on in Germany. The name Hitler was nearly always the topic and his name brought fierce anger. At one time the rage became so vicious that one of the workers on the barrels, the cooper, picked up his mallet and threw it with all his force at the head of his adversary. This got to be a common scene while I was employed there in 1936.

Now the threat of war was real. Hitler had trodden down, imprisoned, or removed all opposition to the ideals written in his book *Mien Kempf*. His name would be in the newspapers and he would scream over the radio about the Aryans being the best people on earth, and the Jews the worst. He accused the Jews of the world's troubles, and dispatched any who opposed him. The whole of Europe was now very uneasy about this tyrant's rise to power. In the British government the greatest opponent, Churchill, often sounded the alarm about Germany's new leader. The Baldwin-Chamberlain government was pacifist and was following no line of preparation for war. In 1939, Germany began annexing lands trimmed from them as a result of World War I peace terms.

Our baby, Pamela, was four months old now and doing very well. Anne was up and around and doing. The garden was planted, and there had been a shower for Pamela, along with all the excitement about the baby things that it brings. We could go out together as there was a house full of willing baby sitters. We were accumulating a few personal things, such as a baby carriage. Anne had books on baby care, including Doctor Spock's. This was a busy time for me. I was best man for George Todd and Mae Hanson. I was also best man for Anne's brother, Norman and his bride, Addie when they were married on September 20, 1937. I remember Norman and Addie's wedding being somewhat marred because some guests got sick from some contaminated chicken. Norman and Addie went to live at 1078 Rae Street, and George and Mae with Mrs. Hanson at 7 Block Rae Street. It was a lovely summer in 1939 and life was better because we had work, were married and were busy with families.

Anne and I used to scan the daily papers looking for a place to live. It wasn't easy since our finances were small. Things were a little better but the depression had not ended. As the summer wore on there was deep concern among the people about the possibility of war. Germany had walked into countries and had simply taken them. There was talk of an invasion of Belgium and indeed a threat by Hitler to take the whole of Europe, perhaps the world. Hitler seemed mad with power. The British government was now following a plan of appeasement, and Prime Minister Chamberlain journeyed back and forth to talk with Hitler, striving to stem the ambition of this power-crazed individual. But he was not able to do so. I recall how tense the radio news became and how bleak were the contents of the press.

Germany under Hitler had built up a mobile force unequalled in the history of man. There was such power in their tanks' long-range guns and automatic weapons. No other nation had anything like them. The air force had *stukas* equipped with cannon that dive-bombed at very low altitudes. It was too late to stop him, and he screeched at any who would be an adversary. The British government failed and the country was beginning to believe Winston Churchill. There was no one to stop Hitler! He had been allowed to develop a power that would not stand for opposition.

In the meantime, Anne and I had seen an ad in the paper stating that Mrs. Young, a widow who lived at 964 Garnet, had her house for sale. She was asking eleven hundred dollars on time, or nine hundred dollars cash. We didn't have that much money, but we did go and look at the house. The lady was quite interesting. We had a nice conversation with her. The house was old-fashioned with a picture-plate shelf going all around the living room. There was a bathroom and toilet, a kitchen and one bedroom on the same floor, a full basement and furnace, hot air heating, and an attic. It looked nice from the outside and had a spare twenty-five-foot lot on the south side, all hemmed in by carragana hedges. The front door was entered by coming through a glassed-in veranda. There were steps to the front and back doors from ground level. The house was nicely furnished. We left to talk about it.

We soon decided that we both liked the house and wanted to see if we could acquire it. Our total cash was seven hundred dollars, so we talked about raising two-hundred more. Anne's sister, Gladys, was able and graciously put up a loan, which enabled us to go to Mrs. Young with our nine hundred dollar cash offer, every cent that we had. We spent the whole evening discussing various aspects of the deal, the deeds, the time of occupancy, and finally it was done. We gave her the money, the house was ours, and she would expedite matters so we could move in during September 1939.

So things were set into motion to get everything ready. Mum and

Dad and the family helped. There wasn't much to move because we didn't have big pieces of furniture. The busy part was cleaning and preparing the house. There were some things we wanted to change, but they could wait. I was particularly happy and thanked the good Lord.

At the end of August 1939, efforts to keep the peace in Europe failed. Chamberlain had gone to Berchtesgaden, Hitler's residence in Germany, and come away with a rebuff to his peace proposals. People on the street already knew there would be war, the atmosphere breathed of conflict. War was declared on September 3, 1939, when German forces under Hitler and his cohorts invaded Poland. With his new mobile army they overran the country with little opposition. War was declared on Germany by Belgium, France, Great Britain and Holland. Italy, under El Duce Mussolini's dictatorship, had been doing its own plundering of smaller states such as Ethiopia, and Haile Selassie was asking for help from anyone. The battle lines were drawn and countries took sides. Canada and America had not made any statement, but Britain was dispatching troops to the continent.

Once the war was on, sooner or later Canada would join. Anne and I talked about the war, as did everyone else. I knew the country would be asking its citizens to go to the aid of countries resisting Hitler and Mussolini. I said to Anne that I should go because our relationship with the old land was so strong. We felt it was the right thing to do. And if it must be that I go to serve my country and the country of my birth, then Anne and Pamela would at least have the security of our own home while I was away. The time was drawing near when I should be joining up.

There had already been some action in Regina. Airports and essential services were being guarded as a precaution. The peacetime militia, NPAM, had been alerted. Key persons for mobilization were being called up. On September 9, Canada declared war on Germany and Italy. The armouries were being made ready for recruitment. The Canadian army would be composed of volunteers.

In those days, I had a chum named Tommy Hogg, who was a civil engineer. He had come to Canada before I did, but I never saw him until I came to Regina. He told me that he had been employed by the Saskatchewan government and had played an important part in their large irrigation systems designed to solve the drought. He was also in the peacetime or reserve army of the Royal Engineers in Regina. Because of an ailment, chronic asthma, he was ineligible for the engineers, but was commissioned as a captain in the newly forming District Depot in Regina. He was also married to Violet Madden, Norman Tindall's sister-in-law. Tom got in touch with me and asked if I wanted to join this recruiting unit. He explained the mechanics of the unit, that there would be a major and driver, a captain, a pay sergeant, a regional quarter master sergeant, and a lance corporal. It would operate out of the Regina Armouries, meaning I could live at home.

I talked this over with Anne. She realized I had strong feelings about the war. It was something nobody wanted, but it was difficult and could not be avoided. We had to decide, and with this lead and knowing Tom, we decided now should be the time. So, I told Tom that I would join the Twelfth District Depot Unit, and made an appointment to see him at the Armouries. I told him that we were moving and it would be a few days before I would be available. So we moved into 964 Garnet Street in September 1939. This was home for us, and we both liked it very much. We had a bed, and had acquired a few other things. There was one thing about it, we were starting from scratch. Anne would have great scope in choosing new things for the home. We had plenty of work to do, but we were living in our own home and we loved it, even if it was bare.

CHAPTER NINE

In the Army

AFTER KEEPING MY APPOINTMENT with Captain Tom Hogg, on September 9, 1939, I joined the Twelfth District Depot Unit as Private Frank Proctor, serial number L22002. As with all individuals joining the services, a medical examination was important. One was sent from the Depot office to the MO, or medical officer. There were always funny things to say about the MOS. A person had to be A-1 to be enlisted. One could be turned down, as indeed many were for one ailment or another. There was usually a queue but it wasn't too long for me as I was early. Since the MO wasn't rushed, he gave me a good going over. "Strip naked, bend over, cough. Ever had this? Ever had that?" Samples of blood and urine were taken. In the end, there didn't seem to be much concern about me, except my teeth were bad. After receiving the urine test results, he asked, "Are you a drinker?" This was something I wasn't, so I asked, "Why?" He said, "Because of the acid content." He assured me it was nothing unusual but added that he didn't think I would ever be troubled with arthritis. That was it for my medical exam to join the Active Service Canadian Army.

So now the staff consisted of the O/C, Major Driver, Captain Hogg, RQMS Sneddon, pay sergeant Henning, and me, Private Proctor. RQMS Sneddon issued me a uniform. There was a shortage of everything at the beginning of World War II. We had World War I khaki coats, pants, forage cap along with army boots, underwear, socks, shirts and sweater. I signed for everything issued to me in a kit bag. Kit inspections were held regularly and if any shortages were found they had to be paid for, but anything worn out or in disrepair could be exchanged.

I went back to Garnet Street, with my kit bag over my shoulder, my hat in my hand, and with a week off before returning to duty. Anne never did show much emotion but we both knew the implication of war. I was home for a week with Anne and Pam, working and trying to get things the way we wanted them. We were so happy and Pam was growing. Anne gave her great care.

Trying on the army uniform had its humourous moments as Anne had a critical eye on the whole get-up. The hat was good for a laugh. I never thought I'd wear one of those things. I guess the little bit of training I got as a night porter at the Kitchener Hotel wearing a porter's hat helped me. Anne took all the wrinkles and creases out of my army jacket and pants, so when I reported I looked smart. Indeed, if clothes make a man, at least I looked like a soldier.

Duty hours would be 8:30 a.m. to 4:30 p.m.. I was to stay at home as there were no accommodations at the Regina Exhibition grounds where there was messing for soldiers billeted on the grounds. I only had lunch there, and had breakfast and supper at home. Army pay wasn't bad and Anne got cheques from the government, except for a little pocket money which I drew from the unit pay master. The army had its own rates for married couples and children. I was fortunate, living only a few blocks from the Armouries as it was like going to a civilian job; out in the morning, back for supper, and sleeping at home.

There was plenty to do, as I was the store-man, under RQMS Sneddon, and each day we would outfit, feed and accommodate those who had joined up. There were daily orders posted for training, reports, and dispatches, those taken on strength, those taken off strength. This gave us the number to be fed or provided for promotion or demotion. There were two daily orders, one dealing with happenings of men, the other with things. Part II was the work sheet. Once there was a call to the District Depot for thirty-five men to fill a shortage in the Saskatoon Light Infantry. Some officers and men in Regina were from the reserve army and had been guarding the Regina airport until the active forces took over. These reserve soldiers signed up at the Depot to *go active* and were dispatched to the Saskatoon Light Infantry on standby to move to Britain. They were enroute in a matter of days.

The Regina Rifles, a reserve battalion, were not as yet mobilized, although they had quarters, or rooms in the Armoury. In the meantime, the exhibition ground adjoining the Armouries was filling with other units. A gun battery from Yorkton, Saskatchewan was in with one hundred and eighty men and officers; the Tenth Field Ambulance was in, the Eighteenth Field Artillery was in, and the Fourteenth Field Engineers were in. And believe it or not, the Royal Canadian Navy Unit recruited and drilled those joining the Navy. This was a daily spectacle. They had a petty officer who, when he shouted "AT-TEN-SHUN" to his guard, everybody in the Armouries came to attention. It was comical, but he was impressive. People had paid money and seen worse shows.

My new way of life involved new relationships with our own staff, and a new way of seeing individuals make important decisions. The *blooming* army was something I was learning about daily. The depot staff was unfit for jobs other than this. Major Driver, the O/C, was too old; Captain Tom Hogg had chronic asthma; Sneddon was too old to go overseas; Sergeant Henning had eye trouble. However, we stayed busy with the war effort.

It was nice that I didn't have to sleep in barracks. I was thankful that I could go home to my family. Captain Hogg would, when he could, give me weekend passes so I was able to help Anne get the home shipshape. Anne was a resourceful homemaker and knew what she wanted so we got things together bit by bit: dining room furniture, living room furnishings and floor coverings. It was really nice to go home, and I looked forward to day's end.

We listened to the radio for news of the war and heard how German pincer movements were swallowing up small countries in Europe. We had feelings about the war but looked on the bright side as we loved our little home, we loved each other, and we adored our baby, Pamela. One night in mid-May 1940, the Germans overran a huge chunk of Belgium and France, bursting the infamous French Maginot Line. The German tanks were swift, making war appear easy, and they advanced impressively.

In Regina there were a large number of Germans, some second generation. They had a German-Canadian Hall and their own printing press. On Eleventh Avenue, east of Broad Street there was a German shopping area: Fuhrmans Meats, the Viennese Kitchen and a number of European-style eating establishments. Through working with Germans at the Adanac Brewery, I knew they had fierce arguments about the goings-on in their fatherland. Some were Hitler supporters and others did not like him. Often I would hear them talk of *Der Tag, The Day*. Hitler's book, *Mien Kempf*, had people, even as far away as Regina, all teed-up for *The Day*, the day when Hitler and Germans would conquer not only the Allies but the world. And now on this May day in 1940, the Germans were running over everything and everybody. When the news hit Regina, the whole of Regina's east end went berserk with joy. They went on a rampage until five o-clock in the morning. *Der Tag* was here!

There were approximately two thousand soldiers living in the barracks at the Exhibition grounds. They didn't like hearing of the Germans' success. The next day, the soldiers talked among themselves and spread word to assemble at the corner of Eleventh Avenue and Broad Street at 7:00 p.m.. There was no compulsion; just be there if you wanted to. Not me, my home was five blocks away and so I went home.

The soldiers assembled at that famous corner where a strong, tall, sergeant major of the Eighteenth Field Artillery took the lead. At 7:00 p.m. sharp he lined them up in columns of three, turned them to face the east end, and quick-marched them into where the German supporters had celebrated the night before. Over eight hundred took part and they wrecked any establishment lending support to the enemy. It was said that even Mounties joined in. They went on to wreck the printing presses and there were some who went a second night to finish the job.

The o/c Twelfth District confined all the soldiers to barracks. No one was to leave; no passes, except to essential personnel. Most of the citizens of Regina applauded the actions of the soldiers, but the top brass had to show they were in control. On their third day of confinement, an elderly lady came nosing around the Depot office seeking someone she could talk to, so we ushered her into the orderly room to talk to the captain. She wanted to know when the soldiers were going down there again as she knew a place that they had missed. Needless to say, that quelled things down, but it did more than that, for the authorities sought out all those who were known to be pro-Hitler and interned them. It was surprising who they got, some highly respected citizens, lawyers, businessmen, dentists and people from all walks of life.

Twelfth District Depot became busy as the Canadian First Division was marshalled and dispatched as quickly as possible to Britain. I was kept busy fitting and issuing army outfits. Gradually there was a better supply from the "ordinances." These were warehouses, from which units' needs were supplied. Indents had to be submitted on proper forms. I was learning on the job. A course on Quarter Mastering became available. I applied and took the ten week course.

RQMS Sneddon had just about given up on feeding the troops. Food had to be provided every day. The cooks in the kitchens got rations from their own units. There were five or six kitchens operating at the fair grounds. These were the food concession buildings in peace time. It became my job to do the indents from the feeding of the Depot personnel. This included all staff and all recruits enlisted and awaiting placement. It was difficult at times for I had to indent for the next day, and I didn't know how many would be enlisting, sometimes ten, sometimes two hundred, depending on the movement of troops. I managed fairly well working in close relationship with the cooks and kitchen staffs.

My QM course was proving interesting. It was based on Active Service and methods different from peacetime. Our present staff and officers were somewhat slanted toward World War I methods and reserve type regulations. There was still a lot of paperwork, but the forms and procedures for being on Active Service were very different. In other words, the O/C of any battalion was responsible and accountable for everything a soldier ate, wore, used, and everything that was issued had to be accounted for by the O/C. It was quite different in battle where loss of men and equipment were written off as casualties.

If living at home, army personnel were entitled to subsistence. This was an entitlement laid down in the regulations. But as a rule, headquarters was always trying to get personnel off subsistence and into service housing or barracks. So officers made quarters in improvised rooms under the grandstand at the Regina Exhibition grounds. The rest of us used a large hall that had been a curling rink fitted with double-tiered, portable, metal beds. So we drew *palliasses* and bolsters, stuffed them with straw and slept in makeshift barracks. This meant the end of subsistence pay. However, it was easy to get a *sleeping-out* pass so I could still go home. It seemed to me awfully silly to be sleeping at the fairgrounds when my home was only five blocks away.

Major Driver was a World War I soldier and had the idea that a person had to be a tough guy, with salutes and clicking of heels. He liked to stay in barracks himself. He enjoyed the mess and the extra messing. Sneddon and I liked to be home with our wives and family. There were some weekends when I had to take my turn on duty, when I slept in the barracks. Other weekends I would get a pass for the weekend at home. I must admit that I was fortunate compared to others whose homes were far away.

I remember a lad who had been around the Armoury for a day or two, trying to make up his mind about joining up. These decisions came to some more easily than others. We were recruiting for a unit needing two-hundred men so for two weeks we had been steadily filling our quota. There was usually a time limit of two weeks to do this. When the first ones sign on, they get their kit, go home and report the day before a set date. Later signers of course got less time at home, and the last ones, like this lad wouldn't get much time at all. He was one of the last three to make up the two hundred. He was hustled from the orderly room to the medical, to the QM, and never did go home. I really felt sad for him. The whole contingent entrained the next morning for the east. I often wondered how he made out, but then there were so many.

The Quarter Master course finally came to an end. I had completed the part for writing and been up before the Ordnance examiners for the oral test. Word did not come down to me, but to the Depot and it was out that I had been successful. It was official when my name appeared on Part I orders that Private Proctor, serial number L22002, was certificated as a QM. For this I was raised to the rank of Lance Corporal, one stripe, *a dog's leg*. The course was very important, particularly in the new and different ways of Active Service, Canadian Army Service Force (C.A.S.F.). Since I was in the QM stores, we had no issue at this moment for battle dress; it was for other reserve people turning in their old khaki for the new battle dress, the new uniform. So often there were better army jackets and pants turned in, better ones than I was wearing, and consequently I would latch onto the better ones and take them home for Anne to fix up for me. It was quite a joke and we had good laughs, especially when I asked her to change the *Dog Leg* for the third time. She said, "Definitely that's the last." Anne was now pregnant with Joanne. Pam was saying "Daddy" and "Mummy," which was exciting.

The war was heating up, and the First Division had gone to Britain. The Second Division was in the process of being formed, and some of these troops were in the exhibition grounds, notably the South Saskatchewan Regiment. Incidentally this was Walter Barker's Regiment. He was their Armourer Sergeant. They came up to strength and moved east.

Major Driver was still issuing orders that the staff, including himself, would have to get down to real soldiering, like sleeping in the barracks. I never did agree with his philosophy of soldiering, since it certainly didn't fit at all with the things the course was teaching.

There was also a vast difference in the QM's attitude towards his men and materials. I used to gawk at Sneddon when a service man would come to the QM store to exchange a worn-out kit. He would take a defensive role and start a diatribe as to why he couldn't do it. He would examine the pants' seat and knees, and almost accuse soldiers of purposely making holes in their clothes. Fancy a guy who has joined Active Service, laying his life on the line, and finding himself faced with such ridiculous negativism. Honestly, one would think the army stores were actually Sneddon's. That store was there for one purpose only, for the soldier. I never could feel that Sneddon knew his job, at least not in the Active Service. Give Sneddon his due, though, after his twenty minutes hassle about why he could not do it, he would change his mind. Nevertheless, he taught me something and that was the way *not* to treat people, especially ones who were offering their lives. I've found that every situation is a learning situation. You either learn the way to do or the way not to do. But I liked Dave Sneddon. He was a Scotchman, canny, and pro-establishment.

During May 1940, there were rumours that the Regina Rifles were to be mobilized. It proved true that Military District Number 12 of Regina had received orders that the Regina Rifle Regiment be mobilized forthwith for active service in the Third Division, Canadian Active Service Force.

Thus, on June 1, 1940, the Regina's began to recruit their battalion: nine hundred and sixty men of all ranks. Lieutenant Colonel Quinn opened battalion quarters across from our depot in the Armoury. The Reginas had a nucleus of reserve personnel to begin the recruitment. There was a good supply of men coming to join. Their regimental sergeant major was Tom Sharp, and their regimental quarter master was

Al Simpson. It was taking a bit of time to get them going as medical examinations turned down many key personnel.

Pam was now fifteen months old. We had much fun with her. Our neighbours next door were Mr. and Mrs. Chapman. They had two boys. Mr. Chapman worked at the post office in Regina, and had done so for many years. They were lovely people. Mrs. Chapman was Pentecostal, a devout Christian. We often talked with them at the fence when working around the garden. The boys joined the services; one was in the army pay corps, the other in the Navy. They were the kind of neighbours that gave me some comfort knowing they were close to Anne when I was away. I was also thankful for good neighbours like the Baumbers. Mr. Mark and Mrs. Baumber were beautiful to Anne and the children.

The Armouries were now fairly jumping with soldiers. There was terrific enlistment going on at the Regina battalion offices. They had enlisted cooks. The establishment of cooks for the battalion was fourteen with two sergeant cooks. One sergeant named Rainbow left his job of being chief cook at the Boys' Industrial School. The other sergeant cook's name was Proctor, same as mine, but his Christian name was Bill. He had a cafe at Watrous, Saskatchewan. They were in charge of the R.R.R. kitchens, and the numbers of men to be fed was increasing every day. We at the Depot were recruiting strongly and had two hundred enlisted from other units. The Reginas were having trouble feeding an increasing daily number. Doctors had rejected Regina's Quarter Master Sergeant Simpson, who could not pass the standard set for active service.

Regina's O/C, Colonel Quinn approached the Depot O/C, Major Driver, with the idea of transferring me to the Reginas. Major Driver refused. Quinn recognized the Depot feeding, which they never had any trouble with, would be in chaos. So it went on for one week when he once again went to see Major Driver. Quinn's offer was to promote me to company quarter master. Major Driver still stalled, but since I was fit and medically ready for active service, he couldn't hold me for long, so Major Driver and Colonel Quinn made an arrangement which placed me in the Depot office, and feeding the Reginas for two weeks, then taking over the Reginas as their QM and being on loan to the Depot to feed them for two weeks.

It was something that only one with my knowledge could possibly do. It was particularly peculiar because I was absolute in that there was no one who knew enough to criticize me. I really believe had this arrangement been any other way, there would have been riots, especially in the Regina's outfit. Sergeants Rainbow and Proctor knew nothing of the quantities. Sergeant Rainbow would get rations for the number of men the Reginas had on strength, then after lunch he would look for me, wondering what to do for five hundred men for supper. It took him weeks to learn how to use his unit's rations for the whole day. He would haunt me. "What am I going to do?" he would say. I would find out what it would take to get him on with his meal and how to use the rations he received.

Rations in Canada were ample: twelve ounces of meat, potatoes, bread, and jams. Lamb was never appreciated, neither were prunes, C.P.R. strawberries, as they were dubbed. Funny, these two were always plentiful and appeared often.

Another fact that influenced feeding was the number of troops. The Depot might have two hundred men expecting to be fed. Sometimes while rations were being drawn, there would be a call for men. Consequently, at times rations in the Depot kitchens would build up. I would discuss this with the Depot's corporal cook and we would share the rations in a pro-ratio basis. Officers' messes got the same as the men, as did the sergeants. Only once did I have to correct Sergeant Rainbow, pointing out that the steaks were not always for the sergeants. Officers had extra messing accounts of their own, to which they all subscribed and bought supplies outside their military rations.

As time went on, the Reginas were coming up to full strength and the time was fast approaching when I would have to leave home. We were not looking forward to this, but I was definitely with the Regina Rifles now. I had taken over the QM stores and had a store man named Jack McGraw and a Captain Quarter Master named Austin Hunt. The company commanders were about, and now the need for recruitment was six hundred. It seemed within a week or so that number would be reached as we were busy outfitting and feeding recruits. I recall shortages, especially of badges and chevrons for the N.C.O.S, and how I had instilled into McGraw that everything issued had to be signed for.

Mac took his job seriously. One forenoon Colonel Quinn's batman came into the stores saying the colonel had sent him for a cap badge. Mac, sincere soul that he was, said that he'd have to go back and get the colonel to come and sign for it. When I got there, Colonel Quinn *had* come down to sign for the cap badge. It was a bit embarrassing, but the colonel should have known that he is responsible for property issued under his charge. Mac was a load of fun, and we were *thick* right from the start, for we both were corny, only he more so. He really suited his name, McGraw, tall and skinny, dour and Scotch. Anne and I got a laugh that she didn't have to sew my stripes on anymore because they had a tailor at the Armouries. We had the wedge cap now for head gear. Sergeant Major Sharp would look in on us sometimes, like when some of the soldiers would be improperly dressed. He would check to see if there really were these things marked N/A, or Not Available, on the regiment's indents.

On July 4 and 5, 1941, the Regina Rifle Regiment entrained for Dundurn Camp, twenty-five miles south of Saskatoon. I left on an advance party to make preparations. The men had been issued denims for summer wear and they didn't look too soldierly in them. We had been given quarters for regiment stores, eighty bell tents for the infantry, and seven marquees for messing. Now the battalion of the Regina Rifles Regiment comprised six companies, one company from North Battleford, one company from Prince Albert, and four companies from Regina, with one hundred forty men each. Four companies were to be front line troops: one a support company, who support the line companies with tracked vehicles, tanks, mobile guns, Bren gun carriers, and Mortar platoon.

Headquarters company included Pioneer Platoon, who built things and operated mine detectors. Medical section included stretcher bearers who operated R.A.P.(Regimental Aid Posts) and and MO (Medical Officer. There was an Armourer and his workshop, technical stores, precision instruments, catering and cooks. Also, QM and QM stores. Telecommunications, signal platoon and military police, along with the whole of transport together, formed a fighting unit called a battalion, which could operate on its own and maintain itself. Being a Quarter-master is an important position because all others are dependent on it. Everything the battalion has or uses comes through the QM. Everything a soldier wears or uses—food, guns, sleeping accommodations—all these things come from the Ordinance Supplier with whom the QM deals.

At Dundurn we were on wartime alert, with every need to be indented out of Ordinance. There was a publication for every unit, although it was somewhat secret, that listed all the things necessary for operating, training and battle. This booklet listed our war entitlement, and gave us the authority to apply for things from Ordinance. Since we were still in Canada, everything we received from Ordinance had to be entered into a ledger book. The unit could not write anything off. All units within the battalion had to sign for their articles. Later Ordinance would send inspectors to see if anything was missing. That's the way it worked in Canada.

We were exceedingly busy at QM. Besides Captain Hunt and RQMS McGraw, Joe Jean became QM Clerk. Little Joe and Big McGraw, these were my constant companions and fellow workers. We had to draw all the canvas tents in advance, along with all the cooking utensils and rations, all the folding tables and forms for the mess. Of course, that took a lot of time and the RSM, Tom Sharp, ensured that we got it. Everything came out on orders of the day: fatigues for cleaning up, for latrines, for moving whatever. We asked for vehicles from the transport officer. The companies provided the men. They had their own O/C, a captain, and a lieutenant for training.

Each unit of the battalion had its Officer Commanding, or O/C, a second I/C, five majors, one captain second I/C, three lieutenants, one company sergeant major, three platoon sergeants, three corporals, and three lance corporals. Non-commissioned officers were: one RSM, one RQMS, six sergeant majors, eighteen sergeants, twenty-one corporals, and twenty-one lance corporals.

At Dundurn, the biggest obstacle to training was the terrible shortage of equipment. Training weapons were especially needed. However, there was a war on and as Ordinance would say, "Things have to go where the greatest need is." The unit, however, was hard at work keeping fit and improving their skills. They had rifles, and lectures about their role. At Dundurn, breakfast was at 7:30 a.m., lunch at noon, supper at 5:00 p.m.. The evening was free time.

The QM staff didn't go out on drill as there was too much to do. Food at meal times was by queue. Soldiers had new mess-tins which held everything served for an entire meal. Each battalion had sixteen cooks, two as sergeants and fourteen as cooks. When the unit was together we ate from one big kitchen. Later cooks would be assigned to their own company. Lining up for meals was not easy because of so many men in long lines waiting for cooling food.

I managed to get a weekend pass at the end of July 1940. It was lovely to be home, even just for a day or so. Anne was pregnant, but I didn't know if I was happy or not. We wanted a family, of course, but leaving Anne with two babies to care for and having to worry about being away, I believed might be too much for her. But she was strong, and although she must have had the same feelings as I, she never let me leave downhearted. Ours was a tender love, I was certain, and nothing would ever come between us, even war.

The Reginas were trained as an infantry regiment, a first-line battle unit. The realities of that did not escape us, but hope and faith were ever present and helped make the burden bearable. So as with thousands of others in similar circumstances, we carried on, each in our own way, with a common cause to defeat Hitler. But it was so hard to leave home, after just getting started in our own house. Even so, I felt grateful that we did have a place where Anne would have a roof over her head and could plan for improvement.

Naturally, there was some competition for promotions. The Officer Commanding, Colonel N.J. Quinn, selected the major for the North Battleford Company (Coy), Major Sharp, and he was to be second in command. For the Prince Albert Coy, he selected Major Matheson, for "D" Coy, Major Scot-Calder, for "C" Coy, Major Waterman, and for "A" Coy, Major MacNutt. There was competition for other officers, especially lieutenants, as there were so many, young and eager.

When the unit left Regina and the two companies from North Battleford and Prince Albert came together, I was appointed acting RQMS. I suppose I was on trial, but I had taken the QM course and knew about stores, rations, ordnance, echelons, Army Service Corps, and about the war effort in general.

The quarter master of the battalion holds the rank of captain and he was Austin Hunt. In civilian life he had been a chartered accountant. He knew little about the QM job, but he was a quick learner, and we in the stores liked him, even if he did swish his officer's cane. My store man was Jack McGraw and my clerk was Joe Jean. Besides these men, there was an ammunition store man, Barney, and we had establishment for a ration clerk, but didn't have one yet. Colonel Quinn had spoken to me often, and naturally since everything worn or used by a soldier came through the "Q" branch, I was familiar with most of the officers. When they wanted anything, they came to the Q, usually to the acting RQ. In due course it became official; I was the regimental quarter master of the Regina Rifles Regiment, the RQMS. Mostly I was addressed as "Quarters." Sometimes I was referred to as the "RQ" or "Quarter-bloke."

It was quite evident that Dundurn was just a jumping off spot, a place to get the unit molded into a fighting force. One irksome situation was the scarcity of chevrons. When a soldier got promoted, naturally he wanted to be paid, and he had to put his stripes on, but the Regina's red and black rifles regimental colours were hard to get. Ordnance always said that they were "on order."

Soon it became known we had orders to move. It had been a dusty, hot July at Dundurn, filled with great activity and preparations. There were some reserve units in for summer training, and Norman, Anne's brother, was one of them. I saw him a couple of times in his K.D.s (summer dress). We were slated for a new camp on the eastern Atlantic coast, a place called Debert, Nova Scotia. Getting the regiment ready for the move to eastern Canada was a monumental job.

It took two special trains to accommodate the move. However, once aboard, the event became restful and pleasant, for the "Q" branch was not responsible for feeding. This was done by railway personnel, and their food was good. I remember travelling with the regimental sergeant major and sitting at meals with him. I think Tom enjoyed the benefits of his rank, which was the highest of the NCOs. He handled his privileges and authority well, but nevertheless the soldiers pinned a name on him, as they often do. Tom's was Grey Ghost. He had a pallid complexion and was soft-spoken. We never had any dealings that were not convivial. We had the same quarters for living, we ate at the same table, and we worked well together.

The train journey was without incident, except for times when we stopped, sometimes for as much as half an hour. When this occurred, the soldiers would pour out to stretch their legs. Indeed some stops were laid on for the purpose of exercise, and it being lovely August with warm weather, there was much fun, with bantering and fooling around. Getting to Debert was a four-day journey and most of us were glad to get off the train.

When we reached Camp Debert at the end of September 1940, it was not ready. The buildings were up but there was much work to be done.

The drains and water pipes were laid, but not filled in, and there were open ditches everywhere. Huts were laid out for the battalion. Headquarters corps and the A,B,C,D and support corps all had their own area huts and marquees. There were huts for dining with kitchens in the middle. The camp had four officers' messes, and a sergeants' mess separate with its own kitchen, cooks and eating hall. There were buildings for the QM and stores. There were also buildings for the medical officer and rooms for the shoemaker and postal clerk. The huge parade ground remained rough and unfinished. We had a padre, Reverend Steel, of course nicknamed Stainless, and we had a regimental band, all from Headquarters coy. The four line companies each had their own huts, as did the support coy, Bren gun carriers, mobile weapons, and the three-inch mortar group and the two-inch mortar group. At full strength, our total number of officers and men was nine hundred and sixty, divided into approximately one hundred and forty-five for line corps, one hundred and fifty for supply, with headquarters corps having the rest, which included the transport section. The regiment would be equipped with a total of one hundred and forty vehicles. We currently had sixty-CWT trucks, eight station wagons, two Bren gun carriers (tracked vehicles). We would have sixty-six Bren guns, four three-inch mortars, twenty-two two-inch mortars, twelve *piat* anti-tank guns, and every soldier had a rifle. There were twenty motorcycles for dispatch riders, and eight bicycles for coy runners. Officers were all equipped with revolvers. These were all the men and equipment that came together at Debert. Laundries, shoe repairs and other services had to be contracted out until the military services were set up.

We were now getting ready to use all these men and materials in a war, a real war, and I had much to do. I think by virtue of the place I held in the battalion, I knew more of the men personally than did any other individual. Shortly after reaching Debert camp, several cases of measles broke out and the whole battalion was confined to quarters. Special permission had to be obtained for anyone to leave the barracks. However, supplies had to be kept moving, so I and a few others were granted permission to leave the premises. In that regard, I, along with my station wagon driver and a couple of fatigue men, became the first soldiers to go into the Nova Scotia town of Truro.

I remember driving to Truro for the first time and how its populace greeted us so warmly. My task was to set up civilian laundry contracts, schedule days and times of delivery and pickup, and to set up contracts for shoe repair until our own regimental services were in place. The people must have expected the soldiers from the west. We were received in a friendly manner every place we went. People would crowd around us and offer us gifts. I recall one woman pressing us to accept an apple pie; this was great apple-growing country. The Annapolis Valley was full of apple orchards. So for two weeks while the confinement to barracks was in effect, a few of us enjoyed the Truro citizens; naturally, we were envied. However, when the ban was lifted the troops descended in hoards to get a look at Truro, Nova Scotia.

Debert was capable of accommodating a whole division or approximately thirty-thousand troops. At first it was tough, but we were busy training, obtaining weapons and strengthening our G-1098 authorization, which still was below 50 per cent. Route marches kept us busy at the stores. We received our first Bren gun carriers, and we had two and three-inch mortars for training. Also, rifle range training occurred regularly.

Wedge caps were changed to berets, and battle dress was now worn, with *gaiters*, but no *putties*. Identification discs, or dog tags, were issued to every person, and were to be worn at all times. There were a few injuries because of the open ditches, but all in all the unit functioned quite well.

Halifax was eighty miles from Truro, and I was making this journey with a convoy of three sixty-CWT trucks. The route to Halifax followed a coast road around Bedford Basin, and the scenery was beautiful. I learned a lot about the country. I even had an occasion to go to Dartmouth by ferry. I remember meeting an old undertaker at the C.P. Hotel in Halifax and he told me of the harrowing sinking of the Titanic and how he buried three-hundred bodies from that disaster. I also heard from him about the explosion in Halifax harbour caused when two ships carrying explosives collided during World War I. The undertaker told me that he handled over three-hundred deaths on that occasion, too. That terrifying blast caused the sea to flood the surrounding land and bodies were washed back into the sea. He said it was awful. There were tales that a small cannon on display in Truro was blown there by that powerful explosion. It was hard to comprehend such a horrendous happening.

During trips from Camp Debert to Halifax, we noticed convoys in Bedford Basin being set to sail to Europe. On one of these occasions we counted one hundred and fifty ships. These freighters, besides carrying their own crews, had special anti-aircraft machine guns manned by trained soldiers. The ships were usually guarded by destroyers. It was fascinating to park and watch them as they glided into the darkness. Only God knew what might befall them.

For recreation, the Regina Rifles, the Canadian Scottish, the Winnipeg Rifles, and the Seventh Brigade had boxing and soccer teams. The Canadian Scots were out in front in soccer. They hailed from Victoria and most were big, burly men. They were by far the best as they beat the Regina and Winnipeg teams by huge margins.

Once lads from the merchant marine put a team together. So one Wednesday afternoon there appeared in the orders of the day that a football match was to take place. Such publicity made for a good turnout, as most everyone liked soccer. When the players came onto the playing field, it was almost comical. The Scottish team were in new jerseys, looking quite capable. By contrast, the pick-up marine team were small and didn't all have the same team jersey. They wore whatever they could find. There was a referee and a linesman from the Canadian army. Once the game began, these little men, soon in their queer-looking outfits, practically waltzed around the Canadian Scots. It was no contest, a rout if you like. One goal, two goals, three, four, five goals, six, seven, eight goals, then nine, ten, eleven goals. Wow! It was sport and fun, not exactly for the Scots, of course, but since they had beaten the Reginas and the Black Devils by similar scores, we thought it icing on the cake to see them get a dose of their own medicine. They took it well, though, and all had fun afterwards at the canteen.

Another unforgettable sight was the Annapolis Valley. The proprietor of the facility where we took the battalion laundry took us one Sunday afternoon to see this marvelous apple valley. The ground was knee-deep in apples. It was the fall of the year and there was no way to transport them, let alone pick them. Strange world, I thought; so many people in want, no pickers, no ships, and apples rotting on the ground.

When we moved to Debert quite a few of the married soldiers' wives joined their husbands in Truro. Freddie Thornton, Ted Fowle, Bob Armstrong and several other men were fortunate.

At Debert, the RSM, Tom Sharp, and I had sleeping quarters in a hut next to the QM stores. I remember an incident related to my dispatching three CWT trucks to fetch coal from the army depot. When we needed fatigue men, we had to put in an order for them to the RSM the night before. He would direct the line companies to detail the men to report to us at the time needed. So far, the coal fatigue consisted of twelve men, with headquarters Corporal, Pops Campbell, in charge of trucks and men to bring back the coal. It was quite a job, and a long way to go, so they were late getting back. There was a shed to put the coal in. After unloading the coal, Corporal Campbell let the men go, leaving behind a large heap needing to be shovelled in.

This shed was not very far from the RSM and my billet. At about 12:30 a.m., both Tom and I were awakened by the noise of shovelling and scraping. We didn't know what to make of it. The next morning the RSM got wind of it and sent for Corporal Campbell. I was with him when the story unfolded. It seems one of the twelve fatigue men deserted the coal party soon after it left the barracks. When they got back with the coal, the corporal had the men leave a fair sized heap of coal outside. The corporal explained that he waited for the man who skipped away and then made that man shovel the remaining coal into the shed. When the RSM asked about his method of getting a job done, the corporal answered, "No one is going to pee up my back and call it sweat." That was the end of that.

I also remember nights when the store men and I were in the stores. In the evening before turning in we would make toast on top of the heater, along with a pot of tea. There was Mac McGraw and Bill Morrison, little Joe Jean and sometimes Barney, the ammo man. What I remember most was Little Joe, whose toast had to be black on both sides. Old McGraw used to say, "When Joe *farted* he made smoke."

The boys had bunks in the store building and kept a box of tea and snacks from the parcels they received from home. At times Captain Austin Hunt would be with us in the evening for a cup of tea. We had many discussions about the stores as they were in camp and how they would be on active operations.

The messing at Debert was better than it had been at Dundurn. The H-shaped building with the kitchens in the middle and the big dining halls on either side where the men could sit at a table allowed us to eat "home-style," as compared to a queue system. Obviously, there was much less waste. Ordnance provided cups, saucers, and plates. Soldiers had their own issue knives, forks and spoons. The orderly officer of the day, as one of his duties, together with the RSM and sergeant cook, would have a tour of duty to visit the mess halls and kitchens at mealtimes. They would ask the men if they had any complaints, and would submit a report at the end of the day. Sometimes there were complaints, especially about lamb stew. In my experience, Canadians did not care for lamb stew, nor did the cooks know how to cook it. It always looked unappetizing.

Bill Proctor was a cook for the officers' mess, since his kind of cooking was right for them. He could make special dishes from the extra messing provided to the officers. These items were bought outside of what the army provided. Bill, at times, would save meat and I would get to share a filet mignon dinner. He stayed with the regiment to England and then went to Seventh Brigade Headquarters to be cook for the Brigadier. Most of the cooks originally recruited had been replaced by the catering corps, although two or three old ones were still around.

A couple of incidents stand out in my mind. One of the cooks named Brunskill, a nice chap, had been a blacksmith in civilian life. The orderly officer always came in after meals to solicit complaints. I, being the Quarter bloke, at times went to the kitchens to see how the cooking was going and to talk to the sergeant who was in charge. We knew what was cooking because there was a menu made up weeks in advance and it hung in the mess halls. This day I visited the kitchen about twenty minutes before noon. Dinner was at noon, and there was much going on. Rice was on the menu and Brunskill had a couple of six-gallon containers cooking rice. What a schermozzle! Rice was running over the brim of the containers and Brunskill was trying to push it back in. He evidently had put too much rice in the pots, and it wouldn't go back in. No matter what he did, it ran over, down the sides onto the tables and floors. "What are we going to do? What *are* we going to do?" he yelled. By now, the men were in for dinner. They began making snowballs from the rice and pelting each other. Riots can sometimes be awful, but this one was a real laugh-riot. Poor Brunskill, this surely taught him a lesson about rice. There wasn't a grain of humour in it for him.

Another thing which had its funny side, concerned Roy Maters, one of the assistant cooks. He also was a nice chap. In the kitchen cupboards there were items which were designated extra messing, meaning not army. These items had been bought, if and when available. After all, cooking needed additives. Among these items were bottles of extract of lemon. Roy could not keep away from this stuff. The sergeant cook had locks and keys and everything that could be done was done, but Roy somehow would be stoned by ten o'clock every morning. He was a problem and he had a problem. He was never violent, just stoned and silly, always promising to do better, but never quite successful. We worked with him and kept him with the regiment until, because of his age, he could no longer go with the battalion and was transferred to a holding unit at base.

This training in peaceful Canada was in a way like living in a new home. A soldier's day began at 7:30 a.m., with breakfast, training, workshops, ranges, then dinner from 12:00 to 1:30 p.m., followed by training schedules until 4:30, when the soldier's day was over. Supper was at 5:00 p.m.. The rest of the evening was free time, except for necessary duties such as guards, latrine sanitation, and fatigues. For others there was transportation to town. Trucks took the soldiers in and out. The town had lots of things going for the troops and the residents' homes were open to those who found friends. There were parades for the soldiers, such as medical, trousers down, shirts up. Feet lice became a problem. Special attention had to be applied where such a number of men camped together. There were clothing parades, rifle inspections, and gas mask drills. Haircuts were enforced. The cleanliness of all depended on the cleanliness of each. Strict discipline was essential to the fighting force of the units. We also had occurrences of syphilis, gonorrhea, athlete's foot, mouth sores and others as part of normal happenings.

The line companies were busy training in weaponry. The support company was training with newly acquired Bren gun carriers. Other infantry-supporting weapons were three-inch mortars. All facets of the battalion were in full training with weapons, of which there were never enough.

At the QM Stores, there were changes as we could adapt to field warfare. There would not be a building for stores. The stores would have to be moved in vehicles wherever the unit went. We had many discussions about this and it was decided to conduct an experiment. Boxes were mounted one upon another on either side of the sixty trucks available to the QM. We had lots of exercises and practice in the ways we would operate in the war zone. Debert camp was filling up to its divisional capacity: three brigades of nine battalions each, with all the ancilliary forces, ordnance corps, services corps, tank corps, headquarters, etc., approximately thirty-thousand strong. There was a certainty this was a buildup for overseas movement. The army also did a lot of clearing of brush and trees and a rifle range was built, along with a parade ground.

Barney was the person in charge of ammunition. He was at times sullen. He was also responsible to the QM for issue and custody of ammunition, with regular reports required. In fact, the RSM was the responsible person, and it would be his responsibility totally when the regiment was in action. Barney would always come to me if there was a problem. He took me into his confidence, and I understood and trusted him. So, although he was quiet and a loner, he joined in with us for snacks or tea and was counted a member of the store group.

There were issues of revolver ammunition to the officers whose issue weapon was a pistol, a Smith and Wesson, with six barrel chambers. Due to the scarcity of revolver ammunition, strict restrictions were imposed. Naturally, the officers wanted to do some shooting. Strange that they shouldn't all agree, but every week there was an inspection of the ammo and these young officers would have to produce the six bullets in their revolvers. There was fun and anger at this, because invariably the officers could never resist the temptation to shoot. However, the top brass was adamant that ammunition be kept for emergency use and not used indiscriminately. These officers really were Barney's lament as ammo for rifle training was more plentiful and it was issued to companies on authority of the RSM.

A battalion would have two two-inch mortars for training, a few Bren guns, a smattering of the things that they would use when in a real war. So we had to improvise. Everyone had rifles, though, so there was lots of work at the rifle range. The division did what it could with what was available. It was estimated that it takes five persons to keep one soldier in the line, twenty-five thousand men to support five thousand in the line.

It was December 1940, and the buzz around camp was about Christmas leaves. Permission had been received for half the battalion to go on leave for Christmas, and the other half would go on the return of the first group. Special trains were laid on to handle so many troops. It was a monumental job to provide all the passes, tickets, times and instructions for long journeys. For some it took four days to get home from Halifax, then four days to return, leaving only six days to be at home.

I found my journey across Canada very beautiful. The train and coaches were rough but going home for Christmas was a happy break and I looked forward to being home with Anne and Pamela, who was now twenty-one months old and talking. Anne had become a member of the Regina Rifles Ladies Auxiliary and met many women whose loved ones were in the army. My marriage to Anne was the sweetest thing that happened to me in my whole life. I loved her and I loved our home and baby Pamela.

My furlough was all too short, but at least I felt that Anne was comfortable and secure should anything happen to me. She enjoyed making our home a place to be enjoyed. We had Christmas together, a warm little family. We attended Christmas services at St. Peter's Church. Reverend Creal was still the minister and wrote to me. Joyce, Anne's sister, was living in Moose Jaw. She had opened a small cafe and called it The Spitfire Lunch. Anne, Pamela and I visited her by going on the train from Regina Station.

My furlough went quickly and it was hard to say good bye. But there really was no problem about going. Anne and I understood what was expected as clouds of war descended on our country. It was not difficult for the country to raise its First Division, because of widespread unemployment following the depression, the services afforded an income for those who had nothing to do for years.

Regina station was packed when it came time to leave. The atmosphere was charged with emotion as the great steam engine heaved and puffed. Winter had set in across the prairies. Steam from the hissing engines, and the noise of those tremendous engine wheels, created a formidable and awesome picture. Even with so many soldiers travelling, it was a lonely ride for me. One's thoughts were silently private and full of all sorts of intimate family things. We had four days and nights on the train, watching and listening to the craps games that some of the lads loved to get into. It was always exciting coming into the big cities. No matter the time of day, the stations were loaded with people, love and kisses, holding tenderly, wartime and uncertainty. The loved ones didn't care who was watching. People's true self came to the surface; it was no time to be bashful. It was heart warming to see folk being themselves.

Back in camp it was rowdy for a while as half of the unit was coming back and the other half was taking off. A cover of snow gave the camp a ghostly look. Several evergreens in the area presented cold, unfriendly outstretched arms that sent shivers through one's body. But one good thing about Debert camp was that there was lots of fuel for the stoves. We heard that those who spent Christmas in camp and in Truro had parties and special Christmas Day dinner in the mess halls.

Once the snow gradually disappeared, training began at the battalion level. About this time large numbers of infantrymen were having trouble with their feet and boots. At the stores we would take time to properly fit boots, but the men were complaining. They would come back to the stores for different boots after only having had them for a week. Their boots were not even worn, nor did they need repair, yet they hurt the men's feet. It was so bad that we simply told anyone who complained to report to the medical officer who would issue authority to obtain a new pair. As a consequence, we accumulated a staggering heap of unworn out and undamaged boots. We reported all this to the brigade and ordinances and after many weeks two inspectors came to inquire about these Canadian-made boots. After taking the boots apart, they found the instep was shattering, or splintering, causing a breakdown of the instep. They condemned thousands of pairs, even all the new boots. Every boot that had come from that particular source was ordered to be turned in. We had a heap like you wouldn't believe, and it was a month or so before we had orders to take them to Halifax and there deliver them to the Army-Navy civilian or surplus store. They would get them for a song. We at the stores were glad to see the end of this episode and happily it was the end of ill-fitting boots.

Battalion and brigade exercises included the movement of men, timing it with transport and motor vehicles. This war was to be a war involving movement, not sitting in trenches as in World War I. While we were infantry, we would advance in tracked vehicles. However, there surely would be ground fighting, therefore the need for training to move masses of men. Of course, we only had limited numbers to train with at Debert. When ready for real war we would have over one hundred and thirty vehicles of one kind or another. I remember when the regiment got its first Bren gun carrier, a tracked oval-shaped tractor-like thing, with a mounted Bren gun that could swivel all around. I had a feeling I'd rather not be a Bren gunner. One weekend RSM Tom Sharpe, CSM Knobby Clark, CSM Hinchliff and I got an army jeep and driver and we went sightseeing around Nova Scotia. I remember how impressive it was to sit on the high bank and see The Bore where the incoming tide would squelch itself into the narrow passage and seemingly boil, or bore itself into the opening. Looking way down there and watching the sea rush in faster than a man can run was fascinating, such an awesome surge of the power of the sea and tide. As the earth is red in Nova Scotia, the scene was more memorable.

On another weekend we visited the coal mines at New Glasgow. Being the top brass of the N.C.O.S, we sergeant majors had access to freedoms which were not available to lower rank, especially regarding the use of vehicles. The RSM, Tom Sharp, asked me if I'd like to go along one nice Sunday afternoon when not much was doing in camp, Sunday being a day off. There wasn't much amiss in filling in the time in this fashion, so we went to the New Glasgow coal mines. The manager had consented to us going and met us at the mine. Having worked in the coal mines in Durham, England, I was doubly interested and after noting all the things on the surface, we were taken down into the mine. Their methods were a little different, but the atmosphere around the mine was the same. Incidently, there had been two terrific disasters in this mine in the form of explosions from accumulated gases.

Towards the end of March 1941, I got news of the birth of a baby girl, Joanne, and that both mother and child were doing well. On compassionate grounds, I was granted a leave of absence. I could hardly wait to get home again. The regimental O/Cs never refused me a request, for which I was grateful. The staff at the QM stores teased me, but they were happy for me and gave me a God speed journey home, back to Regina. Again, the tremendously long journey, but I was full of hope and joy, and bubbling over with anticipation. Four days to think about a lot of things.

Finally, I arrived home. My, what joy, a lovely little baby girl and Anne doing so well. The baby was born March 21, 1941. She was three weeks old when I saw her. We celebrated and were so thankful that we could all be together, at least for a few days, before my leaving for Europe. I cherished us just being together. I know Anne had her own deep feelings: she was brave.

The time came that I had to kiss Anne and baby Pam goodbye. By now, Pam could sing along with me so we sang to console ourselves that it would soon be over. I promised I would write often as we sang . . .

"I'll keep your picture near me, a tender souvenir
I'll hold you tight and kiss you, and say
God bless you dear."

It was so lovely to be home, and the four days were valued by us all. We were all so much in the hands of the good Lord. We shed no tears at saying goodbye, but our hearts were full of hope that things would turn out right and Anne always with that faith. There was no foreboding, but on the journey back to Debert I was subdued.

There were all kinds of rumours when I rejoined the regiment. This sort of thing was always going on in the army, especially, "When are we going to move?" There are none more restless than army blokes. However, there was some excitement in the form of a V.I.P. inspection of the brigade. It was to be by the Governor General of Canada and Princess Alice. These occasions usually meant a headache for the QM. The soldiers were all in possession of cleaning materials kept in a bag called a *hold-all*. They never seemed to have much need for them until an inspection. Then they bugged the "Q" for Khaki cleaner, "Blanco." I remember when the regiment had the honour of providing a special guard at Division Headquarters, and there wasn't a blooming tin of Blanco anywhere. However, we managed to scrounge enough to get the fifty-man guard smartened up with new uniforms, boots and gaiters. This sometimes seemed more important than the war itself.

Since I had my Quarter-Master's course at the beginning of the war, I was now to go for a refresher course, about Field Warfare. It was geared to the movement of the whole army, including the movement of every single thing used by men or machinery from England to army base, to brigade, to unit. We would begin with full complements and anything lost or destroyed would be reported and the job was to replace it. If the coys lost a vehicle or whatever the CQMS brought his requirements to "A" Echelon and RQMS. RQ would go back to "B" Echelon, requests would go to the brigade who would go back to division; and so it went throughout the action. Map reading was a very essential part of war's events, such as a clothing parade, trying on gas masks, or fun with Sergeant Armourer when we had rifle inspection parade. The whimsical sergeant was a character and able to speak seven languages. He was of Swiss descent, and he certainly spoke English strangely.

We at the QM stores were close regardless of rank. We were therefore sad when we heard the news that Captain Hunt was leaving the regiment. In civilian life Austin had been a chartered accountant and very quick on anything to do with bookkeeping and ledgers. Army headquarters needed Austin's talents in the ordnance systems, which we all knew was in a mess, particularly in Halifax. Austin had to make a decision because he really did want to go overseas with the regiment. It's funny how your regiment sort of becomes your home as a soldier. It's the place where the ones you know are. You are sort of on a team and feel the spirit of what a team is all about. Austin's new job was a big one: head of the inspection department for the whole of Canada, and it carried the rank of colonel. What a lift from captain! He was needed and he had the qualifications. I remember the last night we spent together. I had discovered that his favourite poem was Rudyard Kipling's "*If*." So we pitched in and purchased a nice copy of the poem, had it suitably framed, and presented it to Captain Hunt. I think he still has it at home. I felt sorry for him. I know how it hurt him to part with his comrades. But then we were happy for him too. No doubt he would serve best where his unusual gift and brightness would be needed, to straighten out the lackadaisical ordnance in Canada.

Captain Hall replaced Captain Hunt. He came to his Quarter Master appointment from "C" Corps. He had been in the Militia before war broke out. We at the stores had dealings with him as we did with all captains who were in charge of a company. Captain Vassar Hall was quite different from Austin Hunt. He was methodical, calm and collected in all he did. He had no previous training as a QM, but he understood a lot about the army, was easy to get along with, and anxious to learn the "Q" side of the army's function. Captain Hall was a good replacement for our comrade-officer, Captain Hunt. We kept him busy with what he should be doing, and why. He learned by doing, and got himself familiar with stores, men and the job.

It was now the end of May 1941 and there came to Truro a midway called "Elliot's Shows." There were the usual food stalls, ferris wheels, rides on hobby horses, coconut stands, shooting alleys, and games of chance. Everything was fine except for one night in June when an incident at the hoopla stall caused a disturbance. Apparently, three soldiers of the Third Division, Seventeenth Royal Canadian Hussars were playing at the hoopla and claimed one of them ringed a watch. An argument resulted with the stall keeper and it got nasty. It was claimed that the stall keeper pulled out a gun and threatened the soldiers. The following evening hundreds of soldiers descended on the show-ground and literally turned everything over except the ferris wheel. They took hobby horses off their stands and carried them down the streets of Truro. They got the blankets and other prizes and gave them to kids or anyone else who would have them. My what a schermozzle! They wrecked the whole fair good and proper. Of course, when the brass heard of it they immediately confined the whole division to barracks.

Our division got word on July 3, 1941 to prepare for overseas movement. This meant turning back to local Ordnance all the articles drawn for camp use, such as tables, forms, chairs, cots, china ware, and kitchen ware except those things carried by a soldier, such as his kit-bag, pack, weapons, and mess tins. Regimental records would be all packed for shipment. The men would draw their last pay before moving, and all documents regarding everyone on regimental strength were to be crated. We at the stores had to box and crate only those things necessary to replace what a soldier might need, such as clothing, boots, knife, fork, and spoon. All else was to be returned to local Ordnance and the ledger cleared. It was a tremendous job.

We were notified that a sub-conductor was to be present and that it would take some time as camp paraphernalia was to be used after we had gone. So it was all checked and accounted for by Sub-Conductor Robinson. He was a nice man, very understanding, and patient, for things were not altogether in one place. For instance, we had hundreds of tables, folding or otherwise for dining rooms, and lounge chairs of every description scattered all around the area. It took three weeks to complete this phase of *marching-out*. There were thousands of articles on our ledger, and needless to say some of them were hard to find or account for. For example, the dining halls and messes used home-style messing, that is, food was served from bowls from which the men helped themselves as opposed to being dished out from a queue. Imagine all the stuff required to serve nine hundred and sixty men in two great dining halls in addition to the officers mess, the sergeants mess and coy messes. When it came to accounting for more than a thousand cups, saucers, plates and bowls, we found hundreds were missing. However, generally speaking, the Ordnance Sub-Conductor was quite happy and gave a clean bill with few discrepancies. Crockery took the biggest toll although expenditures were allowed for home messing. With soldiers on their way to fighting zones, a few broken dishes were not much of an issue.

Once soldiers were back from embarkation leaves, the Regina Rifle regiment got official notice on August 19, 1941, to prepare to go to war. On August 24, at three o'clock in the morning, we entrained for Halifax. A huge crowd gathered to say Godspeed and good luck. The battalion then embarked for England from Halifax on the eighteen thousand-ton Empress of Russia.

Just when everything was in readiness to leave, a couple of habitual A.W.O.LS strayed back into camp. They belonged to "D" (Dog) Company, whose sergeant major was CSM Knobby Clark. He was a tough hombre. When he confronted these two recalcitrants, his immediate reaction was to get rid of them, so he literally chased them away. So when "D" Coy climbed aboard the transport vehicles, he left these two behind. The sequence to this occurred about one month after the unit arrived in England, when who should pester Knobby again but these two renegades. The Provost Army Police Corps picked them up and shipped them over. They were Kobby's problem boys, and when we finally got to Aldershot he provided some grim entertainment having them execute his particular brand of "full-pack drills" at Ramillies Barracks, where perhaps history had provided for such offenders in previous years.

Aldershot was famous as a military camp. Its old brick buildings and iron beds literally breathed, "You are in the army now," and Knobby and Aldershot were synonymous. Nevertheless, I respected Knobby, as did most others; he had some humour, too, and maybe that's what we all had in common. But really, I could never be like Knobby Clark. He was fair-minded, but unforgiving to those who crossed him.

Home on leave for christening of Joanne.

CHAPTER TEN
World War II

THE EXCITEMENT OF BEING on a troop train was something to experience. The atmosphere was crackling as the troopers found their places aboard this crowded train. Everyone had a designated seat in a specific coach. On battalion journeys, I was usually seated with the RSM, or Regimental Sergeant Major, and the Regimental Quarter Master Sergeant, or RQMS. The three of us roomed and ate together.

During the journey, some of the troops rested and some reflected. I thought of home, of Anne and the wee girls as they were ever with me.

We detrained on a dock at noon on August 25, 1941, and boarded the Empress of Russia. It was an old ship and not ideal for carrying troops. Here again, accommodations had been allotted, but this time there was plenty of room, although it seemed crowded with so many servicemen aboard. Besides the Regina Rifles, there was a small unit of the divisional mobile laundry, some Empire troops, quite a few British army personnel and some British officers.

The regimental band played cheerful music on the "A" deck. Watching the cast off was fun as the great ship edged away from its moorings, assisted by tug boats. Finally, we were on our own, heading eastward into the great Atlantic Ocean. As always, the unit orders, Part One and Part Two, were hung up for all to read. These contained various instructions for what to do and what not to do. The Reginas were in charge, and

I was named ship's Quarter Master. There was much to do, hammocks to be rigged, inspections to be made. Fortunately, the ship's crew provided the meals, but the sanitation was awful.

I became acquainted with a few of the stokers, one in particular, a bewhiskered seaman whom I thought I knew, and he thought he knew me. Lo and behold! It was a chap named John Beaton, who had been in the A.Y.P.A. at St. Peter's Anglican Church in Regina. We talked of familiar things, then he told me quite a tale about how he had become a stoker. I had noticed as we boarded that a group of mixed nationalities was being escorted from the hold of the ship, in irons, chained together. Beaton told me they were the ship's stokers who, when they heard that the ship was going back over the Atlantic, rebelled and refused to go. So they were shepherded off the Empress and replaced by Canadian stokers of which Beaton was one. He told me the Empress of Russia should have been in dry dock, but she had been pressed into service even though she badly needed an overhaul. The British army chaps had been picked up in the Mediterranean. The Empress had crossed the Atlantic and landed at Newport, USA, to take on fuel. This was when the stokers rebelled and were placed in irons. The British personnel stoked the Empress from Newport to Halifax. One of those British officers was Prince Philip and he had actually helped to stoke the ship. Now, Canadian seamen were stoking her. Beaton and I met casually once or twice, but then I never saw him again.

The RSM and I shared a cabin, which was better than hammocks, but cockroaches were everywhere. The ship's plumbing was in disrepair and we had to muster a twelve-man fatigue party to bail water, twenty-four hours a day. This was not a good voyage for me because I got terribly seasick. On my initial crossing of the Atlantic, I had stayed in one place the whole journey: by the rail. Now, thirteen years later, I was again sick, and to make matters worse, this time my job as RQMS required me to be all over the ship. The smell was most unpleasant below decks. I really didn't have time to be sick, nevertheless I was, yet somehow I managed.

There were two other ships in our convoy. All three were fast troop ships that could hopefully out-distance the German submarines infesting the waters. The three ships were escorted by seven destroyers and travelled in line-abreast. Destroyers formed up as a very large arrow point, one at the head point, then three others at each side of the three troop ships. In this fashion, we raced along day by day. Twice there were alert signals warning of foreign or enemy vessels, possibly submarines. Each time this occurred, the destroyers, at least one or two of them, would leave the formation and go after the sub with depth charges. I remember watching the lead destroyer during daylight hours. As I watched it go from side-to-side, up-and-down, almost out of sight in the huge waves, I thought about those poor sailors and how rough serving on a destroyer must be.

During hours of darkness the ships would run with no lights at all, and the three troop ships would come frighteningly close to one another. It was weird, three mighty ships ploughing the angry waters like ghosts. About two hundred miles out from Ireland there was an air-raid alert. We strained our eyes to see the tiny speck, everyone and everything in readiness. Then the word came that the aircraft was friendly, a Sunderland Flying Boat assigned to guide us in and spot for subs.

As the convoy approached western Ireland, I marveled at how beautiful the land looked from the sea. We skirted the north of Ireland and entered port in Glasgow, Scotland, in the mouth of the River Clyde. It was a lovely, sunny day, and the excitement aboard the ship was something. It was a delightful cruise now that we were in friendly, calm waters, and one could hardly refrain from being happy and relieved. The scenery on this bright morning was unforgettable, and everyone was on deck to enjoy it as the Empress of Russia gently eased into Gourock Harbour just before noon on September 1, 1941. We were officially welcomed and then taken off the ship by a tender.

After we disembarked from the tender, special trains awaited us. There were two trains for the troops; one left during the dark hours of

September 2, the other left in daylight. The Scottish people waved and cheered, and the youngsters tried to get the pennies and nickels thrown by troops hanging out train windows. There was much speculation as to where our destination might be. Later we found out that our trains were headed for Edinburgh.

I was somewhat familiar with English rail because as a boy I had watched the London-to-Edinburgh pullman express. I knew that we would go through Newcastle and Durham. The trains travelled in total black out, so it was darker inside the train than it was outside. We had passed through Berwick and were approaching Newcastle when the train suddenly stopped. A German air-raid was in progress over Newcastle and we were delayed for hours. I was so disappointed when the train backed up and went by a devious route to Carlisle west of England and from there to Aldershot. But there were no further incidents. It was an awfully long time to be on a train and I didn't get to go through Durham. I had been really looking forward to that after having been away for thirteen years.

Our assigned barracks at Aldershot was named Ramillies. They were ready for us to *march in*, as it was called in the army. This was the method of all troop movement to barracks or any other accommodation, whether schools or houses. This was my job, with an officer and a representative of the barracks authority, usually a caretaker, attending. We would go into each room of every building. Inventory sheets would already be posted, listing everything in the room or building. So in we would go, checking and counting to see that all the linen, chairs, tables, beds, pots and pans were in order as stated. If one wasn't aware and knowledgeable, it could be costly, so we really had to make a list of anything and everything not in order *marching-in*. For instance, we listed every crack in the walls and windows and any broken locks, as all shortages and damages were chargeable to the o/c regiment.

Five days leave was to be granted to everyone in the regiment. We couldn't all go at the same time, of course. The groups were staggered so that the unit could carry on. For example, the Captain QM and the RQMS were never away at the same time. The captain knew that I had relatives in England, so he insisted that I go first, and indeed I was excited to go to dear old Durham, and Ushaw Moor, where my mother still lived on Station Road.

Soon my leave and railway pass came through, I packed my haversack and found myself on the train for London. Once there, I would change trains for the L.N.E.R., London to Edinburgh, via York and Durham. I really was enjoying not only the anticipation of seeing my mother and family again after so many years, but the English countryside as well. My eyes stayed glued on the patchwork fields, rivers, copses and soft colours. I was naturally elated to be on leave and to see my homeland again.

I well remembered Durham Station. We often took a train to Ushaw Moor in the earlier days before busses were available. The fare was then three pence, and the distance was three miles. Often we would walk. So I lingered a bit in the old station, filled with nostalgia, then walked down to the bus depot. Durham Station was situated on very high ground, on a steep hill above the town streets. Walking down past Wharton Park, I remembered happy hours I had enjoyed there, mostly listening to band concerts. In those days every village colliery, and there were scores, had a brass band and they would compete with each other in judged band contests. I was always thrilled by the sounds of the brass bands. The music made the hair on the back of my neck fairly *crackle.* The vibrations of the trombones and bass instruments always got to me.

The road from the station was still cobbled, although the sidewalk was cemented and smooth to walk on. I was lightheaded as I boarded the Ushaw Moor bus. I looked to see if I knew anyone as I sat watching the folk and listening to the familiar *Geordie twang*. There were people that I thought I knew, but I didn't say anything to them. At Ushaw Moor the bus stopped near the old Empire theatre. I had memories of that, for it was there where I first saw Charlie Chaplin comedies when I was a teenager, and before that it was a music hall with Vaudeville shows.

Inside the theatre was a wooden railing about one third of the way up, on the side nearest the stage. The price behind the railing was three pence, but the rest of the seats downstairs cost six pence. The cost of a seat in the balcony was nine pence. Rounding the corner past the Empire, memories of my schooldays flooded in on me.

Finally, I found myself on Station Road. I had lived there for twenty years, so the memories nearly overwhelmed me. I had gone back and forth to school up and down this road for eight years. Station Road was so named because it was the road to the railway station. Going down from the Empire theatre was a continuous row of houses from top to bottom, with two breaks; one at the big working men's club and the other at Lough's Shoe Store. There were a fair number of stores along the street: Lowery's Confectionery and Ice Cream, Ross's Millinery, Cawthorn's Bakery, Sheval Fruit and Vegetables, Tommy Gate's Barber, Parkinson's Butcher, Denniston's Fruit and Vegetables, Watson's Bicycle Shop, Chilton's Fish and Chips, Smithenbank's Watchmaker and Jeweller, Lloyd's Bank, Foster's Confectionery, Salvation Army Hall, Beach's Fruit, Watson's Confectionery and Newspapers, the Albion Club, the Working Men's Club, and Millburn's Draymen and Cartage, near the station, the Station Hotel, Mr. Wood owner, then Harrison Woodmakers and Jolly's Blacksmith. On the other side of Station Road were hedges and fields. The hedge was hawthorn, and I remember the beauty and fragrance of the May blossom. In wintertime we would sleigh down the road. Often we got into trouble when caught by police.

This morning these things occupied my mind fleetingly for my footsteps were light. There I was on my way down the familiar road, a soldier in Canadian uniform. People looked at me and I just said "Good morning" to everyone until I reached Number 33, Station Road. Meeting Mother was very emotional. She had said when I left for Canada that she would probably never see me again, and now here I was, thanks to the war. Obviously, Mum and I had lots to talk about. She wasn't doing too well, but was able to get along. I went to Hedley's Provision store to get Mother's rations. These rations really struck home to me, emphasizing the belt tightening of the British people because of the war. The whole allowance consisted of a few ounces of this, a quarter pound of that, six ounces of meat, half of which had to be canned meat. In our khaki uniform the trousers have two large pockets on each leg, and her total ration fit easily in those two pockets.

Naturally, I spent most of my leave time at home, but I did have a chance to visit the Reverend John Welby. We had been warm friends. I also visited the Lowery family in their shop. Bennett and Mary, Thomas and Lizzie, Hilda and Sister Amy came to see me from Langley Park. The days went by like a dream and soon my time was up. But I had hopes of coming back in the not too distant future.

The trains in England were terribly crowded, particularly with servicemen. There were bans on travel for civilians, and all unnecessary journeys were discouraged. I felt sorry for the people, but the war was real and there was a strong patriotic spirit. Ladies would be in the stations when our train stopped to provide servicemen with hot tea and snacks.

Back at Aldershot, the unit acclimatized to its new surroundings. This was a real military town and the barracks had been built at a time when discipline was the order of the day. The buildings were cold brick and stone. I stayed busy learning routes and roads. We were issued maps which were highly important to us, for if you were without a map and asked your way, the civilians would not tell you. They had been warned not to talk about places to anyone, even people in uniform, because they could be spies. Road signs had been removed, so maps were essential and were treated as secret documents. These military maps were very detailed.

Many in the Regina Rifles had never been out of Canada, and some had never been out of their province. Most took off to explore London. The sights and thrills of being in London were something they would never forget. The underground system of transportation, known as the tubes, was fabulous. It provided many humourous adventures.

Sandy Black, quarter master sergeant of "B" Coy, told me of one lad who had gone to London for his five-day leave and had a hair-raising experience. This lad, being from the prairies, had never been away from the farm. His parents were immigrants to Canada and schooling was secondary to farming. Consequently, some of our lads were naive. Many Canadians didn't speak or understand English well, especially the rapid-fire Cockney dialect spoken in parts of London. I also had to be alert in order to get around, so I believed Sandy when he told me the tale of Joe Marachuk.

Sandy said Joe got into the subway, which of course was very crowded because of the war. One had to be very quick to board the underground trains. They would come into the station at tremendous speed, stop quickly, the coach doors would open automatically, and people would pour out onto the platform. Then the uniformed porters, usually women, would yell out the names of the stations where the train was going. There would be a rush to get aboard before the doors closed sharply and the train sped away. Joe Marachuk wasn't so lucky. In fact, he didn't get out of the subway for three whole days! With only five days leave, he had spent three of them in the underground. He couldn't get anyone to understand his English and he didn't understand the porters, even when they tried to tell him where to go. He nearly went crazy while everyone laughed at him. Apparently, he got on the wrong train and continued changing at the wrong stations.

Another chap told me that back home in Saskatchewan his neighbour, when he learned that the soldier was coming to England, gave him the address of his brother and his wife who lived near Southampton. He asked the soldier to look them up and say hello for him. Since the soldier had no relatives of his own in England, he went for a long weekend pass to Southampton. There he found a taxi driver who took him to the address. The taxi driver looked at him and said, "You sure?" Of course, he said *yes*, and was taken to a most rundown part of the city. The taxi driver said to our boy: "I'll wait for you to see if it's the right place."

The chap said, "Oh, no, I'll be okay." He told me that when he got to the door of the neighbour's relatives, a lady opened the door and he told her he knew her brother in Saskatchewan, and how he was getting along and so on. After listening for a few moments, she said to him: "So? What do you want?" This really shook him up. He wasn't the only one who got these kinds of rebuffs, but there were many British, Scottish, and Welsh people who would take in Canadian soldiers who were there without relatives and made lasting friendships.

Our barracks, which had been in existence since the Crimean war, didn't lend themselves to comfort. Our quarters fairly rang with the clang of soldiers boots and the metallic sound of mess tins along the corridors. My sleeping area was in the stores. Lots of nights I would lay awake with my thoughts of what this war was all about. It seemed strange that I should be here alone, my wife and children five-thousand miles away. I often listened to Churchill's broadcasts, and I constantly thought about the air-raids, the blackouts, the preparation, and especially the waiting.

In Ramillies Barracks, one of the first things we had to contend with was blackouts. The importance of this was instilled into each of us, even to striking a match or flicking a cigarette lighter, which could be a clue for enemy aircraft. There were to be no cracks in window blinds, and no headlights on busses except for their ghostly blue slits. It was astonishing to be on a curb and see these great double-tiered, ghostly objects coming out of the gloom with their two little blue lights. Even walking was hazardous because one couldn't see the pavement edge. We literally groped our way around in the nighttime hours. There were quite a few accidents caused by the blackouts. Once a member of our unit was walking in the street during the blackout, smoking a cigarette, and he saw someone coming towards him, also smoking. When it looked like they were going to collide, our boy stepped aside and went right through a store window. It had been his own reflection that he was seeing.

Aldershot was where I first heard wailing air-raid sirens. I was to hear them frequently. Aldershot was surrounded by searchlights whose silvery beams crisscrossed in all directions searching for enemy planes which could sometimes be identified by the peculiar beat and low thump of their engines. The regiment was in a war zone now, at least the air war. Things had changed for the Regina Rifles Regiment. We were trying to get used to British rations. Some complained they would never see the war before starving on British food. Rations had been cut drastically, especially meats, from twelve ounces per man per day to six ounces per man, half of which had to be canned meat. There were little or no eggs, fruit, or pies. The British desserts were primarily puddings, which most Canadians hated. British bread was heavier than Canadian bread, but there wasn't much anyone could do about it since everyone had the same rations. Our stomachs shrunk to the same size as everyone else's in England. After a while it was no longer mentioned; we simply got on with our jobs.

We were now on the field system of accounting, so there were lots of new things to adjust to in the first few weeks. There were no ledgers per se. When the regiment was completely filled with its requirements per the G-1098, we had to repair or replace in order to keep up to our authorized quantities.

Near Aldershot was Farnborough, the air centre where there was always the drone of flying machines of every description. Identification of aircraft was taught to the troops. There was a beautifully kept parade ground, called Queen's Parade. Our brigade, that is, Reginas, Canadian Scottish and the Winnipegs were inspected by their majesties, the King and Queen, and by Lieutenant General A.G.L. McNaughton. These parades were quite impressive turnouts. We were now getting more vehicles, and when we got our full complement they would number one hundred and twenty-seven, including Bren gun carriers and tracked vehicles.

One thing the soldiers loved about Aldershot was the sports. There were many playing fields of all sorts. Another thing they liked was the pubs. There was nothing quite like an English pub.

After six weeks in Aldershot, from the first weekend in September to October 20, 1941, the regiment was moved to a place called Runfold, about six miles to the south. The *marching-in* and *marching-out* procedures were the way we moved. Advance personnel were dispatched to the new place. This advance party usually consisted of a captain and me, with vehicles and drivers, and we would go one week before the move. *Marching-in* takes stock of all houses, quarters, property, rooms and contents, inspected with a civilian engineer who worked for the British government. While the unit was leaving Aldershot, I went back and conducted the *marching-out* routine. Everything was noted against us to see if anything was missing or damaged while we were in occupation. Fortunately, there were no damages or missing articles discovered during our *marching-out* from Aldershot.

At Runfold, our accommodations were houses and large requisitioned country mansions. It was beautiful countryside, and provided a bit more freedom than living in barracks. Once we went back to Aldershot to a special parade on October 22, to be inspected by Hon. J.L. Ralston, the Canadian Minister of Defence. The regiment did not stay in the Runfold area very long, but before we left for Haywards Heath, we had a change in Officer Commanding. Lieutenant Colonel Hewitt was promoted to brigade commander and Lieutenant Colonel Harry Sharp was named o/c Regina Rifles.

I was instructed to be an advance party to Haywards Heath, representing the Regina Rifles in taking it over from a British regiment. We had two weeks to effect this *marching-in* job. The transports sent me a fifteen-CWT truck and driver who supposedly knew the way from Runfold to Haywards Heath. After a mile or two down the road he lost all sense of direction. Luckily, we finally arrived. As guests of the British, we were treated well. To see how my counterpart, the British RQM, worked was quite educational. He and his RSM had large quarters together, and the RSM had a cot fixed for me. He had it placed between their two beds.

The British were much more strict with their men than we Canadians. It was always "sir" to the RSM by those under him. Every morning at 6:30 the RSM's would be awakened with a large mug of hot tea. I went down to the British Ordnance and ration point with their RQ. He took along his rifle and when he got a chance he would shoot anything falling within his sights in the park lands along the way. He once told me that when he had a weekend pass to go home he would shoot rabbits or ducks. "Those buggers are supposed to be for the rich," he said, "but here's a few they won't be getting."

Haywards Heath was a lovely place, containing a great house on a large estate. They had Nissen huts, although more were needed. Our own transport hauled in tons of brick to build a foundation and dry walkways, as this was mostly grassland. The gardener explained to me that this small village of Nissen huts would be removed after the war and the land would be put back as it had been.

I had a very interesting time during the two weeks I was with the British. On December 6, 1941, when the regiment moved by motor transport to Haywards Heath, the British had all gone except for a few officers and "Q" in rear party to clean up and square away. The local people of Haywards Heath had gone to considerable trouble barricading their store windows in the streets and shopping areas. They had taken this action on hearing from some sources that the Canadians wrecked things and were a rough lot. I suppose that there was some justification for this because the First Division had some near riots in Aldershot earlier on. I think not knowing money values and being short-changed caused most of the trouble. However, the Reginas had not been in Haywards Heath two weeks when all the boards were taken down. As a matter of fact, there were more true friendships made by the soldiers and civilians in that lovely town than any other. They loved the *Canucks*.

Haywards Heath was very convenient for London and Brighton, being situated about halfway between these two glamour places on the main railway line. "All aboard for 'aywards 'eath," the porter used to call. One listened for his call, for there were many stops and sometimes we would not even be at a station. It was common for some eager soldiers to step off the train right into nothing, just the blackness of the night. I always waited for the call, *'aywards 'eath,* when returning to camp.

The army camp was just outside the town on an estate, with large acreage and a great house called Borde Hill, a huge building. Except for a small portion, the whole of the building was occupied by the regimental officers quarters and messes, with only portions of the east wing used by its owner, a man nearly eighty years of age. The servants quarters were separate, and housed the gardener, the chauffeurs and the vehicles. The gamekeeper, along with the gardener, built homes on the estate.

QM stores and personnel were accommodated in the servants' area, as were the transport corps. We in the stores struck up a close acquaintance with the gardener who often gave us things from the gardens. He also told us about the estate, which contained over two hundred species of oak trees, each of which was tagged for identification, and must not be harmed. I concluded that the owner was a consultant to the forestry department of the government.

The gardener had a problem with the owner. Every time the old man wanted the gardener, he would tap hard with his stick on the pavement. I thought it a queer way of communication. It appeared all other employees of the estate lived in rent-free houses with free fuel, except for the gardener. He told me that every time he confronted the old pharaoh about it, asking why the others had this privilege and he didn't, the only answer he ever got was "Because you've never had it." This answer left him in despair. I confess it was a hard one to take. The gardener was a good worker and loved the soil. We liked him and often shared a cup of tea when the old titan wasn't around.

Another thing about the servants' quarters was the facilities. There were billiards rooms, darts rooms, skittles, and a big yard for outdoor fun. At least it seemed the owner had some empathy for his servants. No unions existed to extract conditions from the boss. There were two levels of these extensive servants' quarters, a ground floor, part of which was for garages, workshops and game rooms, and a second story which was mostly rooms and accommodations for living.

My thoughts on this lead me to a sad occurrence. The regiment had lots of specialized personnel in its formation, such as armourer sergeant, signals sergeant, and an important technical sergeant whose name was Freddie Thornton, a clever worker on precision instruments. He also repaired watches in his spare time, which undoubtedly enhanced his army pay. Freddie had his little workshop on the second floor of the servants' quarters. Outside the upstairs windows was a long glass cover running the length of the yard. This glass cover was partially covered by moss. Often the windows were open and the lads would call to each other. On one of these occasions, Freddie was leaning out his window talking to some lad below. He had a watch in his hand and dropped it onto the glass roofing. Unthinking, Freddie stepped out onto the glass to recover the watch and fell right through the glass onto the concrete yard below. He had the misfortune to break his legs and was in terrible pain. He had to be evacuated to hospital and we never saw him again. I suppose he was sent home. This was a sad incident both because of his injury and because the regiment lost a valuable technician.

Winter was closing in. Fuel, along with everything else, was rationed. The troops in the Nissen huts were unaccustomed to the shivering cold of the English climate. It was to their credit that they accepted and endured this grim experience. Their coal ration was one bucket per day for every stove in each hut. As Christmas neared, arrangements were made to have as cheerful a Yuletide as possible for the troops in camp. The good people of Haywards Heath, on finding out the Canadians were not wild savages, opened their homes and enjoyed the boys. Lots of them would be out to these new-found friends for Christmas. For those staying in camp there would be extra rations for Christmas fare. On

Christmas day, there would be a real treat to begin with, an egg for breakfast. For dinner there would be soup, turkey and ham, dressing, sprouts, carrots and potatoes, Christmas pudding and tea. The townspeople entertained half the regiment at Christmas parties, and the army auxiliaries brought in concert parties and of course there were beer and cigarettes. So Christmas away from home wasn't so bad.

I got a short leave to Durham to be with my family, Mother, Amy and brother Rob who was on furlough from the British army in Africa. We had a great time together in spite of the clouds of war. I remember Rob and I thought we should make a quick trip to South Moor to see our last remaining Uncle on Dad's side of the family, Uncle Bill. We also wanted to see Jenny and Jack King who worked at the Colling Underground. He had been exempt from service because coal was more important.

On the bus ride to South Moor, Rob and I wondered about Uncle Bill. Would he be waiting at the bus stand? I made a wager with Rob that I could state our uncle's first words when meeting us. I remembered what he used to say regularly when meeting folk he hadn't seen for some time, so I said to Rob that Uncle Bill would say, "Why yer bugger," as this was a common saying of Durhamers. So the bus pulled up to the pavement outside the South Moor pub and there was Uncle Bill. When he saw us, he ran to us and his first words were, "Why yer bugger," with tears rolling down his cheeks.

We didn't have far to walk to Uncle Bill and Aunt Maggie's home from the bus stop. They were dear people to me. I had visited with them scores of times in earlier years. It was sweet to be with them, they were always such fun, and the dialect of South Moor folk was very much like Tynesiders. Town was "toon," work was "wark." "Why away man," was "hurry up," be quiet was "ad thee gab." Together there was fun. Aunt Maggie was a dyed-in-the-wool liberal and an ardent worker for the cause. Rob and I also visited uncles and aunts on Mother's side of the family, Uncle Thomas and Lizzie, Uncle Bennett and Marg. They would meet us at the working men's club and pubs.

I recall witnessing a unique dart game in one crowded pub. A local man whom they all knew was into a wager for a sum of money. His task was to go around the doubles slot of the dart board, one to twenty, then the twenty-five spot, and finally the bull's eye. He was to do this in three minutes, picking out the darts himself. To my amazement, he did it. I don't think I ever saw such precision; it was fantastic.

When furloughs were over, the battalion was equipped for real action training: schemes and manoeuvers in the fields and countryside with company vehicles, field rations and cookers. We were being trained for any eventuality, such as German invasions of para-troopers on the high grounds. The winter of 1942 was slowly passing. Early in the year there was a shift of personnel. Some senior officers and warrant officers were taken from the regiment because of their age. These soldiers were originals and it was sad to see them leave. Among them was RSM Sharp, with whom I had been very close, and CSM Knobby Clark, Majors McNutt, Waterman, Scott-Calder and Bone. I had a lot of respect for these fine men. The war was like that; they were with you and then they were gone.

The battalion was ordered to a new area, and we were to be totally under canvas in the Lower Beading area. We had to draw all those tents and marquees from Ordnance at Ryhill. What a job. With over nine hundred men, we had ten to a bell tent, feet to the centre, and a trough had to be dug all around in case of rain. In May 1943, the regiment was ordered to Newhaven, Sussex. Striking all the canvas and getting it returned to Ordnance was a major task. In Newhaven the battalion was on beach patrol on the English Channel, Eastborne, Newhaven, Peacehaven, Brighton, Worthing, and Lewes. *Schemes* were the order of the day now and the battalion was involved in one called *Tiger*, which was just that. It was a gruelling experience, with extended marching. At the stores we had many problems with shoes and proper fittings for the soldiers.

There was a very good sports program in the battalion. I recall the trainer of a score of would-be pugilists. His name was Jackie Lewis. In civilian days he had been so good at his profession that he had been the heavyweight boxing champion of Canada. He used to come to me for all the needs of his boxing team as it was doing well in competition against other regiments.

While the battalion was still in Newhaven, our stores or "Q" branch was in Lewes on the southern coast. It was there that the deficiencies of unpreparedness for war were ingrained into me. I learned that the great big guns on high ground pointing threateningly out to sea were actually tree logs. There were no guns. The six strategically placed defensive cannons in the cliff rocks were actually wooden decoys as the real guns had been removed and sent to Hong Kong.

Winston Churchill said of the airmen in the battle of Britain "Never did so many owe so much to so few." He could also have said "Never did a country have to face so much with so little." We still did not have all the weaponry we needed for training. It took me some time to convince some of the officers in our regiment that these things were in short supply. When at Ordnance, I would ask questions and they would say to me, "We have to work on priorities; there's no use letting armaments out for training when they are so short at the front."

It was said by some Canadians about the slowness of getting things, that they wondered if the English really knew a war was on. The English knew only too well. Every week, boots needing repair would be tagged and sacked, and I would at times have forty or fifty pairs. Although the regiment had a regimental shoemaker, he was not fully equipped with all the necessary tools, so shoe repair was contracted out. Ordnance informed us where to go. While at Lewes we had to go to a shoe-repair cobbler in Brighton. I was on friendly terms with all my civilian contacts in war service.

One time I was in the shoe-repair, casually talking and chatting with the cobbler, when a young Canadian officer came in with a fine brown pair of his officer shoes. Officers had to provide themselves with shoes.

He asked the cobbler if he could repair his shoes. The shoe repairman was an older person, unfit for active service, and his helper was lame.

"Yes," said the cobbler, "I'll repair them for you."

"When can I expect to pick them up?" asked the officer gruffily.

"It'll take about ten days," said the cobbler wistfully.

Well, I could hardly believe my ears. The youngish officer berated the old man and said, "You British! I sometimes wonder if you know there is a war on." The old cobbler let him blow himself out and then explained how many pairs of army boots he had to work on; we of course had to wait weeks also. After the unthinking officer had gone out, I didn't interfere, although I felt like booting the brat. But as for the old man not knowing about a war going on, he told me that he had three sons in the war and that two had already been killed in action. It was enough to break your heart, how some people can be so self-centered and tread on the feelings of others by their ignorant remarks. Yes, he knew there was a war on.

After the regiment was on the southern coast for two months, everyone suspected it must soon be time for a move. And so it was at the end of July that we were ordered to move to Highden House. It was a beautiful wooded area about ten miles north of Worthing, Sussex. My memory of Highden House is of wonder and doubt. Captain Cyril White had the Pioneer Platoon, which was in charge of ammunition and explosives. Of course, we all knew there had to be experiments, but the methods were sometimes startling. So it was one day when Captain White and his merry men managed to get an old wrecked car hauled to the top of a hill behind the camp. They loaded the car with a time bomb and explosives, and then pushed it down the hill to see what would happen. Everyone wanted to know what the terrific bang was all about. It was a wonder that no great damage was done as this could have been serious. I had my doubts about Cyril White. He was always trying something offbeat and getting great fun out of cooking things up.

I had been away from my home in Canada now for almost two years.

The war became a waiting game, patiently for the policy makers, but for the soldiers it was a restless time. It was always, "When are we going to move?" even after we had just gotten moved. "When is the big shove we're training for going to begin?" I suppose there had to be a build up of materials necessary for an invasion, and I knew from my lowly observations and experiences with supplies that it would take some considerable time. At this point they barely had enough to keep the fighting troops in supply, so there had to be a long wait until the whole war effort could be bolstered to even equal that of the enemy. Day after day we prepared and trained with what we had, or could improvise, to supply all these men, so eager at their own level, always wondering why it was so slow and tedious.

Mail was eagerly anticipated and parcels from home were always a big deal. I know that from my own yearnings. Anne and I kept up a regular correspondence and I sometimes got compact parcels from her. There could be disastrous wastage if parcels were not securely wrapped. Anne would tell me how little Pamela and Joanne were thriving and how she was involved in the work of Regina Rifles Ladies Auxiliary. She spoke often of the Baumbers and how this family had adopted her and the wee girls. Anne's letters were always cheerful, trying to reassure me, and her parcels were bundles of love between us.

There were times when I would awaken and wonder why I was so far away from home, waiting and waiting, when I could have been at home with my wife and kids. Then I'd think about the thousands like myself, probably doing the same thing. Anne was at home raising the children and I was way over there fighting to preserve country and home. In retrospect, would it be worth the trials? It really does give one pause to consider, even today, what might have happened to Canada. In Europe almost forty years later, foreign troops are still in occupational roles. How would we in Canada react to foreign soldiers on our street corners, armed to the teeth? The war might have been in vain for some, in that not much was settled, and there were refugees everywhere, but it was not in vain if it preserved our way of life. Our country was free in the sense that we could have a home and do our own thing. In any civilized country there must be laws of curtailment against the idea that one can use freedom to do what he or she pleases. That was the very thing that got us into a war. There is a difference between license and freedom. So one consoles oneself and writes encouragement to loved ones. I suppose the soldiers on the other side did the same things, so really we all suffer when others, no matter who, press for individual or corporate power. One has to understand that every able-bodied man in Britain was on active service and out there holding the lines. The less able-bodied men were in home defense in things like home guard, fire fighting services, bomb disposal, and air-raid wardens. The women were also in much evidence in these services. They were expected to work at their jobs of keeping the country going, like trains, buses, munitions, and so on, and they were called to court to explain if they didn't show up. And then when their civilian work was over, they filled in all these other jobs. It was often, as when an air-raid was on, which was frequent, that a person would work all day and be up all night as the sirens wailed. In my opinion, these people were magnificent. They took it on the chin, as the saying goes, and came up for more. Yet one couldn't get into his beloved pub or train or bus for servicemen of other countries being there.

Our battalion day began with breakfast at 7:30 a.m., then scheduled training, dinner at noon, more training, and the soldier's day was over at 4:00 p.m.. Supper was at 5:00 p.m., with the rest of the time free except when on manoeuvres. If it hadn't been so grim, it would have been like holidaying, in a restricted way. The soldiers could stay out until 10:30 p.m., then they had to be in barracks if they didn't have a night pass. There was no such free time or rest for the English civilian, and my heart went out to those people. In my opinion, they were the unsung heros of World War II.

On September 20, 1942, the battalion was settled in Steyning, Sussex, a quiet and picturesque little town with a long winding main street. At one end stood Wiston House, once the huge historic home of Oliver

Cromwell. Wiston House, with its ancient architecture, turret, and extensive grounds, looked like a castle. I remember a huge oil painting of Oliver Cromwell, bigger than life-size. Wiston House was situated at the bottom of the sunny South Downs on top of which was the famous Chanctonbury Ring, a huge circle of trees. It was believed that if the Germans wanted to attack England from the air, landing by parachutes, it would be on the South Downs, and the battalion had patrols around the area frequently.

There was a very old church in Steyning. The site of this was the original one founded in the eighth century by St. Cuthman. Steyning in ancient times was a port, inland on the river Adur. Shoreham was along the south coast from Brighton and Worthing and Port Slade. All these places were in the battalion area of operation and exercises were conducted on ammo supplies, map reading in darkness, and compass experiences.

In October, there was to be a sports fest. The unit was very competent in ice hockey and boxing. There was an ice rink in Brighton. The regiment had a very exciting boxing team also, and was successful in winning the army competition. The Reginas all enjoyed their few months' sojournment in this little place.

One quiet Sunday morning, artillery gun shells began landing near the churches and schools. There were confusion and mayhem. The shelling kept on for about an hour and a half and did considerable damage to the buildings. No one seemed to have any explanation. Most of our lads said it was the Limeys, others said it was the bloody Home Guard. But it was the same beleaguered Home Guard officer who ran over two miles to get some Canadian gunners to stop shooting. They were having practice and were off-target. This left the Canadians with red faces. Fortunately, no one had been injured. How wrong can you get!

Another situation concerned our QM store corporal, Jack McGraw. When we were in the stores and conversation got around to girls, Mac, who was single, would run for cover when being teased about getting himself a girl and getting married. McGraw's retort was always, "That'll be the fine frosty morning when any girl will snare me." Well, it had to happen. There was a little tea shop on the main street that Canadian boys used to frequent. It was easy access to our accommodations and Mac, Bill Morrison, Barney, and I sometimes would go. Two girls worked in the shop. One girl named Molly ruined all Mac's previous ideas about girls. He fell, hook-line-and-sinker, for Molly, and eventually they were married. Molly returned with him to Canada after the war. Anne and I had lots of fun when visiting them in Regina. Mac took a lot of ribbing for his about-face on girls.

It was nearing Christmas and the Canadians were again accepted warmly by the English people. Many in the regiment had places to go for weekend passes and for Christmas. Of course, I would be going north to Durham to be with my mother. Christmas for those remaining in camp was a happy occasion. The battalion entertained one hundred and fifty children on Christmas day. This practice of having big parties at Yuletide with the local community was followed by most Canadian units. There were always some extra rations for these special annual events. In fact, the soldiers got the best. The locals didn't fare so well, but they always made the best of it.

The war seemed to be stalled somewhat. Air-raids could happen anywhere at anytime, and the sound of wailing sirens and Klaxon horns kept people either up or awake all night. Fortunately, the discovery of radar somewhat remedied this situation. Before radar, if an enemy aircraft crossed the coast of England anywhere, the sirens would go off. After radar, they could track the aircraft, so the sirens would go only where the bombing was going on, and people from that time on did sometimes get a night's sleep.

After Christmas, it was bleak, and in January 1943, we moved from the friendly village of Steyning to Denne Park, practically in the town of Horsham in Sussex. The unit headquarters were housed in a mansion.

Troops and QM stores occupied Nissen huts, scattered widely in the area. The camp was on high ground about a mile south of the town. Between the military camp and the town were lovely recreation grounds, beautiful cricket pitches, and tennis courts. At Horsham, there were scrambling nets, used in training for cliff climbing. The nets were erected forty feet high, and eventually every person in the battalion had to climb up one side and get down the other side. It was a formidable obstacle, especially for those not in hard training like line soldiers. This included cooks, clerks, medics, and so on. But everyone had to go over the scrambling nets, from lieutenant colonel to buck private. Since an army has to be fit, you were either on parade for the routine, or if not well, you reported sick and were put on sick parade. The sick parade reported to the MO, or Medical Officer. Accordingly, one might get a half day's rest, or perhaps a day. For more serious things, soldiers were sent back to army hospital. So if the MO assigned a day's rest, it meant the soldier went back to his company quarters and laid down. The majors had a saying, "Into bed or out of barracks." There was no in between. They didn't muck about, and soon found out those who *swing the lead*. On the other hand, if one was really sick and sent back to hospital, he was *struck off strength* and the battalion would get a fit replacement from a holding unit. If you were sick in hospital, then when you were better you would be sent to a holding unit, usually at army base. The thing that kept many from reporting sick was that they might not get back to their own unit when they became well. Perhaps the unit was at full strength, and one might be sent to a unit where he wouldn't know anyone. The battalion became home to the infantryman. He called it "his unit." He joined up with them, they were his pals, and he tried to stay with them.

So, back to the scrambling nets. The QM staff all went over nicely. There were those who failed the first time and had to try again. In a way it was more difficult than a real action climb, for in training the forty-foot net was hanging free, barely touching the ground. And no one held the net down to keep it tight, therefore it swung, making it difficult to climb. If a number of men were going to scale a rope net on a cliff, for instance, the ones on the bottom would keep it taut and start right up after the others. It would have been much simpler to climb if taut. Probably there was more fun watching about ten men spread out along the net, struggling and swinging, with no one holding it at the bottom. I recall these exercises were all scheduled for dawn. In the half-light the soldiers looked like spiders in silhouette, with their rifles swung over their shoulders. There would be cat calls. No one really knew who it was halfway up the net, twenty feet or so, struggling and getting nowhere. If you let your feet get too far apart you got stuck. One chap managed to get about twenty-five feet up, then froze. There was much yelling and teasing, typical of soldiers. It turned out to be a bigger laugh when it was discovered that this was the Second I/C! There were very few Regina Rifles who wouldn't remember Exercise *Mable* and the scrambling nets at Horsham.

In the grounds at the mansion were lovely gardens and a huge glass house containing many wonderful specimens of flowers and plants, especially orchids. They were not my favourite flowers, but they were rare specimens. The old gardener showed us all around. There was also a pond with geese and ducks and the farmers had cattle grazing in the area, which was quite rural at Denne Park. On the weekend the unit used to invade Horsham. The unit transport would lay vehicles on for the boys wanting to go to town, and fetch them back before lights-out at the camp. Bill Morrison and I used to walk down to the recreation grounds. Usually there was a cricket game on Saturday afternoons, and tennis matches, the players all dressed in white. The people were most friendly and when they would see us they would ask us to join in. We enjoyed the fellowship of these friendly people.

There was another incident with some army humour, but it was no laughing matter for the civilians. Captain White was still officer of the Pioneer Platoon, but was also officer in charge of gas training. An order was in effect that all personnel were to carry gas masks and wear them every Tuesday morning until noon. White had noticed that the order was not being fully followed. One Tuesday morning he decided to catch the lads by surprise, and without warning released clouds of tear gas. He not only caught the troops, but there was a breeze and it blew the gas far afield. The farmers, the people and the police were all up in arms and at Denne Park the old gardener was found lying down by the edge of the lake laving water over his face. The cows' tongues hanged almost down to their knees. In the glass house, the plants were all flat, the orchids hanging limply. It was awful. It took quite a while to get the thing quieted down. People suffered as far as ten miles downwind, and undoubtedly there were claims made.

Another hypothetical war was upon us, called *Sparton*. It was a massive affair involving five divisions, three Canadian and two British, and it covered nearly half of England in Oxfordshire, Berkshire and Bedfordshire. This exercise lasted about two weeks. The Reginas had great success against the British. They evidently got news of the British location at a small village called New Bradwell, a few miles north of the town of Oxford. From about 9:00 p.m., the Reginas were busy with messages, alerts, and preparations for a surprise attack on the unsuspecting British. There was a real air of excitement, and by better strategic moves, the Canadians had the British in a trap. Most of the British officers were in a large school house. At midnight, while they were all in bed, the *Canucks* attacked with mock fire power called *thunderflashes*, extremely noisy, fiery bangers. There were yells, screams, and pandemonium broke out. The anger and arguments went on for a time, but it was no use, the referees decided that the British had been fairly captured and taken as prisoners.

These thunderflashes had burned some of the officers' clothing. They were like the real thing when let off in great quantities. So bully for the Reginas. They had caught and taken captive a brigadier and his headquarters staff. I don't know if the British officers ever lived that down, but it was a feather in the caps of the Regina Rifles. It was peaceful the next day, and the New Bradwell townspeople literally fell for the Canadian lads. The mock war was over and the villagers opened their houses to the Regina Riflemen. I think seeing the Canadians gave them something to cheer about. It was new scenery for the unit too as Canadians had not been much further north than Sussex. Fortheringham and I were invited into a home for fish and chips on one evening, and so were all the others being entertained in someone's home. This only lasted one day, though, then the unit had to withdraw. The townspeople waved goodbye. We were all back in Horsham after about twelve days.

There were changes that kept me busy. We were issued new MK-IV rifles with a different way of fixing their bayonets, and we had parades. The regiment often moved around Sussex, either down to Newhaven or south, just to get used to moving. For a brief spell we were in Lewes, almost on the channel. Not far from our billets was a Church of England, so I got to the Sunday evening service a couple of times. Of course, as always the people were friendly, especially to Canadians in uniform. On coming out from the service one Sunday evening the rector, a short man with rounded stature, asked me to wait for a few minutes until he'd bid his parishioners good night. He told me that he had served in the Navy. He noted that I was a Sergeant Major, RQMS. After we had talked for a little while, he invited me to the rectory. So I went to his home, met his wife and we had tea and talked. He and I had quite a talk about life and war, then he told me that he was still in the service. I wanted to know how, and he took me into a separate room, all equipped with modern listening devices. This was a listening post to intercept things on the airwaves. He was a government appointed secret decipherer, and certainly a surprise to me.

Before I left, he asked me if I would come to a missionary meeting. The church ladies were having one the following Wednesday afternoon and he asked if I would say a bit about what I had told him about church vans going to northern Canada and so on. I had some knowledge of the Foreign Missionary Society, so I agreed and in good faith attended. It was a nice afternoon, and there were approximately thirty ladies present, along with the rector and another Canadian officer, a padre. The meeting was held outdoors on the lawn. It was lovely. We had tea and a few words from the rector, then he introduced the captain. I didn't mind that; *fair enough*, I thought. But darn it all, the captain simply said all that I had prepared. I couldn't believe my ears. I felt awful. He had taken my plank from underneath me. I nearly crept away before he finished, but I didn't make it. Indeed, it was interesting, but now the rector was introducing me. I changed gears fast and told them how I got to Canada and about some of my experiences, such as all the railway engines having bells. I thought the Canadians must go to church regularly, the darned bells were always ringing. I told some truths, some corn, and my fears soon vanished. They all had a good laugh at the green Englishman, but it went over well. I suppose the good Lord knows best. Sometimes one is best when unprepared. The ladies seemed to enjoy what I said better than the padre's talk. So one never knows.

The war still consisted of waiting and training as the unit was moved back to Denne Park, Horsham. It was now August 1943. The fighting personnel of the unit, line companies along with support and some of Headquarters coy, entrained for operational training at Inveraray, Scotland, on the shores of Loch Fyne. This was a rugged experience and in rugged terrain. The idea was to become familiar with landing craft and various sea-craft such as L.C.A.S and L.S.I.S, which would be used in the invasion. These were the men who were to actually meet the enemy nose to nose. The administration and service part of the battalion did not have this hazardous work. The remainder of the regiment at Denne Park had an order to move to Bournemouth where the unit was put together again on September 1, 1943. This was a relaxation period and the battalion was left to itself for a while. The men were given leave, and it couldn't have been in a more beautiful place. It was here that our equipment and stores were brought up to date.

One night in Bournemouth we were sitting around in the stores looking at a newspaper when an item caught my eye. It was about eight Canadian sailors who had been arraigned in court for causing a disturbance in a local pub. They were spending the night in the local jail. Among the eight men named was one Robert Chapman. This aroused some curiosity in me. The Chapmans next door to us on Garnet Street, Regina, had two sons in the war, and I remembered one was in the Navy. I mentioned to my comrades that perhaps I should pop down to see him. Then I thought better of it. If he knew that someone knew, then it might get back to his mum and dad who were lovely, law-abiding people. He might have thought that I would tell them, so I decided to stay away.

After the war, Anne and I visited the coast of B.C. and went to see the Chapmans who had moved from Regina. While we were there, we met Bob and his wife. This was the first time I had seen him since joining up. When we were alone for a few minutes, I asked him if during his stint in the navy he was ever in Bournemouth. He said he was. I asked him if he had a good time there. He said he had. Then I told him that I had seen his name in the evening paper, and he laughingly told me how it all happened. I told him that I was only a few blocks away from him and had been tempted to go and see him. I never knew if his parents found out about it. I didn't want them to be worried, but he said it was all a mistake anyway. There was a mixup and it really wasn't serious.

There was a feeling amongst the troops at this time that things were beginning to gel. The army was trained to a profession and was efficient and aggressive. After we had been moved to Hillsea Barracks at Portsmouth, exercises were all on landing and landing crafts. There was an exercise called *Large Pirate*, geared to demonstrate how things were going to be. I remember Portsmouth to this day. I had never seen so much pulverization of any place. All the docks and dockside were out of bounds to the civilians. The air-raids had devastated this city, especially the waterfront. Just to see so much wanton wastage struck home to me the horridness of war. Things become valueless as destruction becomes a way of life.

There I was in the midst of a struggle for whatever it is men struggle for. It seemed so ridiculous to have the world at war. Hitler had some strange ideas about the common good. I suppose, as the scripture says, we can only assess people by what they do. It's rather difficult to understand that Hitler loved even his own people and countrymen, since he had millions of them killed. How far does a person have to go to get his own way and satisfy his own whims? Hitler certainly had a great talent, but never was there a greater misuse of it. In Roman times, great men would lead into battle and often would fight as individuals to settle conflicts instead of everyone else getting killed. I was witnessing the modern version: flatten everything, kill everyone in opposition. The world had to stop Hitler and his factions. I know God works in His own way and men cannot be gods in their own way, so wars occur. How long will it take? How much more destruction and killing will it take before we get wise and good enough to envision peaceful living?

Anne and I had often talked about my joining up. We realized that it was inevitable what I would do. We could hardly expect another to go to protect us. I didn't want to join, having never cared for the military. So there was Anne at home with our two kids and here I was, five thousand miles away, a mere speck of dust in front of a rolling tank. Could it be stopped? Can the freedom of mankind be overrun by martial steel? To look at Portsmouth dockside sent shivers down my spine. Getting used to such sights, the roar of air-raids, rationed food, witnessing death, these were normal phenomena. As individuals become a team, the teams become a league, and as leagues become legions, and legions become might, might versus might. The result was that many Portsmouths on both sides were lost. History shows the presence of God and his involvement in mankind, but the present is always hardest to understand. To be free costs, and it is worth more than life and destruction.

Hillsea Barracks was old, something like Aldershot. Aldershot was a soldier town; Portsmouth was a Navy town. At this time there was a great concentration of service personnel. The southern part of England was jam-packed with build-up forces readying for the invasion. The Germans working at Adanac Brewery had always talked about *Der Tag* or *The Day*. Apparently, that was to be the start of Hitler conquering the world.

Now on this southern coast of England the talk was about D-Day, the day of the invasion. No one knew just when, but as in spring the countryside turns green, the bulging mass of soldiers, sailors and airmen from Canada, America, Britain, Poland et al surely denoted the intent to invade soon.

Hillsea Barracks were straight up the main street of Portsmouth, about a half mile. The battalion was together for meals, served in the great drill hall. It was equipped with some cookers the shape of oil barrels, something I'd never seen, heard or read about. They were inadequate. The messing was queue line and things didn't go well. The cooks had trouble with these stoves and consequently the whole setup was unsatisfactory. Meals were slow because of the so-called stoves, and cold because the whole place was cold. Complaints were loud, and a riot almost erupted.

The unit, as with all movement, came under army headquarters. It was necessary to learn how to move such a mass of troops and machines. We were placed in confined areas and imagined the sea-craft taking over the invasion of France. It would be some job. Try to visualize an armada of ships of every size, and thousands of men to board them. It was momentous. The practice was to evolve a workable system of embarkation.

While we were at Hillsea, a permanent barracks town, there was always plenty of recreation, and dances were held in a big gymnasium. I was fortunate at one time to be invited to a British celebration in another dance hall. In Portsmouth there were a lot of anti-aircraft units and these guns were operated by W.A.A.F.S, girls. They were service personnel, called *ack-ack* gunners. One day enemy aircraft came over the area and to our delight and amazement, the girls shot down a spy plane, which was miles high. It was extraordinary that it could be hit at such a great height, and as it was so special, the British authorities organized a celebration to honour that gun crew. So they invited a few of us. I was there when they invested the heroines. It really was a splendid evening of fun and celebration. It was sort of a miracle to hit something so far away, especially a spy plane.

At Hillsea, RSM Harry Denham was lost to the battalion and there was a special parade to honour him. Harry Denham, who had succeeded RSM Tom Sharp, was a great favourite with the men. He was also a great friend and companion of mine. As with Tom Sharp, we ate together and roomed in the same quarters. Our association had been a happy one and I would miss him greatly. He was jovial and fun to be with, yet strict or firm with the men. With his peculiar way of bringing the battalion to attention, he would shout, "Reginas, CHOW!" I was lucky to have had pals like Tom Sharp and Harry Denham.

If the army did nothing else, it afforded the experience of seeing many interesting and beautiful places. On December 9, 1943, my birthday, the battalion was sent to the Isle of Wight. After the rustle and hustle of these past few months, and especially the hectic exercises along the sea coast, being on this beautiful island was almost a reward. The place was not as full of service personnel as were Hillsea and Portsmouth. In fact, there had been no others since 1942, and we had the whole place to ourselves. The Isle of Wight is not a large island. I believe it has approximately one hundred and fifty square miles. The battalion was spread around in different areas, some at Newport, some at Freshwater, and our unit was stationed at Totland Bay, a most lovely place. We had so much amphibious training that the troops were almost like sailors, so the island was okay. The Johns will forever remember the local inhabitants of the Isle of Wight. They literally opened their houses to the Canadian soldiers. I was fortunate since my official journeys for laundries, shoe-repairs etc. took me almost every place. While there, the troops did some training with the Navy on landing practice.

There grew an affection between the islanders and the members of our regiment. At Freshwater a lady opened her home at any time to the lads. At Totland Bay, my digs faced west, and I saw the most beautiful sunsets. A lot of us went to the local pubs. Drinks were not available in great quantities, but the places were enjoyable with games, darts, etc. A chap invited Morrison and me to a meal with him, and I recall that he worked for a brewery. He knew a lot about making booze and confided to us that after watching the Canadians drink, he was fearful that some of them would fall down by the way they mixed their drinks. In Totland Bay there was a grand dance hall and almost every night the community had a dance arranged, which the Johns thoroughly enjoyed. For these dances, the authorities brought in girls from the place I used to go with the regiment's laundry, a place called Shankin on the east side of the island.

Most of the boys going on short leaves went through Ryde, the main terminal for the ferryboat. When we had to go to the mainland for supplies via truck and ferry, we saw a lot of the English seacoast, the channel and the Isle of Wight. A lingering, haunting memory of Totland Bay, was the lap of the sea on the shingle beach. It lulled me to sleep every night. The quiet rhythm had a soothing quality difficult to describe. It was a great place for the unit to spend their 1943 Christmas. With soldiers and civilians getting on so well, there just had to be a great Christmas party. We had over one hundred and fifty children and their parents. I think this effort by the regiment was the best of any previous event. The local kids were stuffed with little things hard to get in wartime, such as lemonade, cake, peanuts and gum, all contributed by individuals in the battalion.

There was emphasis in 1944 on training with the Navy. On February 28, the brigade moved to Southampton for inspection by General Montgomery, newly appointed General in command of the Twenty-first Army Group. We were very busy at the QM preparing the unit for these events, getting everything smart for a good show. The regiment exercised at Studland Bay getting experience with bangalores, a weapon used to blow away enemy defenses of barbed wire, which was used by the Germans on the French coast.

As spring approached it became apparent that something big was being put into action. The southern coastal areas were closed to civilians, and reports from the mainland told of roads being widened and tented camps mushroomed all over the place. We at the "Q" knew the time for invasion was drawing near, for a new type of helmet shaped like a scuttle was issued to everyone. We were now under a unit called Movement Control. There was a massive build up going on, consisting of Americans, British and Canadians. On April 25, His Majesty the King, accompanied by Generals Crerar, Stuart and Keller, inspected the Seventh Infantry Brigade. Three weeks later, the brigade was inspected by General Eisenhower. The Johns were a bit awe-struck, but the General was affable and very enthusiastic with the personnel of the regiment.

I, along with everyone else in the "Q," was very busy. The Ordnance was withdrawing all surplus stores, which we considered essential. Every vehicle had its place and carrier, according to the little book called G-1098. All other things above the allotment listed in this book were to be turned in. For the longest time we were nowhere near to having full entitlement, even for training. Now it appeared the chips were down, and all our training weapons and vehicles were to be turned in and new ones issued up to full establishment. Nearly all personnel carried a weapon: a rifle with a bayonet. There were some exceptions. For example, officers carried pistols, and stretcher bearers did not carry weapons. They wore full body-size Red Crosses over their khaki to show that they were non-combatant. Other troops not carrying rifles were the sixty-six Bren gunners, the twenty-two two-inch mortar gunners and the three-inch mortar man. All others, even cooks, carried rifles, except dispatch riders, who had Sten guns.

The regimental establishment for vehicles was one hundred and twenty-seven, composed of tracked vehicles, sixty-CWT trucks, fifteen-CWT trucks, jeeps, station wagons and one staff vehicle for the O/C. We did not have amphibian vehicles at this time. Another item issued at this time was British battle dress. Treated to resist vermin, it was as stiff as a board and detested by the Canadians. However, this was offset by the issue of high-top boots in place of khaki gaiters. These were a great hit. The Reginas were the only ones to have them, and it was for trial and testing for three months. Everyone liked them, and other units envied the Johns. Finally, after a period of time they became general issue. We were a popular QM branch. These boots were in such demand.

The reason the mobile unit was necessary was the compilation of ground troops, Air Force men and sailors. Great areas were made into wired enclosures. The idea was for orderly procession once invasion movement began. Area One would be moved to embarkation, Area Two would move into Area One, and a chain movement would be put into motion. Included in Area One, as we were the assault group, were many familiar faces: the Cameroons from Ottawa, the Winnipegs, the Scottish Beach group. The buzz and activity of the whole southern coast rumbled like a volcano about to erupt. In an impish sort of way it was like when in the fall the robins congregate in large numbers, flying around like crazy eating all the red berries of the mountain ash tree before they head south. The place was alive with expectation; one wondered for what. All our vehicles had gone to an assigned place to be water-proofed. This precaution was taken in case the landing craft (LC), might not get quite to the beach, and the vehicles would have to embark into the water. For those that did, there would be a de-water-proofing area.

Ordnance was caught in an ever-increasing swirl. Our G-1098 establishment, which had never even been 50 per cent complete, was now at 98 per cent. Every soldier and unit was in possession of the things needed for battle. It was a tremendous undertaking. The reserve battalion and company stores were all re-checked and resupplied when necessary. There was strict supervision to prevent any knowledge of these preparations getting outside the area, so there were no letters out, no leaves, and no phone calls. Everyone's life was at stake.

Brothers Ernest (left) and Rob (right), Cousin Arthur (centre).

My staff and I. I'm second from right.

A break in the sun. I'm the one in the uniform.

My wife Anne in "our weekly chat."

Myself and Sgt. Cook perusing the messing circular.

Joe Jean.

All the officers are out to look over our first Bren gun carrier in Debert.

The Regina Rifle Regiment at the Liberation of Calais.

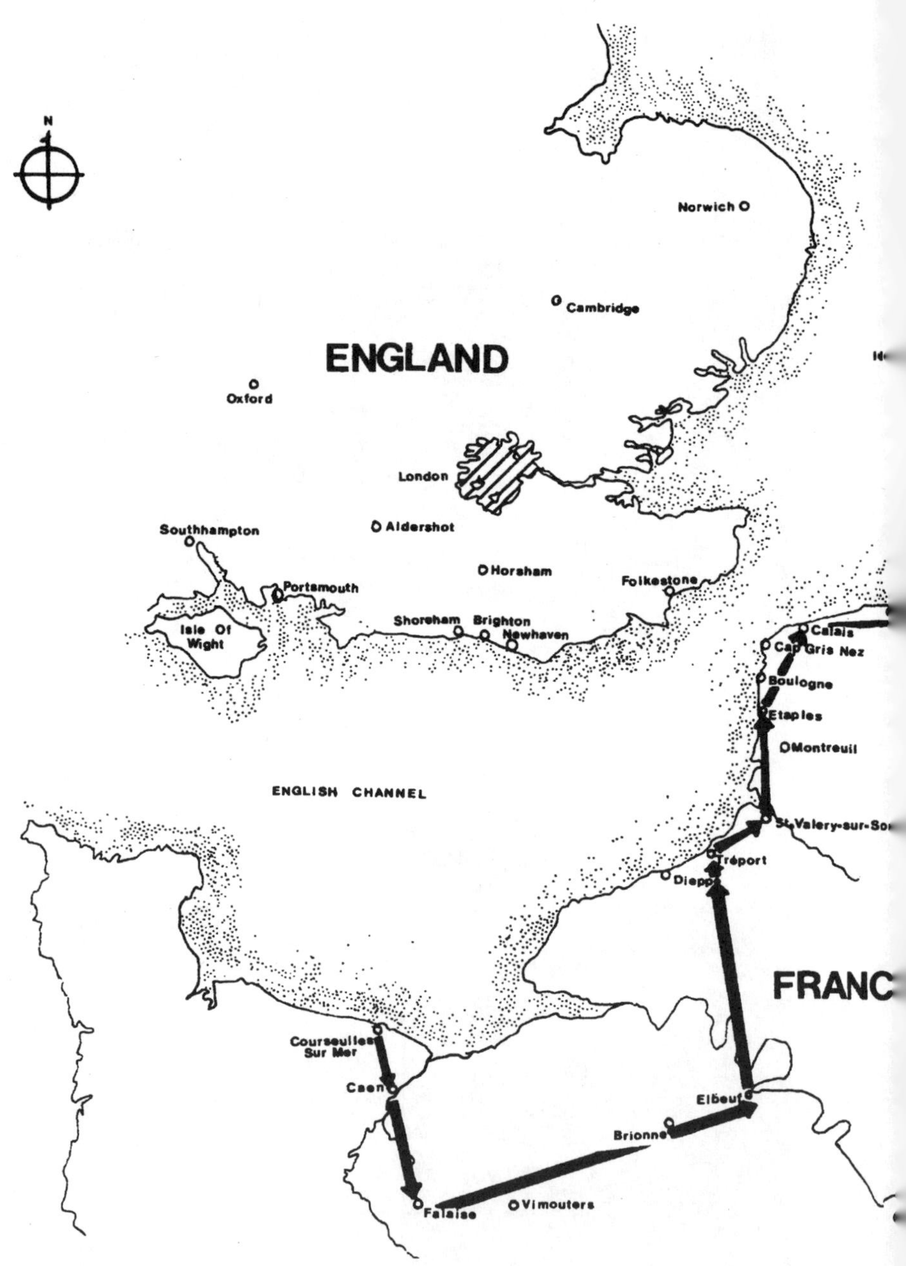
N
ENGLAND
Norwich
Cambridge
Oxford
London
Southhampton
Aldershot
Horsham
Folkestone
Portsmouth
Isle Of Wight
Shoreham
Brighton
Newhaven
ENGLISH CHANNEL
Calais
Cap Gris Nez
Boulogne
Etaples
Montreuil
Tréport
Courseulles Sur Mer
Caen
Elbeuf
Brionne
Falaise
Vimouters

NORTH-WEST EUROPE
1939-1945

CHAPTER ELEVEN

The Liberation of Europe

BRIEFINGS BEGAN THE LAST WEEK of May 1944. The plan was unfolded to those in the battalion at the final meeting on May 30, where everyone was admitted, one company at a time, to a large oversized Nissen hut surrounded by entanglements and guards. Everyone entering this building had to be in possession of credentials. There was a huge map of the French countryside. The briefings followed a familiar pattern: topography first, showing a section of the French coast, the beach, the sands, the mine fields, the marshes, the towns, and the machine gun posts set in concrete. From recent photographs, we could see practically everything. Everyone knew the town that we were preparing to attack. Finally, briefing details were issued for our own specific plans: first the army, then the corps, then the division, followed by the brigade, the battalion, the company, the platoon and finally the section, a group of eight men.

The theme went: "HIT THE BEACH—and go like blazes."

That night in the darkened tents, *Operation Overlord* overshadowed any conversation about air-raids or anything else. There we were after three years of waiting anxiously to get on with a job everyone knew had to be done, and we knew there was no going back. In the battalions, all the familiar markings had been removed. Everything the unit carried into the invasion was marked only with the number "744." Our shoulder badges, kit bags, vehicles, boxes, stores, everything was designed to give as little information to the enemy as possible. *Hustle* took the place of *waiting*. There was, in spite of great dangers and hazards, a relief that battle was about to be enjoined, a sober reflection indeed. On May 30, 1944, the Officer Commanding, Al Matheson, spoke to the whole battalion for the last time before D-Day.

While the unit was embarking in various crafts or vessels, I was dispatched with five sixty-CWT trucks and drivers loaded with spare rations, guns and ammunition. We reported to an assembly area where, with vehicles from other assault units, we were lined up in a convoy. Movement control impressed me with this huge convoy. The convoy started at a point west of London and was routed right through the heart of London to Tilbury Docks where ships awaited us. It was a well-executed exercise; there were policemen at every crossroad. The convoy travelled at fifty miles an hour, fairly racing through the middle of London, never stopping once. The Londoners surely must have wondered what was happening. It was a hair-raising, exciting experience.

As the ships were ready for us, we could drive right onto them and were soon on our way down the Thames and out into the English Channel. The sky was dark and the stars twinkled. Everything above deck was in darkness, but below decks we saw something we had not witnessed for a long time. The meals were really something as they were American rations, meat, vegetables, fruit, anything we wanted.

It was now June 1, and the D-Day landings were planned for June 5. The unit would be loaded at Southampton, with the whole invasion fleet moving in waves. We would dovetail into the main fleet on June 5. So we had three or four days nosing around close to the English coast along the cliffs of Dover. The first two days were fairly quiet. Our ship was armed with six Hispano anti-aircraft guns. These had been installed at the last minute, replacing older type guns. They were manned by American personnel. Although the weather was cloudy and rainy, the aircraft action caused considerable excitement. There seemed to be a constant noise of low-flying aircraft. The Americans manning the ack-ack guns were terribly nervous about these attacks, and when the noise came close, these gunners began firing. Heaven only knew what they were shooting at as they could not see in the dark. Word got around that the gunners had never had orders to shoot at all. They were not enemy planes they had been shooting at but friendly ones. There was a real hassle about it all and there was no more firing at noises. These were curious chaps.

It wasn't really a holiday trip around the White Cliffs of Dover, but it had its moments of levity. The vehicle drivers and I had few chores, just staying with the trucks and waiting until the Navy got us over, so we observed the Americans. I'm afraid we thought it amusing the way they did things so differently from our training, but there they were and the ship was on its way. Everything about the invasion was laid on to the minute for the initial landings.

Headquarters had eleven craft. The first craft was to disembark on the shores of France at Courseulles at H+5 minutes, the next at H+20 minutes, and so on all day until H+9 hours. The feeding for the invasion was thus: every soldier had seven days' rations; he carried three days on his person, two days rations in coy vehicles, and there were two days in "B" Echelon vehicles. These rations were to last until lines of communication were established in France. We would be cut off from all other services and entirely on our own as a battalion when we reached French soil.

Owing to the severity of the weather, there was a delay of one day in the drama of this life-and-death conflict and assault. So we on our LSI (Landing Ship Infantry) had an extra day of lingering on the English side of the channel. There were Morrison, Beaudry, Dursault, Potter, Butler, Smith, Campbell, Howland, Barnes and I, aboard our five sixty-CWT trucks chained to the framework of the ship. On our LSI we huddled together and waited. There were other units aboard with their vehicles, including the Ninth Brigade and British contingents.

I never experienced any cringing with those aboard. I suppose they were all trained soldiers ready to do what soldiers are expected to do. So whatever was at hand we would get on with it, whether it was enjoying the canned fruit, battling the very rough sea, taking cover from hostile aircraft, or discussing the chances of survival. As one lad lightly commented when we were strafed at random by a German aircraft, "I thought one of those bullets had my name on it." It had grazed his cheek. This was a survival game. The soldiers in the infantry were trained not to expose themselves unnecessarily, and to keep their weapons clean at all times.

The weather was awful on June 4, 1944, especially at sea. We had an issue of vomit bags, three per person. I was continually borrowing. For me, fighting the sea, I imagined that the war couldn't have been any worse. Things would get better, even getting shot. All the blokes laughed at me. I guess there's nothing so funny as a fellow *heaving* over the side. One guy, intending to be helpful, said to keep eating something. But that made it worse.

On June 6, at 7:35 a.m., the first flight of sea craft of the invasion began its movement in our sector, Nan Green Beach, at Courseulles Sur Mer. Almost immediately, it was as though all hell had been let loose. The roar of battle became deafening, and we were not even on the first wave of assault troops; the line companies were. It was these men, A, B, C and D Coys who stormed the beaches. Earlier in the dark early hours of the day, British and other paratroopers had been dropped behind the enemy fortifications on the beaches. They were attempting to destroy all communications behind enemy lines, blowing up everything possible to delay and confuse the situation. Navy battleships were off coast shelling the whole area behind the beaches. The noise, the whistling of the huge shells going through the air above, threatened grim death. The firepower of those invading the beaches and those defending was awesome.

The sea was also full of floating and submerged mines, and sea craft were being blown out of the water when they triggered these things. As anticipated, barbed wire was strung everywhere. The Navy with their bangalores had disrupted and spread this system of defense into coils of unfastened wire all over the place. Everything was going on at once, like a terrible cyclone destroying all in its path. This was to be a long cyclone. In the midst of this sight of Hades, men didn't really hear it. The enemy had one thing in common: to prevent landings; the invaders had one thing in common: to make landings. This was what the noise, roars, explosions, cries, and fierce rapidity of gun fire, the wounded and death were all about. Nothing imaginable could have been more savage.

The Germans with their heavy guns were half hidden in the sand in defensive shelters, three to four feet thick concrete, and they fired incessantly at anything in front of them. To silence these guns was the first objective of the infantry. The fierceness of these encounters was beyond description. Storm, shoot, kill, silence the opposition. The infantrymen carried hand grenades and raised havoc whenever they were used. The first assault troops had different sea-craft. Their small L.C.A. (Landing Craft Assault), carried thirty men, their personal arms and equipment. The choppy seas heaved these small craft around fiercely. The sea was worse than the war for some of those Johns who, like me, had no stomach for the dizzy tossing about.

Absolute mayhem was still in evidence when our LSI began its approach, but luckily we were able to land dry. Our trucks were all waterproofed and although the men landed dry, the vehicles had to move through four feet of water between the disembarkation point and the shore. There were fighting men and vehicles everywhere. We were aware that a Beach Group was established, which was necessary to move all incoming equipment and men in from the beach to keep the invasion going. But there wasn't much time to gaze around. At a fleeting glance, I noticed an L.C.A. bobbing up and down and two naval lads struggling to keep it from a floating mine. They didn't succeed, and it blew up. I saw a small craft out from land a few hundred yards blown clean out of the water, then dropped into the sea nose first. Landing craft were everywhere.

We identified ourselves to the Beach Group Sergeant and got directions to the area set up for de-water-proofing. Then the five sixty-CWT trucks of our Regina Rifle Regiment made their way inland from Green Beach. We were in a war, no stops for anything, no meals, no sleep, just shots and shells. Our first mission was to get our vehicles under cover, behind hedge-rows, any low spots, then dig in, a slit trench, anything to keep ourselves beneath ground level. There was to be no movement from one place to another except as absolutely necessary. From the de-water-proofing area we moved to the headquarters area at Fontaine-Henri. The assault troops had advanced a few miles further. We remained there overnight in a hedge-row.

We didn't know much about loss of men or weapons. During battle, an individual soldier knows little about the overall campaign. Lines of communication are in place, platoon to platoon commander, platoon commander to company commander, and so on, company to battalion commander, thence to brigade commander, then brigade to general commander. But all of these deal in large numbers. When there are losses, they are usually reported as numbers, so many casualties, so many guns and so on. An individual gets lost in this overall accounting.

So there I was, as were Bill and Mac and Joe. What were we doing? We were in a slit trench when there was shelling and shooting, and at other times we talked, but never got far away from our slit trenches. In the morning of day two, it was somewhat quiet, with no shelling. A local French chap tried to trade with us: a *poulet* (chicken) for some *savon* (soap), and he succeeded. In countries overridden with Nazis, soap was a nonentity because the ingredients used in making soap were the same as for war materials. So we got the Frenchman's scrawny bird and he was extremely glad of our bar of soap.

From the hedge-row , we experienced enemy shelling, although our chief threat was low flying aircraft, swooping little more than treetop height and strafing us with machine-gun fire. The battalion was doing well, although some of the companies suffered. "C" coy had the most trouble landing. Most of that coy was dunked in the sea and they lost many lives. "A" coy also had heavy losses. But the regiment had by the end of D-Day gained intermediate objectives. Among the losses were three coy commanders: Peters, Love and Goss, all majors. But by now, places like Bernieres-Sur-Mer, Rots, Beny-Sur-Mer (where my brother-in-law, Norman Tindall, was), Thaon, Coulombs, Fontaine-Henry and Le Freshe-Camilly were in the hands of the Canadian and Allied troops. It was night and we were dug-in on enemy soil, but that didn't mean sleep. It meant waiting for what the enemy was expected to do, and that was to try to push us back into the sea. But this kind of break gave soldiers a bit of time to brew coffee or whatever, and explore camp rations.

No enemy attack took place. The night was quiet for the first liners, although bombs, shelling and aircraft were going on in the distance. The word was to advance to the final objective, and we got on the move in a well established and coordinated movement with the rest of the invading troops. At this point, American troops were stretched out to the right of the Canadian Third Division, and they were in trouble. On our left was the Third British Division, also stalled.

We were still on a forward move. The objective was Norrey-en-Bessin and Bretteville. There was tough resistance but the regiment was on target and by 1400 hours we were in Bretteville, a small town with a little church and a courtyard. Canadians were the first to gain their objective, and we were a happy bunch, being the first unit in the Twenty-first Army Group, Montgomery's army, to reach its final objective. Now we had to hold it. As always, we dug-in, defended the position, laid mines, and prepared for counter attack. Then we waited.

For the first time since leaving Aldershot, the battalion was again together: HQ Coy, mortars, and the companies, all around us. We were ten miles in from the beaches, sticking out like a pimple at the mercy of being cut off, for there were no other troops between our regiment at Bretteville and the beaches. It was scary, but never had comradeship been displayed like it was at Bretteville. Our vehicles were parked around inner walls of the square courtyard, the boys like kids with new toys. They brewed coffee, ate hardtack, and talked of what had gone on, who was lost, where was so and so, and wondered how the news would be back home. We talked with a few of the locals who had hidden to elude the Germans.

The town's mayor and our regimental armourer, Sergeant Gene Mossman, occupied the house in the big courtyard. Sergeant Mossman was of Swiss descent and spoke seven languages. Mossman was doing a tremendous job of repairing weapons. At the start of the invasion we had 98 per cent of all equipment, but now that we had time to take stock, we discovered tremendous losses. The regiment had started out with sixty-four Bren guns, and we were now down to twenty. Out of twenty-two two-inch mortars, we had six. We had also lost two six-inch pounders. One of our companies had been issued bicycles, but they were never seen again except laying by the roadside. I began making trips to the beaches to find what guns and equipment could be had. Our erstwhile armourer fixed up so many enemy-captured weapons that he practically kept our lads going. However, the beach groups and supplies eventually caught up, and gradually reinforcements began coming in.

At nightfall on June 7, it was still and quiet, a lull. Everyone spoke in whispers, waiting for the expected counter-attack on our position. No one slept, of course. The attack did come, but a bit later. The line companies, Baker, Charlie and Dog bore the brunt, eventually beating the enemy back. On June 8, there was a re-shuffling of defense, and tightening up to improve positions. On the night of June 8 and the morning of June 9, the enemy attacked heavily, assaulting the HQ, the courtyard and the village with tanks and infantry. The battle ensued with a frightening roar. The attack had begun about 10:30 at night and lasted, and blasted, until after 6:00 a.m., the morning of June 9. A few of us were holed up in slit trenches by an inner wall, and we could hear the huge German tanks manoeuvring, clank-clank then stop, then again clank-clank. Two tanks clanked their way near to HQ and suddenly the fire opened from them; it was mayhem.

The entire battalion was involved with a very strong attack by German infantry and tanks. We were out from the beaches about ten miles with no immediate help. We had had some hours in which to fortify the position; that is, we dug-in. How much the infantry weapons could be relied upon against such a tank force remained to be seen.

The lead tanks of the enemy penetrated to within two-hundred yards of our battalion headquarters and some infantrymen were getting out when our defense opened fire with the anti-tank *piat* guns, killing the German soldiers and crippling the tanks. The lead tank swung around and tried to withdraw when it was hit again, damaging it even more. Then the second tank tried to come to the first tank's rescue and it, too, came under our boys' fire, with some hits. Other tanks entered the village and pounded the whole area with tracer shells. They sprayed the little main street with their tank guns, the shells ricocheting like red-hot potatoes. It was a fierce fight. The tanks did overrun the slit trenches, but somehow the regiment held.

One time we were forced to move from the courtyard. With six of my buddies, we sneaked, crawled and wriggled our way down a hedgerow, and were attempting to cross a small field when we were challenged. In the dark one had to be leery of shooting, because it might be one's own men. For that reason, we had passwords, which were changed daily. The password for this day was "Fish and Chips." So we called to the challenge, "Fish." All we got in the way of a reply was rifle fire, so we squirmed on our bellies while being shot at, and fairly dived into a ditch, readying ourselves for return fire, but there was no follow-up firing. We stayed put until the first light of dawn and then manoeuvred in a circuitous route back to the courtyard. At 4:30 a.m., the German force retired, leaving behind six tanks which had been knocked out. The entire village was burning, with devastation everywhere.

During this test of real war we suffered many casualties and lost several Bren gun carriers, but we had held against a powerful enemy attack, and had inflicted a heavy toll against the enemy infantry. We had also destroyed six tanks, all Panthers, and one armoured vehicle. From my own experience, this was one of the most crucial battles of the early invasion, and perhaps of the whole war.

On the morning of June 8, I had gone from the regiment at Bretteville to the beach-head to get needed supplies. My driver, Joe Bourdray, and I travelled the whole ten miles and back, seeing nothing between the regiment and the beaches except at one crossroad there stood a solitary military policeman. The German tanks could have gone clear to the beach and wiped out the beachhead. They say it's what you don't know that beats you. I wondered what would have happened had the Germans known what I knew, that there was nothing between us and them. Later on it was found that the S.S. General Kurt Meyer led that ill-fated attack. His second-in-command and adjutant were killed. He admitted being badly defeated. This general was a famous tank commander, and after the war he spent years in Canada as a prisoner of war.

Four days had gone by since our landing on Normandy's beaches. We were still in and around the village of Bretteville. It was a time for sorting ourselves out. Everyone was in good spirits and talked excitedly about the previous night's war. Stories abounded. A Bren gunner had picked off the German commander. One of the tanks had its track torn off by a unique defense trick. The defenders had made a necklace of hand grenades and seeded them on the road. This tremendous bang had done the job. The dead and wounded were all taken care of, both ours and the enemies. The dead were laid out on the grass, twenty-five lads that I knew very well. There were also about twenty-five dead German lads.

I wondered how the villagers had stayed alive. Some of them placed flowers on the chests of our dead lads, but none on the Germans. War is a queer game. It was all so sad. There was Shinnon, a young fellow who was a sergeant full of promise. He had been sent to Officers Training School in England, and had come back to our regiment as an officer, so young and bright. And there was C.P.R. Nelson, a superb sergeant major. I cannot name them all. These soldiers who died in the field of battle were placed in a quiet corner, then buried, a cross marking their grave and a soldier's helmet placed on top of the cross. Graves could be found almost anywhere along the roads and in the fields. Later, after the war, they were removed to recognized cemeteries such as *Beny-sur-Mer*.

We remained entrenched at Bretteville. The Germans knew where we were and we had been constant targets for their guns. However, we had gotten used to taking cover when they started shelling. As our regiment was still the furthermost inland, the enemy kept things hot. Our vehicles and drivers were scattered around the courtyard and buildings. I remember there were Bill Morrison, Colin Campbell, Sergeant Smith, Butler, Beaudry, Jack McGraw, Gene Mossman, Huston, Potter, Captain QM Rouatt, and I. We lads were spaced around the tall walls of the courtyard in which there were a few buildings and sheds. Mossman used one of these sheds for his workshop and kept busy fixing all kinds of weapons. He was also very fond of women and wine. Mossman was a very lucky man. On one occasion, Jerry started lobbing shells from four-point-two guns, which were very accurate. One could tell by their sound when they were coming close. One came very close to Mossman and caused him to jump out of his little shed and into a foxhole just as the mortar shell came down with a crump right on his workshop. Fortunately, he received only a slight wound, although his workshop was destroyed. I can still hear him swearing, using all seven languages to curse those Germans.

Driver Potter, Sergeant Smith and I would run the gauntlet and go to the beach every day searching for replacements for our needs. We would still only see one person, the MP. Things were hard to get, and we had lost so much. The authorities couldn't believe how much we were in need of. They said that our Regina Rifles had lost more firearms than all the others. My experience told me why but I wouldn't say. Canadian soldiers usually are not good at carrying stuff. The soldier doesn't want to carry, but when the time comes, he wants whatever in each hand. It was a well-known trait.

Day one, two, three, and four were past. Days five, six, and seven saw the arrival of the priorities required to carry on a war. Large Dakotas flew in, dropping bulldozers and tractors to clear a slice of land for an airstrip. The engineers and pioneers made an airstrip while under constant enemy shelling. This airstrip was essential for medical supplies, guns, ammunition, and food, in about that order in priority.

At the beach we often met vehicles and "Q" blokes from other regiments on our flanks. They would crowd around us and ask excitedly about the Reginas up front and how it was going. The whole beach group tried in every way to alleviate our needs. We had firsthand news from the war front.

One of our greatest worries, when travelling anywhere on the countryside roads, was land mines. The German defense had placed these deadly explosives in many vital spots. It was uncanny how these things would catch our boys. These Germans had placed them on the roads, or in the verges where vehicles would have to turn around. We were so relieved when the engineers of the Sixth Field Unit scoured the areas with their mine sweepers and told us which roads had been cleared. Still, there were casualties from those horrible mines.

Ordnance services had set up as had Army Service Corps Rations Depot. The airstrip had been roughly completed and the Dakotas were flying huge quantities of supplies, so our journey back and forth was frequent. At first we were given a map, showing rations' points where we were to pick up our fourteen-man rations pack. There were no buildings in the half-mile area into which the great trucks staggered. It must be remembered there was always shelling and low flying air attacks taking place. Whenever and wherever we stopped, we would dig a trench, a foxhole, because keeping below the earth's surface was essential for survival. For this purpose, every soldier carried a small shovel in his kit.

On our very first drawing of rations, we got sixty-eight boxes. These boxes were approximately the size of a wooden apple box (fourteen men's rations for one day). Also with us was the regimental *postie*, Doug Howland, who would get the mail, if any. To get this done speedily and get off the point, we drove in, backed our vehicles up and began loading. We had almost half of our boxes loaded when the enemy started shelling, and he was right on target. There was a big crash, quite close to our vehicle. Potter was inside the truck just putting a box down when a huge lump of shrapnel tore through the body of the truck from one side to the other, barely missing him. It was a miraculous escape, indeed for all of us. All the tires of the truck were blown off. The attack lasted about half an hour and when we finally came out from cover we were grounded and had to wait some considerable time to get another truck. The lieutenant colonel of the "S" Corps and his adjutant, who were not on the point but watching from some distance away, had their vehicle hit by a stray shell and they were both killed. There were others too, and lots of damage. It's odd that they were not dug-in, but maybe they didn't think of themselves as line troops. Doug Howland, the *postie*, lost some mail in the blast. This was the second time that my number had come close.

The unit was still in positions, with HQ Coy clustered around the courtyard and surrounding buildings. Moving to and fro from unit to beach every day, we had to pass a place called Bray. German gunners were always cued in on movement of vehicles, perhaps by the dust they created. So daily we ran this gauntlet with them taking pot shots. By then, we were all somewhat used to the sounds and noises of war. We could tell by the sound of the shells whether they were naval, German guns, or our own guns and weapons. It was amusing at times, especially when reinforcements came up front. They would dive for cover and we knew it was our own guns firing, then there would be similar yet slightly different noises, and we would dive for cover. It was amazing how one got tuned in to those sounds. For example, our three-inch mortar being fired made almost the same crump as a German four-point-two gun.

Shelling started one day in the courtyard and we all took cover in slit trenches. Suddenly a round came with a loud swish, then an explosion. Across the yard on the opposite wall, Ernie Adams and Joe Butler were in a trench when the shell exploded. Butler was killed. Adams related to us that Butler, after the shell burst, popped his head up to see what had happened, and at that moment a huge chunk of shrapnel took one side of his head off. Butler had been one of our drivers.

Another time, our liaison officer, Captain Wilson, and his jeep driver, Tom Peach, were returning from the brigade headquarters and got lost. They ended between the German lines and our own lines, fortified by mines. They were spotted heading as fast as they could for our position. Obviously, they didn't know about the mines. There was no way they could be halted. Their jeep hit a mine and was blown into the air, killing them both instantly.

Sergeant Armourer Gene Mossman had done such a wonderful job when we were short of weapons. He had fixed up many of the captured German weapons, and after a while one could never tell whether it was enemy shooting or our boys shooting with German guns. It became so confusing that all captured weapons had to be turned in. By now, D-Day plus seven, the remainder of the regiment had caught up and we were together, those of us that were left.

Another noteworthy episode occurred while the battalion was holding its position at Bretteville. From there to the south, about an eighth of a mile away, was the Paris-to-Benjou railway. Across that railway about a mile away was Norrey-en Bessin, where "C" coy under Major Tubb was holding on precariously. It was a really hot spot, which the enemy must have decided to retake. There were very heroic and courageous men who lost their lives in Norrey-en Bessin. One was Captain White, who earlier had gassed all the locals at Horsham, England. He, like a lot of very brave men in this place, sought no distinction, had no fears of death, and was very virile. To me, he represented all the others who gave their lives. He was so full of life.

One afternoon at Bretteville there was lots of activity. There was machine-gun fire, at short range, and shelling from the long-range guns. We had some captured arms and vehicles. There was one large German truck with camouflaging all over it. There came an s.o.s. from Charlie coy at Norrey that they were desperately in need of ammunition. Our vehicles were all loaded, but there was this German truck which was battered up. But who could drive it? Up spoke Chester Rutherford in his squeaky voice, "I can. I'll go." We loaded the required ammo and Ches boarded this thing, somehow got it going and started from Bretteville. There were shells exploding frequently as we watched Chester go. He was in high gear when he reached the railway crossing, which was raised above the road. When his truck hit the track, it fairly leapt over. I thought he'd blow himself to smithereens. I had never seen such selflessness. Chester was a slip of a lad about five-foot-six, and slender. How such a fragile body could house such guts, I would never know.

The Germans had a frightening surprise for us on June 14. There came terrifying screeching, like a million ghosts on a freight train. It was nerve-racking; no one had heard it before. This was the first time the Germans had used these *Moaning Minnies*. By that night they had secured a hit on our ammunition dump. There was a great conflagration that lit up the sky for miles around. The next day the church tower was shot off by German guns. That was enough, so the HQ was ordered to move to another position, and we left Bretteville for Bray.

In the evening of June 17, the battalion moved to Bray for a well-earned rest. For a few days the unit got a chance to check, reorganize and sleep. Our next action was to take place at Caen. There was a lot of action by our artillery, and we were moved to Villeneuve astride the Caen-Bayeux Road.

The regiment had some tough assignments. There was a build-up to take Caen. There was a one-thousand plane bombing raid on Caen using Lancaster and Halifax bombers. What a sight. The sky was red as some bombers went down in flames. One would wonder how anything could live. This was the time for the infantry to move in, but it wasn't easy. The Reginas had to take the Abbaye at Ardennes which was defended by machine guns. There were lots of casualties during this operation. Charlie coy was almost wiped out; only twenty-one men left out of a hundred and twenty-eight. It took regimental Padre Jamieson four days to collect all the bodies from the long grasses.

Padre Jamieson was a wonderful person. He went meticulously through the kits of the deceased, sending the personal belongings back to their families. He wrote letters to every family; such a selfless man. Everyone loved him and he was rightly decorated, but recognized better as a Padre. I worked with him in moving the dead; it was almost unthinkable, the smell of the decaying bodies. The Abbaye at Ardennes was a tough, fierce battle. The German troops were well entrenched and manned by fanatic S.S. Hitler Youth. This battle was costly, but the clearing of the Abbaye led the way to the breaking of the Caen defenses. The Regina Rifle Regiment in this battle had eleven officers and two hundred and five other ranks killed or wounded.

The battalion next moved to St. Germain on the outskirts. Organization for progressive carrying on of war was in place now. For us, an infantry outfit, it worked thusly: A, B, C and D line companies faced the foe, support coy with tracked vehicles, and mortar, three-inch and two-inch up close to line companies, HQ, medical, headquarters coy personnel in "A" Echelon close with the line coy. "B" Echelon, with stores, water truck and store vehicles was placed a couple of miles behind. All this moved as an entity, sometimes close, sometimes spread miles apart, but always in cohesion.

The division had a division commander and a headquarters. At division headquarters were people who managed the war effort for the division. Also, at division HQ was an administrative group. In this group, headed by a lieutenant colonel, were the Ordnance, the Army Service

Group, food rations, the workshops, and transportation. All materials; food, ammunition, and medical supplies came to this administrative group from the army bases. For the battalion, the RQMS and the QM got the regiments' needs from the unit's second in command. Each line company quarter master sergeant (CQMS), along with his company's second in command, a captain, got reports from platoon officers. These reports plus requirements of any sort came via second in command "A" Echelon. These were daily reports of losses in men, weapons, vehicles, or anything. So the Commanding Officer (O/C) knew each day how many men, guns, and ammunition were needed. These reports came to the QM and the requested forms and requirements were sent to the brigade headquarters and then passed to division headquarters. As the RQMS, I had to work my way through all these messages and dispatches. That was my routine, and it was routine.

I normally laid my head down in "B" Echelon. The QM was at "A" Echelon. The trucks stayed at "B" Echelon. I had a ration truck and driver. Daily I made my way to reference points laid on by brigade. The division headquarters were usually about twenty miles away. The brigade headquarters were five or ten miles back, sometimes closer. We all had detailed army maps issued to us. If the war was stationary, or with not much movement, we drew from these quarters, but when there were advances, naturally the lines were stretched. At times we were seventy-five to one hundred miles from these sources of supply, from division administration to front lines. So this was how I spent my days, taking short journeys for supplies and sometimes very long journeys to reference points. World War II was a type of movement war as opposed to trench warfare. We would see little of the enemy at close range.

A typical morning found me with my truck, driver and ration clerk traveling to the brigade reference point for rations and other supplies. If there were reinforcements coming up to the front lines, we would pick them up also. Then we would forge our way to our own "B" Echelon. At times all the vehicles were used to move the line troops in case of quick advance. Then I, with the truck and supplies and men, went up to the front to "A" Echelon, another reference point, and one that was different almost every day. There I met the company's CQMS's of the line coy. The reinforcements reported to HQ and each of the line CQs had their own fifteen-CWT trucks and I saw that they got their supplies and rations and the news of how it was going. Each coy had a cook, a shoe repairman, and a water truck, since all water was treated.

At this time "B" Echelon was just outside Caen on high ground. We always spread our vehicles, something like the pioneers' covered wagons in American pioneer days. There was much talk about a Lieutenant Bergeron. I think he was of French descent and was taken on by the regiment. He was head of the platoon of scouts and snipers. They patrolled enemy lines during night hours and got inside Capriquet Airport, even with the Germans in occupation. They were made famous by their daring probes into enemy lines. The Maquis (French underground) were very active. By this time we were getting rations and bread, which was a treat after days of hardtack.

One incident I'll never forget occurred one afternoon when I was in the HQ and the Intelligence (I) officer was interrogating a captured German officer. I was amazed at the German's arrogance. He huffed and puffed, saying in no uncertain language that he would soon be released. His armies would shove us back into the sea by nightfall. He certainly must have thought his side was winning, so he sat after the "I" officer had exhausted his interrogation. About that time one Corporal Miller came into the place eating a slice of white bread. The German officer's nearly eyes popped out and he asked the "I" officer if that were white bread the corporal was eating, and got the answer in the affirmative. The change that came over him was dramatic. It seemed to take all his effrontery from him. Germans had nothing but black bread for a long, long time. It was utter disbelief to him that there was still white bread in our countries. Maybe it was a godsend to him that he was captured, since it increased his chances of obtaining white bread.

It wasn't peaceful for very long in our spot near Caen as the regiment prepared to attack the city. We had captured several strong points, Buron, Authie and Carpiquet. When the unit moved into the area, the countryside was lit up with air-raids and anti-aircraft. We cheered as our aircraft attacked. The regiment moved into a reserve position after the rough going of the recent days. This was much appreciated by all. At this point we came under the command of the Second Canadian Corps, having been part of the British army until this time.

After routing the Germans from Caen, the Reginas had been chosen to put on the first ceremonial guard the next day. We got new battledress, epaulets and belts. At the ceremony, Lieutenant General Guy Simonds did the inspecting. This occasion took place in the centre of the city, La Place St.Martin. Here the Canadian flag was unfurled and the civilians cheered wildly. This ceremony seemed so mundane when there we were in the midst of a leveled city, with rubble everywhere, and we couldn't even find the roads, yet jubilation of those people was still alive and so great. It made one wonder what people cherish most. Freedom is indeed very precious. One can only realize this when one finds people who have lost all their worldly possessions, but recover freedom. I felt a lot easier when I pondered this. I still often wondered why I was away from my loving wife and children in Canada. Now, I knew I couldn't be anywhere else. But at what costs and lives lost! The fact that Anne understood why I was here *doing my bit* consoled me tremendously. She worried about me, of course, and in a way it must have been even harder for her. I was too busy to worry. I am sure she would have cheered with great joy to see people so happy as those liberated at Caen. The people of Caen hold a liberation ceremony to this day at the place where the first soldier fell.

There was still a lot of fighting around Caen. The river Orne runs through the city, and the whole Allied army had to cross that river. The enemy made it very tough. The bridges of course were lying in the river's bottom. The field engineers were busy up front with the Regina

Infantry. I knew some of these lads, particularly CQMS Sammy Flatt. They lost several personnel while pondering how best to cross the Orne. It was most fortunate for the unit to have had several civilian guides of the Free French Resistance movement (F.F.I.). They were attached to companies and given Canadian battle-dress, with the regimental colours. And were they proud! They were of great help because they knew the city of Caen like a book, guiding the companies through piles of rubble that were once streets.

We in "B" Echelon were positioned outside Caen on high ground where we could see the war going on. As if losing our men wasn't enough, on August 8, several American heavy bombers made the awful mistake of bombing our men. This really was a sad day. I with others in the "B" Echelon witnessed the whole unfortunate occurrence. There were heavy damages to equipment and several casualties. One was our division commander, Major General Kellar. What a heavy feeling that bombing left with us. In warfare there were always the unpredictable and the unexpected. Things were never the same from one moment to the next. To see bombs reigning down on your own guys, being dropped by your own guys, was traumatic. As if adding insult to injury, on August 14 a heavy air-raid by British Lancaster and Halifax bombers on their way to hit targets in Falaise made the same ghastly mistake. The Canadian-Polish Division and British suffered heavy losses. The Queen's Own lost all their equipment, and the Poles were so devastated they were pulled out of the area altogether. Incidentally, this unfortunate incident could have been worse had not the pilot of a Moth spotter plane hustled up into the air and managed to get to the bombers a message that they were off-target.

Things were so close. Pilots in England got orders to bomb such and such a target in Europe, then the lines of battle changed before they got there. Finally, it was decided that bomber pilots had to make contact with infantry brigade officers on the ground before they could unload their bombs. It seemed the way of things, even life itself, was trial and error.

Caen and the crossing of the river Orne was most vital at this time, since it was the hinge on which the whole allied forces had to swing on their way to Paris and northwest Europe. On July 18, there was a tremendous build up of Allied forces in an operation called *Atlantic*. It began at 0600 hours. Bombs rained from the skies, and shells sprayed the enemy with artillery bombardment. Underneath all this flying death the infantry battalion wheedled, waddled, and dodged, working their way forward. The enemy was determined, and their machine-gun fire was fearful. The Reginas got a patrol across the river, with persistent small-arms fire, although one of our French lads who had been showing the way was killed. The regiment's three-inch mortar, with the carrier platoon finally silenced or neutralized the resistance. By 1700 hours the Regina Rifles were across the river Orne, and by 2100 hours all companies were on their final objectives. Our regiment was the first Canadian Infantry to be on the other side of the river Orne. Soon the whole brigade was over.

On July 19, the battalion moved into an area around Vaucelles. Lots of P.O.W.s were coming in and there were great advances on other fronts, especially by British Armoured Divisions. The Johns were to have a breather for a day or two, but it didn't turn out that way. During the days of July 20 and 21, our own Canadian medium artillery moved into our area, and Jerry was over every night, so while we were behind the front lines, we were still in the heat of war. It seemed like no place was safe and it was here that I first saw shell shock. A captain went wandering around when everyone was in their slit trenches. We jumped out, got hold of him and got him into a trench when another shell burst. Then up he went and started wandering around, nowhere in particular, half-dazed. We got hold of him again, restrained him, and finally got a jeep to take him out of danger to where he could get medical care. In our war they called it *battle exhaustion*. It seemed to me that he felt sure the next enemy shell was going to get him. I heard that some soldiers walked into enemy lines, completely unaware of what they were doing.

A couple of days later, July 22, there was talk of the Germans hitting Caen with a *buzz bomb*, a sort of rocket shaped, small aeroplane that emitted a sheet of flame from its tail. This thing would fly as long as its engine was running, but when its engine cut out it would nose dive to the earth and explode. We got our news from members of the Mobile Bath Unit. To us, a bath was great. The unit would have a soldier strip, throw his underwear and socks into a heap, go through the mobile bath, then pick up clean underwear on the way out. This was good for a laugh, depending on how the garments fit. One time a guy picked up a large undershirt, put his feet through the armholes and pulled the rest up to his head, making two holes for his arms. The spectacle was ridiculously funny.

During our rest from the line, the unit held a church service for both Protestants and Catholics. One wondered about the God we all prayed to as Jerry raised hell with anyone trying to cross the bridge at Caen.

The regiment was always on the move, and next we were ordered to the Tilly-La-Campagne area. The Germans always seemed to know where their foes were, and this night their bombers were out again. Everyone sought shelter in slit trenches and there were some near misses, but no casualties. There was even one spot of humour: Corporal Pretty had a bomb explode so close to him that it piled dirt on top of him, nearly burying him.

The regiment was in a holding position, waiting for something. I saw my CQ every day and heard about lads I had known since the regiment had mobilized, some wounded, some killed. There was a surprise for our battalion on July 31. We were ordered to the back, to Colomby, a rest area near the beaches. Even so, nothing was easy. The Jerries were always out with aircraft and they would drop chandeliers, which as they came to earth very slowly, lit up a whole area, so then they could see to use artillery. However, back we went through Vaucelles, over the River Orne, crossing a class forty bridge which the engineers had laid. And now we were in Colomby, having been in battle continuously for almost two months. We found out that our total casualties were six hundred and seventy-eight, of which one hundred and eighty-five had been killed and eight were missing. But we had taken several P.O.W.s and inflicted heavy losses on the Germans, gaining valuable ground.

The rest area in Colomby was great, even if it only allowed us to breathe easier. The Canadian Legion Auxiliary War Services provided lots of shows which were set up in a natural theatre at Fontaine-Henri. Actually it was a cave where rocks sloped down towards a stage. We sat on the rock floor. There were baths and excursions to the beaches where the Johns could re-visit the scene of D-Day. There was room for some pride walking along the beach, plus sorrow at the graves of comrades asleep there.

The battalion spent a week in Colomby. A few dignitaries visited, among them General Kellar, the one wounded by American aircraft. A lot of the boys, myself included, took time to write letters back home to family and friends. In England, Anne and I wrote very frequently to one another and she systematically sent me parcels of homemade goodies.

Naturally, there was little priority given to mail during the invasion. Transportation of supplies for the war front worked on priorities: ammunition, weapons, war equipment, medical supplies, food, technical instruments, clothing, then mail when and if. We did get news about some of our casualties of the first assault. We heard that the Regina press ran exciting stories about the wonderful successes of the home-based Regina Rifles. One of the first letters I received from Anne while in France told of how one Chief Settee was in Regina hospital with a foot blown off and was enthusiastically telling all and sundry that the Reginas were the most famous regiment in the war, that the whole town was aglow and proud of what the home boys were doing in the war effort. Of course, I knew Chief Settee intimately. He was a professional boxer in civilian life and he boxed in England on the Regina's boxing team. I think, being the RQ, that I had more to do with the lads personally than did anyone else, simply because all their supplies came through me. I was proud of all these fine men.

Our seven days of rest ended quickly. The war was still in full swing at the front between Caen and Calais. After our rest, a new operation was in place to pursue the enemy. There was news of a forward movement. The infantry was foot sloggers, and this was the first time vehicles had been used to move the infantry. There was a pre-attack on the ground by another one-thousand plane Lancaster bomber raid, to soften them up, which meant obliteration. Supremacy of the air by the Allied forces was becoming apparent. At two o'clock on August 10, there was a great concentration in an area south of Vaucelles. The drive was on to Falaise and there was tough resistance on the ground. "B" Echelon was situated at IFS through Caen, over the Orne. The line troops were at Cintheaux and Hautmesnil, miles away, down the road towards Calais.

"B" Echelon was all around the hedges of a field one day about noon. Tom Feica had *soups on* about ready, and the lads were in his makeshift kitchen fooling around and relaxing when a single German plane came low over the trees and fired its machine guns, spraying shot everywhere. Everyone dived for cover. One of our lads, Don Wilson, had his slit trench across the other side of the field, about a hundred yards away. Instead of taking cover where we were, he ran like hell across the open field, everyone yelling at him, "get down, get down," as the plane roared over. He made a ten-foot dive into his hole. Happenings such as that were what kept the chaps going. The kidding, the chiding, the bonhomie, and the *corn* of humour were always part of our daily diet.

Tom Feica was a man slow of speech, with a dry humour. But he was an excellent cook, and "B" Echelon was lucky to have him. He said to me one day, "Quarters, if somehow, or somewhere we could pick up a sheet of iron for a hot plate, we could have hot-cakes every morning." We kept our eyes open, found a sheet of iron, took it back to the workshop and got it cut down to size. The army was using blow-torch type burners for heat, so we dug a one-foot trench, bridged it with a grid, and that became the stove. We got Tom the flat sheet, and it was something. He made up his *batter* the night before, and in the morning he made it into hot cakes or pancakes, the nicest that one could have ever wished for. He was a hero to "B" Echelon, but got no great rewards except in knowing that everyone loved him. In that great war he continued to make delicious hot cakes. Always first up, he got the burners going, then it was "Come and get it, eat it when you can or get it on the run." He was the sort of man who never got official recognition. What were they going to give a cook after all the accolades the regiment received and the medals the officers got? May God bless Tom Feica.

One day "B" Echelon had gotten up close to "A" Echelon along the front lines. No group stayed in one place very long, chasing the enemy on the run. Tom picked his spot to unload and set up his kitchen. It was a little shed at the rear of one of the battered buildings, and Tom was hard at it, but not too pleased with the on-again-off-again routine. Just then, a captain nosed around to Tom's shed. He looked at Tom and said that he was looking for battalion HQ and would like to speak to someone with a little authority. Tom, in his drawly way, said to him, "You sure as hell found the right guy. I don't know anyone who has less authority than me." Dear old Tom Feica. He could get a chuckle out of the whole regiment and provide food for the spirit as well.

The area around Tilly-la-Campagne included Huber, and La Hogue. These were places on a map, but we did not move to place names, we moved to map points, in fields and woods. One such move put us in a field where the stench of dead animals was nauseating. What a mess war makes of things. There were scores of dead cows, and the place was untenable. We got engineers to come with bulldozers. The Germans seemed always to be able to make things difficult one way or another.

About this time a lot of trucks were being blown up by mines. Jerry was using mines fitted with ratchets, which meant that one truck or vehicle passing over it would turn the ratchet one cog only. There might be seven vehicles pass over the mine, then the eighth would be blown up, or the twelfth, depending on the setting of the ratchets. Consequently, to think a place was safe because a dozen trucks had just gone over that road was dangerous. Sly Jerry. We never knew when it was safe. Jerry sure knew how to trip up the works.

The war became intense as the allies tried to close the Falaise Gap. German P.O.W.s were coming in and we were standing by to move forward by bus. By August 23, we were all bussed to Vimoutiers. The roads were rough and rutted, but for the foot sloggers, rides were better, and the Germans were withdrawing in haste. There were discarded vehicles and damaged guns left behind. Our air force was raising hell with the retreating German army. There was great excitement now in the Allied forces because the whole German army was in full retreat back to the river Seine. The road to Versainville, Mandeville, and Vimoutiers led to Elbeuf, between Paris and the coast. This road was a shambles. Allied airmen had field days, harassing the fleeing hordes. There were soldiers, animals and equipment scattered everywhere. Our troops with great gusto, were moving quickly from advance to advance by sixty--CWT division trucks. The great German commander, Rommel, was in one fleeing vehicle and was hit by low-flying aircraft, but he was not captured, although he was believed to be wounded.

My job now took on a whole new dimension as the echelons became stretched to their limits. Division headquarters was miles behind and supply lines were taxed to the utmost. I, along with my QM sixty-CWT truck and driver, Potter, and sergeant cook, Smith, were adrift from "B" Echelon very frequently. We would collect supplies from advanced map reference points or pick up from a cache, miles from anywhere. On these journeys we were alone in areas that line companies by-passed, so there were German soldiers left behind, hidden and cut off from their retreating units. These troops were still armed. On our long trips to the front lines and back, quite often we would have to contend with instances relating to these circumstances. One day, just past Brionne, the local people excitedly waved us down to tell us some German soldiers were holed up in a little copse. These people expected us to go get the soldiers. At other times isolated soldiers would give themselves up to us, having had enough of the war. Some small villages through which we travelled would open windows, upstairs and down, to wave and cheer our presence. If we stopped, they would crowd around and make a big happy fuss. Many young French people were in the Free French Resistance (FFI) and they didn't like to let retreating Germans get away. Usually they nabbed some poor rear guard personnel. They didn't always wait for us before they made efforts to free themselves from Germany's oppression. For those rear positions and administrative groups, the road up to the front saw the appearance of road signs, placed by division provost. "Maple Leaf Up" would keep anyone on the right road looking for Canadians.

It took quite a while to pick up bodies and clear away dead animals. I remember passing through Orbec at a street cross-roads on the way to the front where I saw a German soldier propped beside a wall. Then coming back the next day, he was still there, but in a different position. Life is so precious, yet on the winds of war it is blown about as if chaff. The evidence of a disorganized army was everywhere. They left behind those who were unable to move, as there weren't enough bicycles, horses or anything else that could get them away from their beating. The Regina's line coys' spirits were being lifted by all the transport we had. Every vehicle was pressed into bussing foot sloggers. It was one of the best times the battalion experienced. The country was wild with enthusiasm of a liberated populace. It was like a trek with cognac, cider, apples, eggs and flowers, better than a carnival. Each town was out in force to cheer us on.

On August 25, the regiment came in for a special evening at Epegarde. The whole village had a welcoming committee parade before Colonel Matheson to express their deep gratefulness at being liberated. These celebrations in the French towns were really emotional. The Reginas were next at Elbeuf on the Seine. There the people were also crazy with joy, even though they had a food shortage.

At Elbeuf, units' forward troops were working to find a way over the

Seine river. The Thirty-fourth Field engineers were to have storm boats ready to help with a night crossing. It turned out there was a goof when the Sixth Field showed up to unload the boats, as their motors had arrived in packing grease and with no petrol or oil to run them. Later, the Lieutenant Bergeron's Regina scouts found the opposite bank clear of the enemy and used the storm boats to ferry the whole unit across. It was August 28 before a Bailey Bridge was in place. From D-Day and Courseulles, down to Falaise, up to Elbeuf and now up the coast to Tourville, the Canadians had moved in a huge letter "U," and were now back to the channel.

The war was going well, but always at great cost whenever the Germans dropped back to prepared positions. Thus, when the First Canadian army had to follow Germans to the coast at Tourville, they found fierce resistance and lost a score of men. Farther down the road, Lieutenant Colonel Allan Gregory, who commanded the Queen's Own Cameron Highlanders, was wounded and evacuated. Finally, Tourville was captured, with forty-five P.O.W.s taken, and things became a bit quieter. There was always a scuffle when French towns were liberated, as the Free French would round up partisans and collaborators and *shave* the heads of both sexes, then parade them around the main streets. Whenever we saw a kerchief wound tightly around a head, we knew it as the badge of a collaborator.

The unit had a pleasant move all the way up to Londinieres through Durant, La Pommerays and Rocquement, enjoying accolades, kisses and garlands. It was a pleasant breather for the regiment. As we moved north to the Channel coast, some small towns were liberated without any fighting or resistance. We saw pleasant orchards and wild cherries. Through LeMesnil, Reaume and Monchy, we moved as a battalion onwards towards the sea at Eu.

In the meantime there was a build-up in order to besiege the sea town of Boulogne. Before the town was about to come under our artillery shell fire, there was an arrangement to evacuate the civilians. About five thousand were transported by Army Service Corps Troops to refuge camps at Samer. This was really something to see as people used every conveyance they could lay their hands on: baby carriages, wheelbarrows, bicycles. It was sad, yet they would do anything for liberty.

Sammy Flatt, CQMS of the Sixth Field Engineers told me this story. They were feeding a lot of refugees hard tack biscuits and when these were gone the supply depot sent food to a farm for these hungry people. As was the custom of troops who were bivouacking at the farm, their latrine was filled in and a marker was erected in the shape of a cross with the words "FOUL GROUND" neatly inscribed on the cross-bar. Some few days after they departed from this area, CQMS Flatt had occasion to return for more supplies. Much to his surprise he found that mound of earth marked "FOUL GROUND" carefully tended and covered by loving and reverent hands with a blanket of flowers. Sam said he didn't have the heart to disillusion the people, so he thanked them for their thoughtfulness.

There was a lot of hard fighting for these parts after a great raid of Lancaster bombers wrecked the city and the Canadians took it over. In Boulogne, the troops got into a vacated abattoir that was full of meat. A few sides of beef found their way to some of the Regina John's kitchen. It was the first time in a long time for beef.

It was from the rocket ramps in this area that the Jerries sent *buzz bombs* into the south of England. Some Frenchmen told us with great glee about when the Germans first tried to send these bombs. They would get them on a ramp ready to fire and then run like hell to take cover because on the first few tries, the *buzz bombs* would go only so far, then swing around and come back toward them. The Frenchmen loved that. It must have been fun to watch.

The brigade was next headed for Cape Gris Nez and Calais, still advancing by unit transport. It was a long haul for the supply trucks and tricky to find out where everyone was located. We were shot at more than once. On September 8, the unit was in the Wissant area with Cape

Gris Nez on one side and Calais on the other. Cape Gris Nez was famous for these great guns that fired even greater shells on Dover and the south of England. Operations to gain these coastal places were most difficult. More than a few of our lads expressed their opinion that they were glad the assault was not made at these places because the defenses were deep and those extremely large guns were underground. Their living quarters were like a home, although three-hundred feet below ground level. These shells were nine inches in diameter, and destroyed houses in one blast. Even when our artillery was on target, our shells bounced off the German guns. These Germans could not be blown out and had to be flushed out by foot soldiers. It was slow work and the Germans could kill a lot of attackers, yet be safe themselves. Oddly enough, after killing as many as possible, they would then give up to save their own skin. This was a trend throughout those defenses where we lost a lot of men.

For the whole of September 1944, the division was positioned at Wissant and in a tough battle over Boulogne, Cape Gris Nez and Calais. It was estimated that over twenty thousand Germans occupied this part of the coast of France. Gradually and stoically the infantrymen cleaned out the enemy, but at great cost. There were P.O.W.s daily. "B" Echelon was now going into the little town of Wissant with supply trucks. On the night of September 11, German shells landed on HQ in Wissant, demolishing a whole house. Four men were killed and three were wounded. Our route into Wissant was a roundabout road, inland through Hautville. Often the supply roads were shelled from the big guns at Calais. They could be turned to shoot toward Dover or inland. Invariably we became their targets, especially as we neared Wissant. There was an open area, about a one-mile stretch to cross, and Jerry peppered us every day both going in and coming out of Wissant.

The division brought all its supporting weapons to this bitter struggle: tanks, flails, and flame-throwing crocodiles. In one day's fighting on September 25, we lost ten men, with sixty-one wounded. We also took one hundred and forty-one German P.O.W.S. Montgomery was building up for a great attack on Calais. The town was surrounded by two hundred fifty twenty-five-pounder guns, each supplied with three hundred shells. Previously there was a devastating one-thousand bomber air-raid on Calais. It was estimated that ten thousand Germans were in the town. I remember so well wave upon wave of Lancaster planes pulverizing Calais. How anything could live, God only knew.

On the night of September 26, Monty's special onslaught began. I watched as two hundred and fifty cannons fired incessantly. It was like a massive fireworks display, the sky lit up with spectacular flashes and thunderous explosions. It was almost worth being in the war just to witness this awesome scene - almost. Shells were going over us from a mile back and exploding a half mile ahead, and this went on for hours. Tagged the *Monty Special*, this was a technique he had used in Northern Africa campaigns. It sounded like *bom bom be bom ber bom* and made captured Germans swear we had new automatic artillery guns. After this crushing artillery, the city was levelled and the ground forces moved in. That was enough for the Jerries. Ten thousand prisoners were taken, which didn't seem possible since they were in caves underground. Because there had been a twenty-four-hour period of cease fire to let the civilians leave the city, the Reginas got possession of a liquor store and celebrated.

I saw a weird sight in Calais. The whole staff of a military hospital surrendered and our troops escorted them down the street. A German Captain led them in columns of three, about two hundred in all. They marched , dressed meticulously in uniform,this contrasting greatly with their captors still in battle dress But there they were, the captives and captors, and honestly one would think the Germans were the winners. It was unbelievable how they marched in parade-ground precision towards the P.O.W. area.

It was expected that the battalion would have at least a couple of days rest, but early on October 2, we were ordered to move at first light. Calais had been flattened. Before leaving, Padre Jamieson tried to obtain burial for three riflemen killed near Boulogne. Their names were Darby, Geddry, and Finner. Finally, a French priest arranged for a burial service at which the mayor of Boulogne delivered the following address. Captain Jamieson was so moved by the sincerity of this official that his words were passed to the whole battalion. Here is the Mayor's speech:

Ladies and Gentlemen:

Seldom on this earth is there any joy which is not mingled with sorrow. Thus, today although we are very happy, we must dim the brightness of our joy to take part in mourning and sorrow—the price of restored liberty.

Is it not a gracious gesture of providence to have sent to liberate us from the clutch of strangers, Canadian soldiers, sons of Canada, distant from yet dear to French people; from Canada where the memory of France is always fresh; where numerous are those who speak our language; from Canada loyal to England and faithful to France.

Also it is with deep feeling that I bow my head to the glorious remains of these courageous soldiers, who have fallen on our soil. I do it on behalf of the municipal authorities of Boulogne and the entire population.

Rest in peace, noble sons of Canada, may the soil of France lie lightly upon you. You lie at rest among our ancestors, and near the French and English soldiers who found death on our soil in 1940.

Your remembrance among us is assured, and your more happy comrades who live to carry on the fight, may rest assured that our hearts beat in unison with theirs so valiant. May they soon, victory having been assured and peace brought to peoples of the world, be enabled to return to their beloved country and carry with them a mark of recognition of France's debt of gratitude to Canada. Across the sea we send our sincere and affectionate sympathy to the families of the three soldiers whom we honour today. We salute the glorious armies of the Allied Nations and we look forward with complete confidence to total victory.

Glory to the valiant fallen on the field of honour. Long live Canada. Long live the Allied Nations. Long live France.

So at 1:30 in the morning, the day after Calais was liberated, the battalion moved on as the unit's vehicles marshalled for a sixty-mile move to the Belgian small town of Cleit, near the Dutch border. During these long moves it was quite a job to stay in touch with forward troops, divisional and brigade supplies. Even "B" Echelon, my base, was often miles back of me. There were times when the whole string of communication was thin. We would be in touch by point, or map references, and we left messages at specific places.

It looked like Antwerp and the Scheldt peninsula were ahead. By this time the army newspaper, *The Maple Leaf*, was filtering through to forward areas, telling us of the joy people at home felt about the successes of Canadian troops. I had letters from Anne telling me that she was involved with the Regina Rifles Ladies Auxiliary and how she had companionship with others in similar circumstances. They were a great help to the soldiers of the regiment, always sending their cheer. I always felt consoled and thankful for news from home, especially of the Chapmans next door. Also of Mr. and Mrs. Baumber and their girls Eileen and Doris, who were close to Anne and looked after Pam and Joanne, and Ethel Sparkes whose husband, Doug, was killed on an air force raid on Germany, leaving her with Shorty and Marge. Anne and Ethel had much in common. Our children, Pam and Joanne, were five and three years old now.

Everyone was heartened by the news of a retreating German army, but there was still such a long way to go. Our regiment had lost over one thousand men. We still had the same C/O, Colonel Matheson. There were no company commanders with us who had begun on D-Day. Other officers and N.C.O.s who began the assault had changed dramatically, too, with daily casualties and daily promotions; my storeman Bill Morrison was now a CQMS. The battalion was composed primarily of new troops.

We in the Third Division and our battalion in particular were located near the Belgian border. On October 6, 1944, we moved into Belgium, to

Maldegem and further to Moerhuizen, a quarter of a mile from the canal. On our trying to cross the canal, the enemy resisted with terrific power. They were well dug-in and were there for all-out warfare, so getting across that narrow waterway was going to be difficult. As temporary bridges were constantly knocked out, infantrymen took to canvas boats. Finally, a bridgehead was established, but with many casualties on both sides.

Between the days of October 6 and October 12, the regiment encountered its fiercest battle, losing over three hundred men. Riflemen used up to twenty-five hand grenades per night, and on one occasion twelve field regiments laid two thousand shells on the Regina's front alone. Our mortars used a thousand and sixty bombs in one three-hour period. It was almost hand-to-hand combat, with terrible conditions, rainy weather and in low-lying water. Great precautions were taken, especially to prevent contaminating our water supply. The troops nicknamed this place *Little Berlin*. Our battalion issued orders that personnel were not to walk alone at night when in these small towns of Groede, Oostburg, and Knokke. It was slow slogging and a wet business getting the enemy out of these water-logged places.

"B" Echelon was now in and around Sleydynge, a factory yard area. I remember an order to free some vehicles, so we left two sixty-CWT truckloads of blankets in one of their buildings. We needed the vehicles for troops. On going back and forth to the front line, we went through the small town of Eeklo where I came across Anne's brother, Norman Tindall. He was serving in the Army Service Corps, and so we spent a few fleeting moments talking. The echelon then moved to Wateruliet. The Germans holding Breskens, next to the sea west of Antwerp, capitulated. I remember being there to see two hundred and fifty German prisoners march out, after surrendering to Major George Cooper. After this success the whole Canadian Third Division was given a one-week rest in the large town of Ghent, Belgium.

It was wonderful to be back so far from the battlefield. The battalion was together, with lots of food and kitchens set up, and the authorities in Ghent solved our billeting situation. Their policemen who walked beats simply took our troops to people's homes. Battalion meals were sparsely attended as most soldiers ate with their hosts. The town was festive and being there was refreshing. The people looked upon us as heros.

The thing I most remember about Ghent was their trams. They usually consisted of two coupled, and they were always loaded to the point where people would stand between the cars, hanging on anywhere, and to anything. The ticket collectors would never ask for or take a ticket from a soldier, but they would ask civilians for fares saying "als ter-blief" repeatedly, "als ter-blief, als ter-blief." I guess it meant "fares please." I talked with some of the townspeople who would invariably tell me how their men, their sons and their belongings had been taken away by the Germans. Some of them never heard the whereabouts of their menfolks. Germans used these men to prepare their defensive positions. They called them a *Labour Battalion*, and kept them moving back towards Germany as their armies retreated. While we were in Ghent there was a battalion parade. The occasion was an investiture by Field Marshal Sir Bernard Montgomery who decorated Captain Jamieson, the padre, with a Military Cross, L/Sergeant Armstrong, Rfn LaPointe, and Rfn Leask with Military medals. Leaving Ghent was somewhat sad. The good people of that town never forgot the Canadians.

From Ghent, the unit moved to Sheldrood, and after a couple of days regrouping and relaxing, we were on the move again to Nijmegan Salient. Almost every Regina Rifleman will remember Antwerp, Roosendaal, Breda, Tilburg, Bergen op Zoom, Hertogenbosch, Grave, and Nijmegan. These towns and roads were always loaded with huge conveys and thousands of refugees. It was pitiful to see families with only what they could carry in their arms or maybe on bicycles and in wheelbarrow handcarts. I remember one day we were up near Grave. There were no town signs, and we wanted to check our map, so we stopped an elderly civilian man and asked him about this place named "Grave." He shook his head, indicating he had never heard of it. So, not understanding, we showed him the word on our map. "Oh! Oh!" he said "Ravey, yah, yah."

The people of Europe had a very different idea of proper and improper personal behavior. Their public latrines are out in the open. On one street in Brussels, I noticed that the "Mens" was off the sidewalk, behind a chest-high wall. One simply walked behind this wall where there was a thirty-foot walkway. I saw one gentleman relieving himself while looking and talking to his girlfriend across the wall on the sidewalk side. Another time, our convoy was stopped in traffic, and as was often the case, some civilians were always ready to banter with the lively Canadians. Soldiers were not allowed to disembark from their vehicles, but they congregated at the truck tailgate. On this day, three young women were jollying and the boys were whooping as always when they saw girls. An elderly man standing a few yards away decided to relieve himself right there where he was standing. The soldiers just roared and started calling him all the dirty names they could think of. The girls didn't bat an eye. In fact, they couldn't understand what all the fuss was about. There were some tough lads in the Canadian army, but I never met one who would have done what that old boy did. He thought the Canadians had gone crazy, as if they didn't know what relieving oneself was.

The "B" Echelon did not go directly into Nijmegan. We were positioned at a little place called Overasselt, a couple of miles away. The kitchen that Tom Feica selected was the local blacksmith's shop. Our trucks were spread around the area. My store man now was Gus Sanderson, and we offloaded our trucks and set up a marquee tent for the stores.

We were now near the German border at Cleve. Some of the night patrols boasted of the Reginas being the first Allied troops to have set foot on German soil. In fact, they made frequent sorties into Germany. One of the lads said he had done what he'd always wanted to do, water the grass of Germany. Evidently there was to be an immense build up to attack Germany proper.

While at Overasselt, while on duty riding in a truck with driver D. Perry, I felt sick and vomited a lot of blood. Perry took me to Doctor Olacke . Dr Olacke was in Nijmegan, but he agreed to come and see me. He decided not to evacuate me to hospital,but rather to treat me. So for two weeks he said I would be all right and to just "lay low." (I found out years later that I had an ulcer) I had never been out of the regiment, so the lads, Fred and Gus, looked after me until I got well, but it left me with sinus trouble. Fortunately the war was winding down. There was still some shelling, just to let us know they were still there. Some of the troops were taking leave to Brussels and Antwerp.

The River Waal runs through Nijmegan. The R.A.P. was stationed underneath the Nijmegan bridge, and the other side of the river was German territory. Once more I was in the R.A.P., this time to have Dr. Olacke look at my fingernail which was entirely black from being jammed between two boxes. While I was there, a terrific roar came from two low-flying aircraft. Everyone scrambled, partly for cover and partly to see what was happening. It was a dog-fight. A German aircraft was evidently trying to knock out the bridge and an Allied plane was right on the German plane's tail. Zooms, swoops, roars, ups and downs, what a show and what a racket, as anti-aircraft guns fired. Evidently both planes were downed, for the roar suddenly stopped. Dr. Olacke took the nail off my finger and bandaged it. Before I left, some of our soldiers from Dog Coy spoke with the young German pilot who had been in the dog-fight. Dr. Olacke took a look at his bloody face and asked him what happened. The young lad, twenty-three or twenty-four years old, said that he had bailed out but his plane was too near the ground for his parachute to open and it dragged him into a tree, face-first. Apart from his face injury, he seemed okay.

I suppose the taking of prisoners was the same procedure, whether ours or theirs. Enemy infantrymen who were the ones first taking prisoners usually took money, rings, watches, things he could pocket, then turned the prisoner over to HQ where they were questioned and searched by Intelligence (I) officers. Every time a prisoner was turned from soldier to HQ, to brigade, to division, he had to put everything out on the ground and place his hands above his head. Each inspection left him with less, until all he had left were his clothes and his family pictures.

Now the young German air officer was confronting Dr. Olacke. The officer wore a very good watch and didn't want to give it up, saying it was a keepsake from his family, but it actually was a German-issue watch. He also had to let his wool-lined airman shoes go, and he received in return a pair of gym shoes. Before he left the R.A.P. his face was dressed; it wasn't a serious injury. At this moment a Royal Air Force officer came into the R.A.P. After salutations with Dr. Olacke, he asked permission to question the young German pilot. He wanted to know who had downed him, the Allied Fighter or the anti-aircraft gunners. The pilot answered, the anti-aircraft guns.

There was only casual and desultory shelling at this time. I was up front with our three-inch mortar platoon. They were set up in a low setting and would just answer any German firing. It was a case of hold on for both sides. There was a newspaper reporter and a photographer, anxious to have some front line pictures of guns in action. I guess the mortar men decided they would have some fun. Indeed, they would go through their routine and fire a few rounds for the newspaper man and photographer. So they prepared for loading and firing, got the men up very close for a good picture to see how things worked. It was all set. These three-inch mortars fire with a very loud crunch, and when it fired, the photographer, with his camera set up on three legs, flew backwards about thirty feet. The reporter was knocked down, scared stiff. The gunners roared. It wasn't a nice thing to do, but the news guys had had enough. Action on our front was now relatively low, and there was opportunity for the Entertainment Auxiliary Services. The troops got short leaves. It indeed was a waiting game at this point, late in November 1944. Nijmegan was a town very well known to the Regina Johns. They had time to get to know each other.

In the meantime, we at "B" Echelon in the little village of Overasselt were very well received by the local people. At the end of November, there was a skiff of snow on the ground and a tinge of frost in the air. Most of us would resort to the kitchen in the blacksmith's shop. We had billets for the soldiers, and they would bring new friends they were billeted with into the blacksmith's shop, making quite a gathering. The locals brought their instruments and each night there would be fun singing with the joy of being liberated from the enemy.

I remember when we got orders to billet. I didn't have many to get billets for, about twenty, and once an inhabitant answered my knock on their door, I would, in my best effort from the Dutch-English dictionary, say "Gooten avend; Soldarton for slappin?" Nearly always the answer would be, in good English, "How many?" No problem, they were happy to oblige. The first week in December, the community was preparing for the Dutch Christmas, which is December 6. On December 6, Santa Claus comes all dressed up in the image we know, but in Holland he goes around the homes with another character called Black Peter. They decide who has been good and who has been bad. It all made for a lot of fun.

Naturally, the Canadians were all up for a Christmas party, Holland style, in the blacksmith shop or in the kitchen of "B" Echelon. Food and wine were plentiful. We provided what we could and they brought instruments. The Dutch sing and harmonize beautifully and they are very entertaining. The Dutch people use English as a second language and can speak it far better than we speak Dutch. We sang all the war songs we knew and they joined in wonderfully. I suppose the stable manger was a lowly place for the birth of Jesus, but this forge, its implements, the bricked walls, were most unlikely for us to enjoy not only Christ's birth for which we are ever thankful, but another dimension of liberated folk, both young and old. It was emotional and a great release for them after four years of oppression. They were indeed thankful and were a consolation to those of us so far from our own homes. It was a celebration, however, and it was good for us all.

Things were still quiet at the front. There seemed always to be smoke screens intended to cover the Nijmegan bridge. The word was going around that the battalion would be out of the line for Christmas and the second 1/c, Bob Orr, was setting things up for a great occasion. He found a monastery whose halls were vacant, and the regiment moved in to use it for a rest area. Dances were laid on for the whole battalion. It wasn't difficult to get local feminine citizenry to attend. There was a Christmas Eve candlelight communion for both Protestants and Catholics.

The rest, however, was cut short. We were to move out Christmas night, so the regiment's Christmas dinner was hurried, but it was a good Christmas dinner with all the trimmings. That Christmas night in 1944, the Reginas took up front-line positions at Groesbeek.

There was snow now, and we were issued white rabbit-skins for our scouts and snipers, personal camouflage. There was a railway leading to Kranenburg, and we heard that the engineers were working on a scheme to load a locomotive engine with high explosives, steam it up and hurtle it down the track to German-held Kranenburg. But this didn't come off. At a minute or so before midnight, the Germans fired volleys of tracer ammunition creating quite a fireworks display. Then at a minute after midnight, the Canadians retaliated. The sky was most colourfully illuminated with dark, red, yellow and green streaks. *Happy New Year, soldier*, war style.

A scheme was emerging that personnel who had been in battle lines since the assault invasion on June 6, after six-months continual service, would have a ten-day leave in the U.K.. I qualified for this leave and was given a pass for ten days' furlough in England. A train was set up and the blown-out bridges had been made passable, heaven only knows how. I suspect the Canadian engineers fixed them. Anyway, I bid the lads *adieu* and was shepherded with several other chaps to a railway platform behind the lines. The train coaches were primitive, with wooden seats accommodating four persons on each side of the aisle, and the seat backs were straight up. There was going to be no *hogging* seats, for the military police marched us on and ensured that every seat was fully occupied. We sat on wood and straight up, but no one cared, we were off for ten whole days to enjoy ourselves. The first day was a trial, taking twenty-four hours for the train to finally land at Ostend. There was fun, but oh those hard seats. I remember well, the train never did exceed ten miles per hour, except when *buzz bombs* were flying overhead. On these occasions the lads would cheer like hell, and holler for Jerry to keep them coming, for it seemed they put the *wind up* to our locomotive engineers and we went faster. So we cheered the bombs. The train seemed to stop every few miles, sometimes for long periods of time. I could understand, having seen the destruction of war. They did well to get a train going at all.

We boarded our ship at Ostend, having been provided with some snack rations. The ship journey was a nightmare. It was a black night, the seas rough and the deck crowded. We were exposed to cold, windy weather in a tossing boat. Deathly sick, I was thankful to stagger off the boat at Harwich.

A warm reception awaited us, and we were enveloped by persons there especially to care for us. They had hot drinks and special trains. I boarded a train for Newcastle, with cushioned seats, and train attendants, mostly young women. They did their very best to cheer us. A newspaper reporter spent some time with me, I suppose because I was Canadian, yet born in England. It did get a write-up in the newspaper. As I got off the train in Newcastle, I thought how nice just to be back, even in the railway station. I walked around while waiting for a train back to Durham. I tried to sit up and see everything in the early morning since the train was travelling through country I remembered so well. The green countryside of old England never looked as good as it did that morning. Perhaps the darkness of night made the morning show up brighter. Maybe the stresses of war had been lifted fleetingly from me.

I arrived and alighted alone on the Durham platform at around 7:00 a.m.. Shouldering my kit, I walked down the Wharton Park hill, over the cobblestone road, towards the bus station on North Road. I took a long look at the great viaduct which straddled part of the city, and it occurred to me what a catastrophe it would be if Jerry got a hit on that very high structure. I looked keenly into the faces of all the other travellers to see if I could recognize anyone. I was an attraction in that I was wearing Canadian battle-dress and a Regina Cap and badges. People were friendly and greeted me, but I didn't find a face that I knew. Of course, I had been to Durham on leave before the invasion of France, but now there was new emotion as the war grew fierce and the civilians geared for it. Their sons and daughters were over there somewhere. People spoke to me and nodded while en route to Ushaw Moor. One or two knew me or my family.

It was between 8:30 and 9:00 a.m. when I stepped down from the bus. The weather was bright, but a bit chilly. I saw the Empire Ushaws Music Hall, which had once been a theatre, but now was a Bingo Hall. Around from the Empire to Station Road, the Lowerys spotted me. They had the Top Shop and were busily about their milk deliveries. I chatted with them briefly, then made my way down Station Road, the road I had travelled as a boy. It was familiar, yet changed. There used to be houses only on one side of the street. Now there were houses from top to bottom on both sides. The big oak tree, where we used to play as kids, was no longer there.

It was a complete surprise to my mother and sister, Amy, when I entered the house. There was no way to let them know I was coming. They were amazed when they saw me, but it didn't take long to get settled after some great hugging and embracing. My cold kept me subdued, so I enjoyed being babied. Mother wasn't too well, either. My cold was stubborn, and I thought for a while that I would have to apply for extended leave, but I didn't. I just stayed around home the whole time, not getting to see those whom I wanted to see.

Leaving created a real heart-pull. I had seen some of my school friends, especially Syd Rhodes, my dear chum, and I saw Vicar Welby, briefly. I retraced my steps back to Durham for the train south, to Harwich and landed at Ostend where a much-appreciated unit vehicle picked me up. The drive back was through Bruges, using main routes.

Things were as I had left them except that there now was frantic activity building up for an attack on Germany. We were beginning to see such vehicles as Crocodiles and Buffaloes together. The battalion was compactly situated at Beek where the unit was facing the Germans at Zyfflich. There was low-lying land and canals. An operation called *Veritable* was underway. The Germans knew what to expect so they blew bridges and canals, flooding the areas for miles, leaving little pockets of high land completely cut off from everything. It took some time to pick up the soldiers and people caught by this flooding. They used the amphibious Crocodiles, Buffaloes and Alligators. What a job, evacuating those people. It took some time to get the unit concentrating on Cleve. I remember when at Beek we would watch the extremely fascinating sight of V2 and V1 flying bombs being launched from German soil. In the darkness, these illuminated streaks would go straight up for the greatest height and then level off on their way to Antwerp or London. The V1s would chug along making a fierce racket, with fire flying from their tails. We could see Cleve, and were close enough to see and hear the battle. The sky was crimson with fire and Cleve lay in rubble, devastated by another one-thousand Lancaster bomber raid.

The invasion and assault on the beaches of France had been one great *build up* of every type of men and material required to make the operation successful. First the leaders of the Allied nations decided what the objective was, and then proceeded to appoint top generals and commanders of the navy, army and air force. This group planned where and how this invasion would take place. Then how many men, guns, ships and airplanes were necessary to do the job. This involved massive organization because it was an Allied force, practically worldwide in scope, the British with all their war effort, America with all her resources, along with Canada, Australia, Poland, and other countries. All these hordes of men and materials were brought together in the south and midlands of England.

The build up for this monumental task was almost incomprehensible. It worked by chain of command, from the Supreme Commander down to the foot-soldier in the front line. The Canadian army had five divisions, with thirty thousand men. Each division was broken down into three brigades, each brigade with five thousand men, with a brigadier in command. Each brigade had three battalions with one thousand men, a lieutenant colonel in command. Each battalion had four line companies, with front line infantrymen, one hundred and thirty men, with a major in command. Each line company had four platoons, with a lieutenant in command, and each platoon had thirty men, with one sergeant. The platoons were broken down into sections of nine men, with a corporal in charge.

Since the invasion had begun on June 6, 1944, these front-line soldiers had been in almost constant contact with the enemy, in some way. If the last of the enemy retreated fast, we advanced faster. If he stopped to fight, then battle it was. The stress of the war machine was to keep pressure on the foe, and the infantryman was seldom more than half a mile from the enemy.

To sustain him in the line, there was a support company, a mortar platoon, Bren gun carriers, *piat* gunners and so on. These were used when the linemen needed them. They supported behind the lines. There was also divisional artillery whose job was to soften up the enemy. They fired over the heads of the front-line soldiers. Then there was a tanks division which could come to the aid of the infantrymen. Being mechanized, they moved to tough spots quickly when called upon. The big bombers and fighters of the air force worked ahead of the infantrymen to break up defenses that might be in the towns.

So it was the foot soldier who had to occupy, and it was he who wrested the land from the foe, or lost it. It was he who met the adversaries face-to-face, and it was he who captured prisoners. It was he who had to deal with snipers, land mines and weather. Most others, for instance the lads in the big bombers, if they survived the attack, had a bed when they returned to base. The Navy lads had their bunks. The foot soldier had a slit trench, and never knew where that would be.

The whole force of the war was bent on gains at the front lines. The expenditures of men and materials were of great dimensions and cost. Freedom must be the costliest product in the world. Yet men and women died for it, and the liberated cheered and cried with joy, losing everything else, but free. Free! What a glorious feeling it was to be free. Nothing else mattered.

In mid-February 1945, the whole force was ordered to cross the river Rhine and found the enemy ferociously trying to prevent it. There was terrific fighting at Udem, Calcar, and in the Moyland Woods, and we were experiencing awful casualties. The medical section worked right through without rest, and brought great distinction upon themselves. I knew these lads, Ben Wolf, Moorehead, Allen. I especially remember the German shelling of the wooded area. Shells would burst in the trees and get the troops in their slit trench. It was a horrible situation. It was February 20 before the enemy was beaten back after we had suffered the loss of a large number of men. Colonel Gregory was put in charge of the Ninth Infantry Brigade at this time, and the unit was sent to a rest area at Bedburgh.

It was evident that the Germans were making last-ditch efforts to hold, however there was a concerted attempt to make the Rhine at Xanten where the river was bridged. In German territory, our lads were amazed at the food stocks. Basements and cellars of houses were full. We had never seen so many provisions anywhere we had been. The troops spoke of sealers of fruit and meats. The Germans were not jubilant to say the least, and there weren't any fraternization problems at this time. It's funny, they were just people in civilian life, much like us. It seemed rather odd, though; none that I met were NAZI.

Our brigade had a tough job trying to clear the Germans out of small places west of the Rhine. There was some mixing with British troops and tank men. The Canadians loved the British tank men. They'd had lots of experience with tank warfare in North Africa. Canadians liked the way they probed ahead of the infantry.

We were still in the same area at the end of February. On March 1, we got our Lieutenant Colonel Gregory back from the brigade and we were put into a new operation called *Blockbuster*. On March 6, our unit launched an attack on Sonsbeek. However, there was good news: the Fourth Armoured Division had assisted the Second Division in the capture of Xanten. The west bank of the Rhine was in Allied hands. At the ration points I would see CQMS Sammy Flatt, from the Sixth Field Engineers. He told me every three-ton truck in the division had been loaded with bridge materials, awaiting word when the infantry would have a foothold on the east bank of the Rhine. We had word that the First Canadian Division from Italy was in the area. So there was another tremendous build up among the American, British and Canadian Divisions.

Our next task called for the clearing of the Reichswald Forest, the breaking of the German Seigfreid Line, and the Hochwald Forest strong points, closing to the Rhine. The stage was set for a massive encounter. I remember returning from the front through a wooded area where we found an enormous crater. It appeared that a bomber had been downed with its bomb load. The explosion must have been tremendous. All around the huge, deep hole, it looked like a giant cone had been inserted into the ground, with trees all around the cone above ground sheered off in receding circles. We found parts of the engine and bits of stuff. It must have been blown to smithereens and we wondered about the crew.

By March 10, the enemy had been forced to withdraw to positions east of the Rhine, but they didn't simply run. They took time to blow up bridges at Wesel and other places. The battalion and most of the division were dispatched to a rest area to re-group, train and prepare for the last lap of the war. It was thought that we might billet in German houses and schools, but instead the place was a clearing in Reichswald Forest. Indeed the forest was beautiful, and we learned that it was kept private for Kaiser Bill's hunting sorties. Soldiers being what they are hauled makeshift stuff for dugouts and shelters. Of course, there were tons of materials, doors, etc., in Cleve. This was fun, and it was sunny most of the time we were there. We had a big marquee for meals. We had fun trying to outdo each other in making ourselves relatively comfortable. We had no shot nor shell to contend with, except a few enemy aircraft. The officers even staged a dance, bringing some nurses in from Eindoren. The Canadian Auxiliary Services brought in a variety show.

After two weeks of rest, the unit was moved up to a new marshalling area near Rees. Evidently, everything was in place for an assault. We in the Seventh Brigade, and Canadians in general, were still to be the left wing, with British in the middle and Americans on the right on a very broad front. The engineers had bridges in place at Rees and the Reginas crossed on one construction called *Waterloo Bridge*. All the vehicles crossed on *London Bridge*. On March 25, we sort of all crossed together. Our objective was Emmerich, but the small town of Dornick was taken first with no resistance. On March 29, 1945, the unit was to attack Emmerich. This was a tough proposition because there was still a lot of fight left in the enemy. The battle raged from 8:00 a.m. until the next day and throughout the night. Emmerich fell to the Reginas on Good Friday, 1945. My recollection of Emmerich was of its total wreckage. There was nothing left standing and another extra cause for anxiety was the awful discovery of *Schu-mines*. These unsavory articles were hidden in the ground and being made of wood, the mine detectors didn't locate them. These dastardly things blew the feet off many infantrymen, one of whom was the officer, Ray Sweetman.

After Emmerich, the battalion moved to Wehl, in Holland. Wehl was in the hands of the enemy so another build-up was necessary before mounting an attack. The unit was facing younger Nazis now who fought to kill or be killed. There was a bit of a humourous story of a young Jerry who was brought in for questioning. He claimed he'd left his German unit and was on his way back to Emmerich, to see his girlfriend there. Such was love. He took the news of Emmerich's fall badly.

The war for us now was in the towns up the river Ijssel. There was no holding back the spirit of the Dutch. They were always trying to reward their liberators by entertainment or just plain joyfulness, but the war had to be fought, and it wasn't always safe to rejoice.

In April, the regiment came to Zutphen. The civilians in those Dutch towns had kept low until the Jerries left and now offered their houses to the Canadians. Zutphen held up the advance, and it was the stubbornness of the Hitler Youth who kept on firing until they were killed. There was a lot of concern at one time when I was up front. They told me of finding ten Dutch bodies in a grave. There was evidence that they had been buried alive, and their bodies mutilated. The Dutch had real cause to hate the Germans.

I remember the day that we were on our way back from the front to administration. As we came to a bit of a wooded area, we picked up three Jerries who simply didn't have anywhere to go, the war being away ahead. So we got them into our vehicle and took them back as prisoners. When we came to a small village, all the inhabitants were out and excited. Some buildings were still burning. When they saw the Germans in our truck, they made a rush to get at them, shouting threats. They swarmed around our vehicle demanding we release the Germans to them. This we could not do, so we refused. They made an attempt to mount the truck and take them by force, so we had to get tough and hold them off at gunpoint. They desisted, but I remember how they jumped up and down and spat at the Germans. We rolled out of there amid curses for the Jerries. I can understand their hate, as the Germans had done horrid things to the Dutch families.

In the area around Zutphen, the unit was continually taking in P.O.W.S, some very young lads. Among these sixteen and seventeen year olds was one in particular. He was so much a juvenile that our lads sort of dressed him up to be like a youngster in short pants and sent him back to the German lines. In the context of fighting a war we had to remember we were dealing with people much like ourselves. How personal war became when we had to bring in prisoners. It made one think about our own men who had been taken prisoner, and it was humbling.

Moving northward from Zutphen, there was the Schipbeek river to be crossed and Zijkanaal. These advances were made very difficult by last-ditch stands by fanatical Gestapo Hitler Youth. In Deventer at last, the local people were overjoyed. I remember how we enjoyed a house there. The owner of the house and his small family were in the basement. He was happy for us to occupy the upper floor, which we did. I can still see how he'd make for the basement every time a shell would come.

After about the third day, the enemy had been pushed further on and we were about to be on our way. In saying farewell to the householder, he said to take anything we wanted for a souvenir. I took a four-by-six painting of some sunflowers. To this day the picture hangs on my wall.

On April 13 and 14, we were still moving northeast up the river Ijssel away from Deventer and cleaning up straggling enemy, blown bridges, and road blocks. When we approached Zwolle, we received one of our best receptions. It was expected there would be resistance, but the enemy had gone and the locals were awaiting the arrival of the Reginas. They embraced any soldier in sight and climbed all over our trucks. But our stay was short. The regiment together with the Scottish and Winnipegs (Seventh Brigade) was moved to Steenwijk and Meppel, spread out across several miles. There were no Jerries. It was really nice with no enemy to bother us and the Hollanders so friendly.

I recall being at Meppel railway station when a lady gave me a plate for a souvenir. It hangs in our kitchen to this day. On April 20, the unit moved further north to Groningen and beyond. This place had been liberated by the Second Division so there was no fighting. I had time to observe the citizens, being far out in the country. The national dress of the inhabitants was really interesting. The men in their baggy pants and clogs, the ladies and girls in frilled dresses with tight-fitting waists, also clogs for footwear. The men wore toques and the girls wore bonnets.

One day I saw a sight to behold. It was a funeral, with a horse-drawn hearse and several coaches. The horses were draped right to the ground in black lace, with varied hangings, the undertaker and others all in top hats. It was really class. I talked with some of the bystanders and they explained to me that this was an expensive funeral. You could buy whatever kind of funeral you wanted, and what you got was determined by how many trimmings you could afford.

The unit was centered in Groningen and extended to the North Sea. Our job was to rout out and clear all the villages of stray and straggling Jerries. I was in some of these villages, Usquert,Zant, Roodeschool, Middelstum, and I got to the North Sea coast where I viewed Friesland in the distance. The regiment expected to be moved against Delfzijl, but there was opposition from shelling at Spijk, and we were ordered back to Groningen. An armoured division was going to take Delfzijl.

The next battle was on German soil. On April 29, the Third Division was poised to take Leer, and Leer fell. I recall how the unit had to set up guards to prevent the Germans from looting their own buildings.

There were rumours of peace overtures, but this didn't stop the fighting, although more caution prevailed. To get wounded or killed at this stage of the game was a fearful thought.

The regiment was ordered to prepare to attack the town of Aurich. We had heard that the German army in Italy had been surrounded and that Hitler had been killed. We also heard that the Russians were driving on Berlin. Some of us wondered if we might come face to face with the Russian army.

On May 4, 1945 the unit was set for Aurich. I was to attend a meeting for details. Major Orr stood with a marked map in his hand and said, "Gentlemen, in case you haven't heard the news, this meeting will be a matter of interest. Tomorrow morning, May fifth, at zero-eight-hundred hours, we cease fire and complete capitulation of all enemy on our front takes place."

Phew! What a feeling of relief and release I felt.

The *end* had come. But there was no *ooph ar ra*. Instead, the atmosphere was quiet and contemplative, with solemn relief. This was not a time for great celebration.

But thank God it was over.

CHAPTER TWELVE

The Aftermath of War

THE BATTALION WAS FINALLY TOGETHER in Aurich, Germany. At the time of the cease-fire the situation was quite odd. We could see the Germans and they could see us but there was still no fraternization. There was much activity in the QM department with time for the boys to smarten up their uniforms. Joe Jean, CQMS of "C" Coy asked me if I would like to take a ninety-six-hour leave and go to Paris, France with him. I didn't have any problem getting the leave, so with the blessing of QM Rouatt and the O/C Major Orr, I went.

Joe and I had been together since mobilization of the Regina Rifles Regiment. He, like I, had come up through the "Q" branch, but being French Canadian he spoke French fluently. So off we went with our small shoulder packs. We decided to stay at the Ambassador Hotel in the heart of Paris. It was a long journey through Nijmegan, Brussels, Lille, to Paris. As the train had every seat and corner occupied, we found space in a baggage compartment where we could lie down.

The Ambassador Hotel accommodations were large and plush. There was a huge lounge with several kiosks and concessions. The staff saw to it that we enjoyed ourselves. At the desk they had lists of places to see so we decided to go to the Folies-Bergere first then, to the Arc de Triomphe, and then the Champs Elysees.

Paris and the Ambassador Hotel were so new and a bit bewildering for me, but it was fun. In our room were three push-buttons: one to have shoes cleaned, one for tea, and one for clothes pressed. I was thinking of home, of course, and how elated and jubilant Anne and the folks in Regina would be, thanking God the war was over and their men would soon come home. In the hotel concession I bought a souvenir for Anne and the children, which is still a family treasure.

When Joe and I were en route to the Folies-Bergere, we were surrounded by Parisians. Paris had been liberated sometime earlier and the populace almost worshipped us. I breathed a sigh of relief when I got back to the hotel where all was quiet, yet one could understand their exuberance. When we were in the Folies-Bergere lounge area, one of the ushers grabbed my beret and wouldn't return it. Finally, Joe did some fast talking and he returned the hat, then another usher took us to our seats. The show was really something. The theatre was shaped like a big horseshoe, and from the centre stage a long platform came out into the audience. Joe and I were in the balcony where we had a great view. The theatre was quite full, and we were surrounded by French people, but on the ground level along each side of the platform were mostly Canadians and Americans.

Most people knew that the Folies-Bergere was noted for can-can dancers and scantily dressed girls. When the girls came along the centre platform into the audience, those blighters would shout, whistle, scream and nearly go crazy. Perhaps, since they hadn't seen girls for such a long time, their behaviour was excusable. The French never blinked an eye nor showed any emotion at the gorgeous girls, but the servicemen went wild. The show really had good variety and the innovative way they used the stage was marvelous. I thoroughly enjoyed being at that famous theatre.

Outside, again a group circled us, hugged us and kissed us. I think the fact that Joe spoke their language encouraged them. Finally, we got away and as we walked a quiet street towards our hotel a young "woman of the streets" accosted me. Joe knew what was happening so he kept on walking, laughing his head off. I didn't know what to do or say as she asked me to go with her. I said, "My friend's waiting for me," but the son of a gun wasn't. I then said "I'm sorry," and left quickly to catch Joe and let him know he had embarrassed me.

Back at the hotel we learned that the next day, May 8, was to be VE-Day and that General deGaulle was to be present at the square in Champs Elysees. deGaulle had been in England since early in the war. On May 8, 1945, Paris went crazy with joy. People filled the streets, hanging out windows, standing on top of cars, carrying people on their shoulders, shouting, cheering, waving flags, kissing and hugging everyone, especially us. We were targets for their joy, and it was rough. I heard deGaulle speak that day and it really was a great day for France. Indeed, it was a great day for the whole civilized world.

The next day we visited a puppet show in Tuileries Gardens. The lady at the door, seeing Canadians in uniform, came running out, caught hold of us and got us into the audience of kids and grown-ups. I don't think I've enjoyed a show more in my life. It was hilarious and the audience was part of it as the puppet gendarme was hitting a robber with his baton and shouting to the audience asking if he should hit him again. The whole theatre rocked with laughter. After the show the lady had us stay for a while. We talked and she showed us around, then treated us to free ice cream.

On our last day of leave, we got tickets to the horse races at Longchamps Race Course, about ten miles outside Paris. To get there we took the metro. Fortunately, Joe knew how to get around. People fussed around us and wouldn't let us pay for anything. The race course was crowded, but we could see the races, although we didn't bet the pari-mutuals. After the races there was a special train returning to Paris from a nearby station. The platform was loaded with people and when the train came in, it was packed. Joe had an idea, so I followed him right to the engine at the front of the train. He hollered in French at the engineer, and up into the engine cab we went. Joe got out his cigarettes and received hugs and much bantering from the Frenchmen.

Finally, the engineer pulled the switch and we began to move. People were hanging out the doors and riding the buffers between the coaches, everyone laughing and shouting, and people at each side of the train were shouting and waving at the train. In no time at all, Joe was on the throttle. The engine-man wanted to let him drive a bit. There was a stoker since this was a coal-driven steam engine, so we took turns shovelling coal and stoking the train into Paris. When people saw us up there in the engine compartment they nearly went crazy as we pulled into the station in Paris. What a day! What a leave and what a time, VE-Day, 1945. I will never experience anything like that again. My heart was light during these days because deep down I realized I would soon be on my way home.

Once our ninety-six-hour leave was over, we boarded a train to leave Paris. Joe found a good spot for us to in the baggage compartment where we could stretch out. It was going to be a long ride back to the unit at Aurich, Germany. It was quite warm when we reached Lille where there was a twenty-minute break. As usual, the railway station contained willing people with hot drinks and biscuits for servicemen and women.

Joe and I had our refreshments and walked a bit to stretch our legs. Then Joe began talking with some people. I finally left him and went to the train, expecting he would be along soon. When the train pulled out for Brussels, I was in our place along with everything, including Joe's battle-dress jacket, his small pack and various other items, only no Joe. I thought he would be along soon as perhaps he was in one of the other coaches. Wherever he was, he was in his shirtsleeves. But Joe never showed and so I travelled alone to Brussels where I disembarked hoping Joe might be in the train somewhere. But he was nowhere to be found. There was only one train per day travelling this route, so I decided Joe must have been left at Lille, and so I decided to wait in Brussels until the next day's train. The military police found me a place to stay for the night.

Sure enough, when the train arrived at the Brussel's platform the next day, here comes Joe, minus battle-dress coat. "So, what happened to you, Joe?" I asked. He explained that he thought the coaches near where he was talking with the locals were part of our train. He said he talked for half an hour before he began to wonder when the thing was going to move, then noticed there was no engine on those sidelined coaches.

"Where did you sleep?" I asked. He said the MPs found him a place. I was glad it was nothing worse, and it was good for a laugh. Since I was a witness, we trusted the O/C would believe the reason behind us being a day late checking in. He did.

Back with the battalion at Aurich, we found our unit busy smartening up and rounding up Germans and weapons throughout the area. There was talk of repatriation and how dissembling of the war machine was to take place. The regiment would be in the area for some time yet. There was plenty going on to replace the fighting. Auxiliary Services and Mobile baths were having a lot to do now.

In Aurich on Sunday morning, May 13, there was a Thanksgiving-for-Victory service, and on May 14 there was a parade of the Seventh Infantry Brigade. Lieutenant General Guy Simmonds told us there would be a demobilization plan within a few days. Early in the morning of May 15, the regiment began a two-hundred mile journey to Utrecht in Holland, directly into the City. The battalion settled in barracks, factories and schools. Our QM took up quarters in a school. The school yard was fenced so that civilians wouldn't interfere with our work of getting supplies in and dividing them.

The regiment dispersed throughout the large city of Utrecht. The citizens of Holland had high esteem for Canadians. The work of the battalion was mostly rounding up and disarming Germans, then turning their weapons in to a huge ammunition dump outside Utrecht. The units reverted to peacetime hours: breakfast at 7:30 a.m.; lunch at noon; and at 4:00 p.m. the work day was over. Daily we would draw rations from the Army Service Corps and the company CQs would come to the school and draw supplies for their units, along with mail and ordnance claims. So this was again a peacetime routine. There was a shortage of food however, since the war had interrupted everything. It was a slow exercise to get things going, but during this aftermath things could only improve now that the people were *free.*

We of the QM staff were comfortably billeted in the large school. After splitting our rations, we enjoyed some leisure time, which I spent writing letters, my eyes on home. Around me were Fred Fotheringham, Geordie (Barnsey) Barnes, Tom Feica the cook, Howland the *postie*, Gibson, and Colin Campbell. The school had a small playground from which we would supply the companies. There was always a group of civilians crowded around the fence encircling the yard. It was heart-rending to see those gaunt souls wistfully eyeing our rations. The regimental unit gave up one-tenth of their rations from the depot and the whole army was helping feed the Holland people, trying to get them back on their feet. For the rest of the population there was nothing, no shops, just small rations. I had never seen such hunger in my whole life. At 7:30 in the morning, people who had been there since 5:30 a.m. waited for scraps that might be left from breakfast. Soldiers frequently shared their parcels from home with the townsfolk.

In the house next to the school lived a Dutchman who spoke English. He would stand at the fence watching us. I held conversations with him which started a friendship. He was an interesting man by the name of Bertus Gort. He told me that in peacetime he had worked in a factory a short distance from the school. He also said that he once weighed one hundred and seventy-five pounds, but now was down to ninety-five pounds. I soon began to give him smokes coffee, chocolates and goodies from Anne's parcels. I then began to visit his home and his wife, Lies, and found myself hardly able to cope with the state of their malnutrition. Their three-year-old son, Bartje, had rickets. It was unbelievable what they had endured. Lies' wrist bones were so soft that when I pressed one with my thumb the impression would remain.

We couldn't give away army rations simply because what we had was sufficient only for our own troops, but I had one experience that I'll never forget. The army day was over, supper was finished, and the troops were in their quarters. I was shaving and the outside door behind me was open. Looking in the mirror, I noticed a small figure flash by the front door and make its way around towards the kitchen. We had trouble with intruders and had warned them about being a nuisance, so I chased after this boy to see where he was going. As I turned the corner towards the kitchen back door where there were oil drums being used for garbage, I saw the lad. He wasn't very tall and what I saw first were his feet. His head was down at the bottom of a barrel. I grabbed his feet, hauled him up, and what I saw nearly undid me. The boy's hands were covered with sticky oil and around his mouth was black oil from his thrusting small pieces of hard-tack cracker into it. That broke me up. I escorted him back and scrounged a bit of food for him. How hungry could a person get? Poor little guy. But if they got to know you, you gave. It was an awful situation. Many times in my early years at the coal mines, especially during the 1926 coal strikes, I had thought I was hungry. At one time I had only a stolen turnip for two days, but I know now that I didn't know hunger at all. I had never seen anything that moved me like the hunger I saw in Holland.

On the afternoon of June 6, 1945, there was a divisional parade, with *march past*, General Crerar taking the salute. This was a tremendous event and the citizens of Utrecht lined the streets in thousands. Truly the Third Division of the Canadian army had earned its laurels.

By now some personnel were being moved, some of the unit being returned to Canada for further transfer to the Pacific theater. On June 6, at 7:30 a.m., a memorial service commemorating D-Day was held in Werkspoor Auditorium. The whole battalion was present as well as the One

Hundred and Seventh British Brigade who had been with the Reginas on the beaches. It was an impressive occasion. The Reginas continued to celebrate this date after the war, June 6, D-Day. The Johns, those of us still around, will never forget it.

There was talk of our unit moving out of Utrecht and I was getting ready for a move home to Canada. CQMS Joe Jean, my great friend, was going to take my place as RQMS of the battalion when I left. I was sorry to leave Utrecht and Bertus Gort and Lies; we had become great friends. Goodbyes were difficult. When the battalion moved to Ede, I got word that I was to be demobilized. Being one of the first to join five years earlier, I was to be repatriated on a first-in-first-out method. It would be done in a group camp just as it was during the invasion; a group moved off from camp one, to camp two, to camp three, then to Aldershot England, and from Aldershot to the seaport and then shipped for Canada, thence to Regina for demobilization. I said an emotional goodbye to the lads who would be following soon and embarked on a train at Nijmegan. Before I left the regiment I was presented with a large booklet as a gift from the Holland government. It was called "Holland and the Canadians," and had been written and compiled by the Netherlands people.

The last paragraph of the book's introduction contained these words: "The Canadians who came overseas in the common crusade against Nazi ideals fought some of the fiercest battles in Holland. They found victory in the Netherlands. They stayed as guests during the difficult period of re-establishment and learned to respect and admire the Netherlands' way of life and they return to Canada to strengthen the ties between the two nations that the principles for which they fought may be preserved." To read and see the pictures in "Holland and the Canadians" gave one a real feeling for the ugliness of war.

On my way out of Holland I was conscious of several military Canadian cemeteries where thousands slept, never to return. The price was great. Our journey to the coast was far better than it had been when I'd had my furlough, but we were held up for one week in camp on the continent due to a delay of ships leaving England for Canada. However, waiting wasn't too difficult now; we had done plenty of that, and there were no shells or bombs, so it was good. Eventually we were delivered to Aldershot, there to clear all documents and receive what was to be our last pay on English soil.

Things took a nasty twist after our two weeks in Aldershot. There was another delay, and the troops had spent their pay with still no word of sailing. As always with nothing to do and no money, grumbling began and protests became loud. There wasn't a chance to get any advance pay because the brass said all personnel documents had already gone to Canada. So with nothing from no one, it was a stalemate. There was rumbling, then rioting. And what a riot it was. Shop windows were broken, rocks were flying, and absolute mayhem broke out. The friendly town of Aldershot was devastated worse than by bombs, but fortunately no lives were lost. I felt so sorry about the whole incident because it needn't have happened. Surely some way could have been found to get these boys a few bucks. The citizens who had good relationships with the Canadians now cold-shouldered them. McConnell, one of our lads, observed that we were in the riot (right) place. I wouldn't forget it soon. It was started by about ten disgruntled persons and ended with hundreds on a rampage.

Subsequently, shipping got straightened out and we were ordered to be ready for a special train to Southampton where we would board a forty-nine-thousand-ton New Amsterdam passenger ship. It turned out to be a lovely liner and I got a good cabin. Better still, I didn't have a job. What a difference from when we were going in! The voyage west across the Atlantic was pleasant. We were briefed concerning the terms and settlements of returning to civilian life. There was also a lot of entertainment. I was elated that I would soon be with Anne and our children. Every day seemed so good since I was drawing closer to home. For the second time, I saw the rocks of Belle Isle at the mouth of the St. Lawrence river as we gently sailed past for the two-days' journey into Montreal.

A troop train awaited us and things changed when feeding the troops became my responsibility. Before, I had been just travelling, doing little and being provided for by others. Crossing Canada again was a lift, though, especially seeing the prairies as we approached Regina. Our excitement was terrific, getting ready to detrain, and what a reception as slowly the train came to a halt. We formed loosely in columns beside the train which had stopped near the armouries. Gathering our kits, we entered through the big south doors and walked onto the huge armoury floor. The roar, the cheering and flag waving was thunderous. Everyone seemed to be calling their loved ones. The balconies were full of relatives and friends. We marched around in a circle to get the whole column in. At first I didn't see Anne, but she soon spotted me. Oh, it was so wonderful to be back!

The ceremonies were short, our leave passes were ready: one month discharge leave, then return for discharge. So there we were, relatives and friends crowded around us on the floor of the hall and I was with Anne and my two bairns at last. Oh, what joy for us all at that moment. It was like a dream. They looked so beautiful. There was lots of milling around with friends and well-wishers and saying goodbye to comrades. Finally, we got ourselves together and into a car. To this day I don't know who drove us home to 964 Garnet Street. How beautiful Anne had made our home. She was so excited, and Pamela, now six years old, and Joanne four, what beautiful girls. This was a homecoming I would never forget.

It was so wonderful to be home again, free from army discipline. I gradually got to meet all the lovely people who had befriended Anne and the children while I was away: the Chapmans, the Barkers, the Baumbers, Ethel Sparkes, whose husband did not come home from the war, and George and May Todd. I was content to stick around the house since there were many things to be done. Pam was going to school, but Joanne was still too young. It was a time of incomparable bliss.

Home again. The Lord be praised.

War's over. Home at last with Pamela and Joanne in Regina.

Mrs. Loving with Mark in 1948.

Dressed for work, with our son Mark.

Brother Harry, trainer, Norwich City Football Club, greeted by King George.

What was left of the last Pit Head in the Deerness Valley.

Station Road Ushaw Moor Albion Club, foreground. Taken on our visit.

Bertus and Lies Gort in 1967 at the wedding of their oldest son Bart.

This is the Ushaw Moor Colliery banner at the Miner's Gala or The Big Meeting as it was called, taken on Silver St., Durham.

CHAPTER THIRTEEN

Return to Civilian Life

BEING HOME WAS HEAVENLY but it just didn't seem real, our house, our street, our garden, and time to breathe it all in. The smiles and friendliness of our neighbours were wonderful. Home, with Anne and our lovely girls. I couldn't help but be thankful for such joy. At times I found myself thinking of those who did not return to Canadian soil, and realized how lucky I was. It was going to take me a while to assimilate all that had happened in such a short time. Yet, time seemed eternal. Now here I was by the grace of God, returned to my loved ones, in our own country, and without fear of losing our freedom.

All personnel returning from overseas were given one month disembarkment leave. During this period, after Anne and I got ourselves back to some degree of normality, we decided we would take a trip to the west coast. Mr. and Mrs. Loving now lived in British Columbia at a place called Mission. In her letters, Anne had often mentioned that when I came back we might move out west. So we contacted the Lovings and arranged to visit them. I had never been to British Columbia, although Anne had, so we visited for a week to assess the possibilities. We had to think a long time about a move like that, changing our life style, the effect it would have on the children, and new jobs. But we liked the coast and the week there passed much too quickly.

We had become a part of the Regina community, especially St. Peter's, where I had taught Sunday school. Anne and I had been married there, our children were baptized there, and we were familiar with the congregation. It was our church; we had been members for a long time.

My month's disembarkation leave was about to expire and I, along with other returned soldiers, lined up for discharge at the armories. There were ten or fifteen in line in front of me when I was tapped on the shoulder by a major of the district depot. He drew me out of the waiting line and said, "The O/C wants to see you." So I went with Major Bright Thompson to the O/C's office. There I met Colonel Robertson who put a proposition to me. He asked if I would agree to take the job of RQMS of the Twelfth District Depot, Regina, Saskatchewan. This indeed was an odd circumstance. I told the colonel I was interested, but I would like to talk it over with my wife, Anne.

The terms for the position of regimental quarter master sergeant would be until all returning soldiers were discharged from active service. It was estimated this would take about two years. And then after processing personnel discharges came returning stores, including the barracks, to Ordnance. If I accepted this appointment, I would be on army pay and could live at home with subsistence benefits. And as we only lived five blocks from the Armories, the offer sounded almost too good to be true. The downside was that it meant living on the prairies for a few more years. It would also mean going to work from 8:00 a.m. until 5:00 p.m., with some exceptions.

Anne and I discussed this at length and finally, we made our decision. I accepted and rejoined the Twelfth District Depot where I had begun my army service back in 1939. That it was to end where it had begun was odd indeed. Of course, I was familiar with all the surroundings and understood the systems and workings of the Ordinances, the forms and paperwork, both in peacetime and active service. On strength with me would be one sergeant, four soldiers of lesser rank, a goodly number of civilian typists, a cook and some cook's helpers. I had known Major

Bright Thompson in civilian life since we had played tennis at the same club. So instead of being discharged, I found myself back on the job. But oh, what a difference. My sergeant was Sergeant Gordon Kerly, whom I had once taught in Sunday school. His sister, Kay Kerly, had sung at our wedding.

Our objective was to discharge about fifty returning soldiers per day. In the barracks were sleeping quarters, a kitchen, dining halls, and a fair-sized hospital, all well equipped. It was lovely to have breakfast at home. I would lunch at the Armories and come home for supper. Usually I would be at home every evening with Anne and the girls. I would be home on weekends, too, and could go to church with my family on Sunday mornings.

When soldiers returned from overseas, we usually had received their documents beforehand by mail and had their papers for discharge ready when they arrived at the Depot. This all worked well, except on one occasion there were fifteen returned chaps getting hot under the collar because we did not have their documents. Their paperwork should have been in our hands long ago, but it could not be found. We phoned the shipping source overseas and were told that the paperwork had been forwarded a long time ago.

Since there was quite a rush to get the returning servicemen discharged and home, the Colonel continually looked for more typists. He had recently hired a new girl. It turned out her chair was too low, so she had located a bundle of big envelopes and put them under her seat cushion so she could reach the typewriter keys. Of course, she didn't understand the importance of the documents or anything else to do with the army. She was just a typist. Her seat support was, of course, the chaps' documents. They had been underneath her seat cushion the whole eight days. What a relief! Naturally, we didn't tell the chaps the source of their delay.

Life continued to be good, both at home with my wife and children, and at work. It was pleasant to see soldiers coming back and returning to a life of peace. The atmosphere was relaxed, and many times I thanked the Lord that the fighting was all over.

The depot personnel were not the same ones I had known in 1939. The MO from 1939 was still around, although retired now. I saw him occasionally on the grounds and around the hospital. At this time the authorities in charge of rehabilitation advertised that there would be an examination open to any returned servicemen who cared to enter the Immigration Service for custom officers. Anne and I thought perhaps sometime in the future this might be worthwhile, so I applied and attended. The exam was held in the Dark Hall on College Avenue. There were three hundred men sitting for the exam. It was some time later when we heard the results. I received word by letter that I had passed, and I was placed seventeenth on a list for when the time came.

So time went on. I spent most of my spare time around the house, and what a blessing it was, just to be home with my family. Yet, I still could not help remembering those not so fortunate, those who did not return. Being home for Christmas in 1945 was one of my greatest delights. It was always my favourite occasion, but this time it was really special. We made it a celebration of joy and thankfulness, especially for Pam and Joanne. It was a bit different for them, having Dad around at any time, but especially at Yuletide.

With the entry into the new year, all was going well, except that in January of 1946 I began to have pains in my stomach, and one Friday night the pains became so acute that Anne phoned the doctor. He came, examined me, and quickly called an ambulance to take me to Regina General Hospital for an appendix operation. Apparently it had been about to burst. I remember being on a stretcher and being rushed into an operating room. Some of my army buddies were in the corridors and gave me silent salutations. After the hospital, I returned home and for two weeks Anne looked after me.

I had a leave of absence until I was fully recovered. Sergeant Kerly had done a good job of getting along without me, but they all welcomed me back at the Depot and things were soon back to normal. At home, Anne had become pregnant again and was visiting the doctor periodically. All went well with Anne right up to the final week of her pregnancy. She had seen the doctor and he said everything was fine. But something went wrong, quickly. I phoned for an ambulance and rode in it with Anne to the hospital. Her doctor, who had been away, had rushed back and was there to meet us. There was great concern so I waited in the corridor. After a very anxious time, the doctor came and told me that things were very serious with Anne and the baby. It appeared the baby had turned upside down, and they doubted they would be able to get the baby out of the womb without injuring it. He said we were probably going to lose the baby, and perhaps Anne, too, and that the baby might be injured for life if they did save it. I remember standing there watching as the doctor went back into the room, my life disintegrating before my eyes. This could not be happening.

Later, the doctor returned and said, "I'm sorry. We lost the baby." Anne had to have three blood transfusions and her life remained in jeopardy. Thankfully, she survived. She was going to get well but it would be some time before she got home. There was nothing more to do but go home; the girls were with the Baumbers. The next day, the priest of St. Peter's Church came to visit me. Apparently the baby had lived for about ten minutes after birth. Anne and I had decided to call the baby Jill Elizabeth, and we agreed to have a graveside burial service for her. It was a most trying time for us and it took some considerable time to get over it. Anne finally came home and recuperated well. Mae and George Todd visited frequently and helped out. To add to the awful tragedy of that period, one day word came that my mother had died. There was no way I could return for her funeral.

The number of soldiers returning for discharge began to diminish rapidly and closing the hospital was well underway. Anne and I began again to discuss the possibility of moving to B.C.. It meant breaking up our home and selling our property and it would mean departure from our many and wonderful friends and neighbours, and it was a hard decision to make. The day was near at hand when my job of clearing out the ordnance supplies from the grounds of the Armories would be completed.

In early 1947 it came time for me to sever ties with the military. Having been busy discharging soldiers, I was now to go to Winnipeg depot for my own discharge. This took one week, but being in Winnipeg, a city with much prairie history, was interesting. I was very content to be free at last, after seven years in the service of my country.

Soon after my discharge, Anne and I finally decided to move to the coast. This gave us something to look forward to. Beside our home on 9 block Garnet Street was a vacant lot that we owned. We figured the whole property was worth about forty-five hundred dollars, and we would have to sell everything in order to buy a new place in B.C.. So it was agreed that I would go to the coast and stay with Mr. and Mrs. Loving on Third Street, Mission until we became established. Anne would remain in Regina to sell our lovely little home. I had twelve hundred and fifty dollars in gratuity from the army, twenty-five cents a day for my seven years time. That, along with the savings Anne had been able to accumulate, might be enough to finance our move. So in the late spring of 1947 I left Regina and headed to B.C. to find a place to live. Anne remained in Regina to sell our house. It was difficult to say goodbye to my wife and children again, but this time it was on a far different mission, a happy one.

CHAPTER FOURTEEN

At the Coast

I HAD FRIENDS ON VANCOUVER ISLAND who had served with the Canadian Scottish Regiment, so after a day or so with the Lovings, I decided to have a look over there for possibility of work. However, the minute I got onto the ferry I knew I didn't want to leave the mainland. But I did visit with Fred Fotheringham, who had been with me in the army.

I soon decided it would be best to live in Mission. I had attended a small church that was there between First and Second Avenue and it was there I met a man named Strachan. He was trying to sell a house at the end of Third Street, near the home of the Lovings. It was a big house with spacious grounds and had been occupied by a United Church minister named Hibbard. Mr. Strachan said he was selling this place on behalf of the United Church of Hatzic. I told him I was newly out of the service and was looking for a place to live.

This house was to be sold by bid and he asked if I would like to make a bid. I had to put up a two-hundred dollar deposit, and I bid fifty-two hundred dollars. I, of course, knew practically nothing about buildings except counting things that were in them. In the meantime, Anne was doing her best to sell our house in Regina. She had had several possibles and thought we might have to reduce the price. It was more than a week later when Mr. Strachan saw me again and said, "The house is yours for fifty-two hundred dollars." I didn't know whether I wanted it now and almost told him so, but with great uncertainty I acquiesced. Then I got word from Anne that she had sold our house, getting the full asking price of forty-five hundred dollars.

Anne had the enormous job of getting our furniture and all our belongings shipped after the sale. I had settled the deal with Mr. Strachan and had met the Reverend Hibbard, who was in the process of moving out. Our new house was heated by sawdust burners, one in the kitchen and one in the living room. On the ground floor was a big bedroom and bathroom just off the kitchen, and a stairway upstairs, where there were three bedrooms. Off the kitchen was a sawdust shed. It was so different from our little house in Regina. I said several prayers about the whole transaction. Anne had made me promise to try to be near a school and a church, and this house met both conditions. Anne had been to Mission and had stayed a couple of days with the Lovings while I was overseas, so she knew something about the street.

Anne and the girls had arrived in Mission before the big van arrived with our belongings. Anne said, "Whatever am I going to do with this great big house." Then she said what she almost always said, "Let's get on with it." So, we moved in but it was no easy job. The sawdust burners were something new for us but they provided heat and were self-feeding. We settled in and soon Anne took Pamela and Joanne to enroll in elementary school, a block away.

Mr. Loving was employed at the Imperial Oil distributors where he worked in the office. He was also busy in the Anglican Church, and Mrs. Loving was head of the Altar Guild, as she had been at St. Peter's in Regina. We had quite a surprise when on the first Sunday morning, we attended the eleven o'clock service. The Reverend Oswald was the rector, and amongst his announcements he said, "Mr. Proctor will be superintendent of the Sunday School." Apparently Mrs. Loving had told him that I had taught Sunday school at St. Peter's for several years. Anne and I looked at each other but said nothing. After the service we found out that Mrs. Oswald had the Sunday school. She had pupils from age eight and up, and Mrs. Lane had the young ones up to that age. So we were quickly into the church life.

The next week, as I walked along the street, I met Mrs. Loving. As we talked she said she was keeping a close look out for the chimney sweep. She further explained that every year the sweep came up the valley, and that if she missed him there was no one else to call since no one in Mission was in that type of business. Generally speaking, the prospect for work was not very bright, but when I mentioned to Anne about their being a shortage of local chimney cleaners, we both laughed.

On going around to shops I noticed the shopkeepers cleaning their own store-front windows and so I found out there was no one in that business either. Anne and I discussed this and soon discovered that there also was no one in town in the floor maintenance business. It seemed that I was being drawn into the way we should go. We had great fun thinking about these things, partially because we didn't have a vehicle, and I couldn't drive. I had ridden all over Europe, but always in transport with a driver. It soon became evident that I should learn.

There were driving courses in New Westminster, so I applied. Since it was a ten-day course, I would have to take residence in New Westminster for that time. But after four days they were satisfied with my tests and I received my driver's license. It was nice to be home early, with everything going well. Next came the purchase of a vehicle. This was not easy, since cars were hard to get, but after a while we found a second-hand car to buy. It was not a good one, but it did run.

To learn about starting a chimney, window and floor cleaning service we scoured newspapers looking for chimney sweep ads. I phoned one business in Vancouver and told them about my situation, about just coming out of the service and looking to start a new business. I told the man there were no chimney sweeps in Mission and would he allow me to learn from him what he did. He was willing to cooperate, so I made plans to visit his business in Vancouver.

I booked a room in Vancouver and then began a short course in chimney cleaning. This man was a great help, another angel in disguise. He personally showed me everything I would need to know, and how to use the equipment from ladders to brushes. I stayed with him for a week.

Next, I did the same sort of thing with a city window cleaner, another angel in my life. He too was only too glad to show me his equipment and how to use it. Things were moving right along. For the floor maintenance I acquired the necessary equipment from a wholesaler, including floor machines, buckets, mops, and soaps.

Now we needed a name. The family spent an evening discussing what our name should be. It was a riot. We thought of a window cleaning name, "Let Frank Lighten Your Life." What fun, but we finally came up with the name "Frank's Business and Home Service."

My next hurdle was getting a license, so the following morning I went down to the City Hall. I said a little prayer and proceeded to the clerk's desk, stated who I was and that my business was to get a license to start a cleaning service in Mission. "Hmmmm," he said, looking at my application. "There are three businesses on here?"

"Yes," I said, "but this town has none of them." I then explained that the chimney cleaning would only be in the fall so he quickly wrote out a license for "Frank's Business and Home Service." The charge was ten dollars, and I hurried home to tell Anne that we were in business. We thanked the Lord.

We discussed putting ads in local newspapers and getting stickers for cleaned chimneys. We also wanted to get a single-line telephone for work. Anne would handle phone calls and log the work. From the beginning, I never had to look for work. My first customer was the Bus Depot Cafe. Then the Five-to-a-Dollar store booked me for once a week. Next, the Mac-and-Mac's booked me for cleaning and polishing their hardwood floors at a hundred dollars a month. This provided a solid anchor.

It was about this time that we had to choose our family doctor. Being new in Mission we did not know any doctors personally, but we had heard of Dr. Marcellus, so Anne and I arranged an appointment with him and it was soon discovered that Anne was pregnant again. This brought back the memory of her previous pregnancy. However, this time Anne was in good health and again I heard her say, "Let's get on with it."

In the fall of 1947, many people were anxious to get their chimneys cleaned, so I stayed busy. I soon became so busy that I got Gilbert Smales to help me with the chimney cleaning. The Smales became great friends. We knew Gilbert from our Regina days. He and his wife, Amy, had moved to Mission from Lumsden, Saskatchewan where Amy's dad had been an Anglican minister.

I also had lots of contract window cleaning, including Buckerfields, and the city hall. Since most of my work was by contract, the income was steady. I knew I wouldn't get rich, but it promised to be a livelihood and we were thankful to the Lord.

Anne, who at first had been overwhelmed by the size of the house, was getting settled in, but she missed her friends and companions from Regina. It was quite understandable that she pined a little now and then. Anne found a piano and we bought it for three hundred dollars so the girls could take lessons.

The number of people wanting chimney cleaning had grown quite large over the years and I soon began to set schedules for this work. One of the pleasant elements about my business was that I could plan my own time. I knew what had to be done and I could schedule it as I saw fit. I had keys to get into the stores so I could work anytime between store closing and opening next day. This allowed me to schedule around family events.

A new rector, Paul Wade, arrived in 1948, and with him a young priest, Tom Speed. Gilbert Smales introduced me to Bill Shepherd who was a dedicated church goer. Bill loved the game of curling, and invited me to join the local Mission Curling Club. There was a large membership and I enjoyed it. This also brought me lots of new friends. Curling was a game that suited me since back in my school days we played a similar game called *quoits*.

In 1948, the people of Mission had to worry about the Fraser River which had begun to flood. All indications were that the Fraser River's raging waters would soon ravage the lower mainland. We heard stories of tremendous rushing water taking out farmhouses, riverside buildings, as well as much acreage. A call for help went out to the army, the navy, and the air force for help. The flood waters were now rampaging through Hope, Agassiz, and Nicomen Island. A call went out for sandbaggers, and for rooms for those who were flooded out of their homes. Anne and I talked it over and decided to take in some whose home had been washed away. We took in four adults from Hatzic Island who had lost their house and belongings: Charley McKintosh, his wife, and his wife's parents from Saskatchewan.

It was June 7, 1948, when the brunt of the flood struck Mission. The water was soon over the railway tracks at Mission Flats. One Saturday morning there was a call for sandbaggers to work near the Pioneer Garage. Water was lapping over the railway there and threatening to cross the highway, so I joined about thirty others who were sandbagging. I have often thought about the sandbagging. No one ever asked who you were, or to what church you belonged, or where you were born. You just got on with the job, and everyone willingly worked in good spirit.

Before the flood ended the water had reached a height of twenty-five feet. Soon afterwards the flood subsided and the town began to pull itself together. The flood victims whom we had housed and with whom we had become friendly, went their own way but we often saw them around town.

By the end of June, Anne was preparing to have the baby. She was in constant care of Dr. Marcellus and everyone was excited, waiting for the day. We prayed everything would go well. The girls were out of school and we carried on as best we could. It seemed that nothing else mattered.

Anne gave birth to our son, Mark David, at Mission Memorial Hospital on July 15, 1948. This was an exciting time for us all. I was so thankful that the birth went well, and that it was a healthy boy. Our prayers had been answered.

Things at home were becoming more routine. The business was firmly established. But I had to get a different car. One of my customers was Legion Motors and they knew I was looking for a car. One evening while I was doing the Bus Depot Cafe floors, there came a knocking at the door. It was a lad from Legion Motors. He said there was a country station wagon at the Motors that I might like and that I should quickly go see it. The next morning I went to Legion Motors and it seemed that it would be the car for me, so I bought it. It was an English car and it cost two thousand two hundred dollars. Anne knew we had to get a new vehicle and so she was delighted. Six days after that purchase, the English pound went down under three dollars and the value of the car dropped as well. However, there wasn't much we could do about that but exhale a "ho hum." But we needed the car, and were glad to have it. It was more of a family vehicle and served us well.

In 1950, we decided to renovate our house. We had the whole front verandah removed, and moved the stairs from the porch to the outside, making a three-room suite upstairs. This work was done by the Lightburn brothers. They also enlarged the living room on the south wall. We soon rented the upstairs suite to Sammy Sinclair and his wife, Vilma. Sammy was a partner in the sheet metal business and a very good builder. He and I soon became very friendly. They were the first occupants of the new suite and it was he who put in the kitchen sink, the toilet and the cupboards, making it into a nicer suite.

Since the 1948 flood, the town was busy, building and growing. The church, too, was growing in numbers. Reverend Paul Wade was very popular and the church school was enlarging. There were now about thirty children attending. But he died suddenly in 1951. It was a really sad time and a loss of a great minister to the Parish and community. I was now sitting on the church committees, along with Mr. Bill Shepherd, Mr. Wier, and others, all devoted people. We had to find a new Parish Priest.

At home, we wondered how we could get rid of the sawdust burners. Natural gas was being touted, but we thought that having only a crawl space under the house would render that difficult. We sought two Mission outfits to have a look, which they did, but they declined. Finally, we contacted a furnace man in Whonnock who, to our surprise, took on the job. I've always been thankful for him because installing gas was no easy job. He was another angel in our lives. He and his son installed a furnace and kitchen stove and it has served us well. The house was so different and so much cleaner after this installation.

In those days, property wasn't in great demand, but one evening Sammy Sinclair asked Anne and me if we would sell them the fifty-foot lot on the west side of the house. We were good friends of the Sinclairs so we sold them the lot for two hundred dollars and Sammy began building a house on it, all by himself. This took time, of course. They lived upstairs in our house while constructing their own new house next door.

In 1951 the girls, Pam and Joanne, were doing well in school and with their piano. Mark was an active three-year-old. He and I used to play a game going called "I don't want you." I would be sitting in my chair and he would try to get onto my knee, then I would push or roll him away, saying "I don't want you." This game was loads of fun. We had a little stream that trickled its way down into a drain on the east side of our property, and Mark would spend hours damming it up.

After many meetings with the Diocese and Bishop Gower, it was decided that our next parish priest would be the Reverend John Clarke. He and his wife Georgina were from Saskatoon. Our family and the Sinclairs were sitting under the large cedar tree in our yard having fun with the kids when John walked in amongst us. He was a chap that everyone immediately liked, full of life, jokes and laughter. We took to him and his family and they were good for the parish. John was excellent with children and a very good teacher. Our families got on really well together and we visited often.

About this time, Anne's sister Joyce and husband Bert Moore moved to Kelowna, along with Anne's Mum and Dad who had now retired. Anne's older sister Gladys had served as a WREN in England. On her voyage home she met Arthur, and they were married and lived in Regina before moving to Haney, B.C.. One of Anne's younger two brothers, Victor, had served overseas, and had visited my people in Durham. There he met and married my niece, Joan, and they returned to Canada. They had four children, Melody, Beverly, Lyn, and Ernie, and finally settled in Fort Saskatchewan, Alberta. Arthur, Anne's other younger brother, met a WAC, Dorothy Holloway, during the war. Her home was Ontario, and when they married they to moved to Kitchener where they raised four girls, Donna, Patricia, Shirley, and Nancy. Norman and Addie Tindall remained in Regina where Norman continued to manage his butcher shop, The Grand Meat Market. They had one son, Bill, and a daughter, Norma. The Tindalls were a very close-knit family and always kept in touch with each other.

In the years after the war, I continued having the trouble with my stomach as I did during the war. At times Anne would encourage me to go to Dr. Marcellus. He treated me for ulcers and advised me about the kind of foods that I should eat. So I began taking Gelusil pills and staying away from acidic and fatty foods. I lived with my ailment as best I could and with Anne's tender care I was okay. I then began applying for an army pension. I was turned down at first, but later I was granted a small pension.

Things were going okay with my business. At times when I needed help Gilbert Smales, Ernie Lathrop and George Alexander would work for me. They would help place the ladders and get the chimney cleaning tools out of the vehicle. We would both go in the home to remove stove pipes etc., covering our tracks with newspaper to keep it a good clean job. I would always go up the outside chimney. They would hold my ladder and reach and fetch for me. Going to great heights had come easy to me through my working at the Imperial Oil yard. It occurred to me that through life the Lord is preparing us for things. It was working in a coal mine that gave me a sense of proportion for other forms of work. So, I could climb chimneys without fear and would stand on the top and look down, to brush or scrape the chimney. In the early 1950s, I charged two dollars and fifty cents to clean a chimney. Of course, those were the days when we could get a large ice cream cone for a dime. It cost fifty cents to go to a movie, and fifty cents for a hair cut. All things being equal, the Lord was good to us.

Anne having worked at Barrie's Furs, in Regina was excellent at fur work. She knew all about skins and once had made her own fur coat and hat. News got around of her talents and people began to bring fur coats to her for repair. This kept her busy, besides answering the phone for my work, being a member of the Altar Guild, and also and a member of the A.C.W. (Anglican Church Women). She was great, and I loved her dearly.

Upon the death of Anne's dad in 1960 in Kelowna, Anne stepped in to take care of her Mum. She was to come and stay with us. At this time she was suffering memory loss and often was quite confused. We had dear old Mum for a year. After that Mum went to live in Haney with Gladys.

We had been in business more than ten years now, and we talked about a trip back to England. It seemed that such a trip was possible as both Pam and Joanne were teaching now.

Since we both had lots of family in England, we longed to visit them. Anne had relatives at Hodthorpe, near Worksop, Derbyshire and she had school friends with whom she had always kept in touch. So we kept on talking it over and found that we could make such a trip, and also take Mark, and he could do Grade 9 by correspondence. We would give up our business, since my ulcers were a problem. We decided that if ever we were going to England, now was the time. We further decided that we would buy a Ford Anglia. It was a small car, but would be just right for us to get around in England. It cost thirteen hundred dollars and we would pick it up at Liverpool.

This was so exciting , especially since the family was so supportive. We would be away for almost a year. But it took a long time to put everything into place. Mark was finally set for his correspondence studies. There were bookings for the train to the east coast, and a ship to England. At that time the C.P.R. went from coast to coast and the C.P. Empress Fleet of ships carried passengers. Finally it was arranged that Joanne would stay in our home, with two friends, Mary Mayer and Shirley Arnold.

CHAPTER FIFTEEN
Visit to England

It was near the end of summer 1962, when we sailed from Halifax's Bedford Basin onto the high seas, bound for England. Not being a good sailor, I thought it best for me not to move around much, but Mark toured the ship, fore and aft. Always a curious lad, he explored every place he could, and a few that he shouldn't.

Anne had a relative, a ship's engineer, so upon our arrival in Liverpool she located him and he helped us find the car dealer so we could pick up our car. There was a lot of paperwork, insurance etc. to be taken care of before we got started across the Yorkshire Dales headed for Durham. It was marvelous to see those Yorkshire scenes. Barnard Castle was on our route and we stopped there for a couple of hours to visit and tour the castle. We shopped for a few things there before leaving for Durham.

When we arrived at Durham, I discovered I had lost my wallet. We hastily got in touch with the shop and were relieved to discover that I had left it on their counter and they would hold it for us. Of course, we had to make a return trip of thirty miles to retrieve it. Amy, my sister, was now a widow and lived at Ushaw Moor and she had plenty of accommodations for us. This would be our home until our return to Canada. Amy was still a nurse at Brandon Hospital, about ten miles away. We took her to work and then had plenty of free time to travel to the places I remembered so well.

We frequently went into the city of Durham. We saw Broompark, a place where we lived in the 1920s, past Neville's Cross where there once was a great battle between the English and the Scots, and then down the hill into Durham. Durham is situated on low ground near the river Wear, and is surrounded by seven hills. A very old city, its history could fill a book. The Cathedral there had a famous knocker on its door that was used in ancient years by fugitives seeking sanctuary.

As Durham was the centre of a coal-mining county, every year there was the Durham Miners' Gala. Each village of coal miners had a brass band. They were impressive, especially when marching with their banners. They would assemble on North Road, Durham's main street where people of each village would fall in behind their band and parade down to the race-course, a huge area of playing fields. Once there, they would place their banners side-by-side all the way around the outside of the course. The street would be full of people and families.

We visited the homes of all our relatives, Frank, Jean, Gillian and Ian at Station Road, Bennett and Mary Mac, Robin and his family at Langley Park. I met Tom Henderson who had been a policeman when I was a boy. I remember the day he caught me sleighing in an unauthorized area, and he took my sled. He was now the church warden at St. Luke's Church. I met Syd Rhodes and his wife Bella. He was winding engineman at a colliery and I visited him at his work.

We thoroughly enjoyed all the surrounding country. We had fun at Amy's and time passed quickly. Once the cold of winter bore down on us, we discovered there was no central heating in the house and the upstairs bedrooms were without heat. So Anne and I finally obtained a paraffin oil heater for our bedroom. We spent Christmas with Amy.

In the second six months of our visit to England we visited Anne's village of Hodthorpe. Here we met many people and saw places where Anne had begun her life. Her lifetime school friend with whom we stayed was Elsie Clarke and her husband, Sam. They had a big house and garden. I remember as we were driving from Hodthorpe, how excited Anne was at going down a stretch of road where she used to cycle. She couldn't believe how short it had become, compared to how she remembered it. It was really interesting for both me and Mark, since we had never been in those parts.

Elsie and Sam had two sons, Paul and Martin. We took many trips together, including one to the Duke of Portland's estate. We often went over the small bridge on the railway in Whitwell, which is a fair-sized town nearly 1000 years old.

We moved on from Hodthorpe to Nottingham where we met Betty and Jack Ashcroft and Betty's parents who were great friends of the Tindalls, especially the mothers who were school mates and had worked together in Nottingham Castle. Betty and Jack lived in Malvern, Worcestershire, a beautiful part of England.

From the midlands, we visited my brother Harry and his wife Olive and their children Janette and Martin, for a month. They owned and ran the Railway Hotel and Pub opposite the railway station. Harry had retired there after playing professional soccer for a good number of years. He became an accomplished football player during his school days. He then went away to play for Hartlepool United. Harry and I were great chums.

The county of Norfolk was most interesting and we travelled through most of it. We met some of Olive's relatives, her brother and sister and others, and her Mum and Dad whom I had met in the war years. I remember then that there was an enemy air-raid on Norwich, a frequent occurrence in that particular part of the country. Harry and Olive's home had been hit, but they had shelters in their back yards. During one of those raids, a bomb dropped close to Olive's brother. He was a fire-warden and wore a hard hat which saved his life, but as he had been knocked out he got three weeks leave.

Often we would go around and see the sights of Norwich. One day we passed a big elementary school and Martin said, "See that big school over there?" and we nodded, and he said, "That's where the poor kids go." I have often thought about the differences between living in England and living in Canada. The class distinction existing in England did not appeal to me.

We left Norwich for London for a short visit with Lottie, a nurse friend of Amy's whom we knew in Durham, along with her husband, Syd. They lived in mid London. It was a busy place, but immensely interesting. Their friend, George, who boarded with them took to Mark right away and went out of his way to show him everything. We went to a London marketplace. My, what an experience to be in such a populated area. We walked and bussed most of the time.

We left London to visit Olive Richardson at Southampton. Olive was a teacher and lived in a lovely seaside home at Hythe. We returned to London on our way back to Durham to visit Anne and Mary, Anne's cousins. Driving back, Anne was in the back seat and Mark was in the front seat checking the road map. As I remember, we were thoroughly enjoying the ride. It was such a nice day and we were singing when Mark said, "Dad."

"Yes, Mark?" said I.

"If that river on our right is on the right side, then we are driving on the wrong side."

I stopped the car and sure enough we were going merrily along, but in the wrong direction. That incident has been a lesson to me to this day, as with life. We could be oblivious and be going the wrong way, as was Saint Paul when he was persecuting the Christians.

We got to London and Mary and Anne showed us a lot of that countryside, including Pinnar just on the edge of London, near the school that Winston Churchill attended.

After a really nice visit with Mary and Anne we boarded the plane at London airport for Amsterdam, Holland. The Gort family was there to greet us: Lies, Bertus, and their sons Bart, Frank and Simon. They had named Frank after me. We had kept in touch after the war.We all had such a wonderful time together and the boys, Frank and Simon developed a lasting friendship with Mark. I remember that we had such fun in the house with the shuffleboard. We stayed with them for one week, then returned to England and made our way north.

This was the last of our visits, so we headed back up the three-lane highway to Durham, stopping often to see the sights. We stopped at York and toured its great wall and even greater Cathedral. When we finally got back to Amy's, she had to work but had weekends off, and of course we were home evenings. We spent the days seeking out those places that used to be familiar to me.

I found the shortcut through Armory's farm to Bearpark. The farm was gone now and houses were there instead. The railway line had all been taken away and was now a road, so we walked this road from Ushaw Moor to Esh Winning, a lovely walk. We visited Broadgate, where Fords had an orchard. I remember how we used to try to get an apple or a pear from the branches overhanging the fence. Ushaw colliery had been demolished entirely, and New Brancepeth or Steelburn colliery had disappeared from the face of the countryside. The only pit left in the Deerness Valley was Bearpark. We walked down Station Road to the bridge over the river Deerness, underneath the great viaduct built for the railway between Durham and Winning, and then to the riverbank. It was all so interesting to me.

I remembered going to this river so often as a lad. At one time we were catching minnows in glass jars when someone hollered "Here's Bramley!" He was the game keeper and he rode a horse. He always carried a whip, a short handled stick with an awfully long lash, and he used it to chase away any trespassers. On this one particular day, brother Ernest, like the rest of us, had his trouser legs doubled up above his knees and had his big glass pickle jar in the middle of the stream when the call came that Bramley was bearing down on us. Ernest came up with his jar containing a small pinhead fish, and in running away, he slipped on a stone in the water and fell. His hand fell on the glass jar, which broke into pieces on the rocks, cutting his hand in seventeen places. We managed to elude Bramley, but poor Ernest's hand was in a terrible mess and he even lost his fish.

This Bramley family lived on a place called Brancepeth Estate. They lived secretive lives and were troubled with suicides. The river in those years was the catchall for the disposal of anything: beds, mattresses, drowning of unwanted dogs and cats, a convenient dump. There was a strong little stream of pit-water always emptying itself from Steelburn colliery into this small river. We lads along with most of the locals called it the Cankary Beck, it steamed and smelled and was so black.

On the high ground above the river level stood New Brancepeth, home of the Steelburn colliery band. It seemed that they were always practicing and they really created a lovely sound. One could hardly move away from listening to them. They were noted and won many competition prizes. I knew quite a few of these talented bandsmen.

The pit where I first began to work had vanished, but the memories will be with me as long as I shall live. My Dad, Thomas and Bennett, my uncles, brother Ernest and I all worked there, and we had followed their famous band onto the race-course at the Durham Miners' Gala many times.

In later years, brother Ernest and I had worked at Ushaw Moor colliery. The memory that came to me from there was the thirteen-month strike, the daily seeking for coal on the slag heap, and the scraping to live. I had fond memories of exercising pit ponies in the colliery field. When production stopped for any length of time, ponies were brought to the surface and that's the only time they saw daylight. Sometimes it seems to me that the good Lord evens things out and I believe that suffering brings us together. In prosperity, who needs anyone?

I looked for Number 8 Middlefield Terrace, where I had lived before going to Canada. The house did not exist. In fact, the whole street had been demolished and moved.

We were all quite sad when it came time for us to leave England, but it was time to return to our daughters and home in Canada. The Sunday before we left, we all went to St. Luke's Church: Amy and Hilda, and our niece Anne with her husband Martin.

We took the Anglia car home with us on the ship. Our return journey was uneventful. However, as we crossed the ocean and witnessed the majesty of the sea, Anne and I sat on deck and pondered the events of our lives. For me, I was grateful for all that I had seen and done in my life. I had crossed the Atlantic five times, three of them at someone else's expense, and now I was sixty-one years old and ready for another change in my life . . . retirement.

During this crossing I contemplated what I had seen and accomplished. I had learned a lot about life and about painting from nature, how things grow, how they live and die. The autumn leaves in all their colour and glory die. These leaves, in their last release from the trees that bore them, just flutter gently down to the bosom of Mother earth from whence they came. Just like humans: they are born, they live and they die. *A chance to know the Creator* for a few years, which seems like a bubble on the stormy creek or babbling brook. This bubble then bursts and one would never know it had ever existed, enjoined again in the ever-moving circle of things.

I considered that my life was primarily influenced by four things: First, my willingness to risk leaving my boyhood home to venture to Canada as a harvester; second, the love of my wife, family and good friends that I found in Canada; third, my experience in the Regina Rifles that taught me the price of freedom; and fourth, trusting in God as my navigator never failed me as I was tossed upon the seas of life.